An Olive Branch
on the Family Tree

A History of Canada's Peoples

An Olive Branch on the Family Tree

The Arabs in Canada

Baha Abu-Laban

Published by McClelland and Stewart Ltd. in association
with the Multiculturalism Directorate,
Department of the Secretary of State
and the Canadian Government Publishing Centre,
Supply and Services Canada.

Government Catalogue No. CI44-5/1980E

The Canadian Publishers
McClelland and Stewart Limited
25 Hollinger Road
Toronto, Ontario
M4B 3G2

CANADIAN CATALOGUING IN PUBLICATION DATA

Abu-Laban, Baha.
  An olive branch on the family tree

(Generations, a history of Canada's peoples)
Bibliography: p.
Includes index.

ISBN 0-7710-0715-9 pa. ISBN 0-7710-0714-0 bd.

1. Arabs in Canada.   2. Arabs in Canada –
History.   3. Arab Canadians.*   4. Arab Canadians –
History.*   I. Title.   II. Series.

FC106.A65A28   971′.004927   C80-094162-4
F1035.A65A28

Picture researcher: Jill Patrick

Printed and bound in Canada

Contents

Editors' Introduction

Canadians, like many other people, have recently been changing their attitude towards the ethnic dimension in society. Instead of thinking of the many distinctive heritages and identities to be found among them as constituting a problem, though one that time would solve, they have begun to recognize the ethnic diversity of their country as a rich resource. They have begun to take pride in the fact that people have come and are coming here from all parts of the world, bringing with them varied outlooks, knowledge, skills and traditions, to the great benefit of all.

It is for this reason that Book IV of the *Report of the Royal Commission on Bilingualism and Biculturalism* dealt with the cultural contributions of the ethnic groups other than the British, the French and the Native Peoples to Canada, and that the federal government in its response to Book IV announced that the Citizenship Branch of the Department of the Secretary of State would commission "histories specifically directed to the background, contributions and problems of various cultural groups in Canada." This series presents the histories that have resulted from that mandate. Although commissioned by the Government, they are not intended as definitive or official, but rather as the efforts of scholars to bring together much of what is known about the ethnic groups studied, to indicate what remains to be learned, and thus to stimulate further research concerning the ethnic dimension in Canadian society. The histories are to be objective, analytical, and readable, and directed towards the general reading public, as well as students at the senior high school and the college and university levels, and teachers in the elementary schools.

Most Canadians belong to an ethnic group, since to do so is simply to have "a sense of identity rooted in a common origin . . . whether this common origin is real or imaginary."[1] The Native Peoples, the British and French (referred to as charter groups because they were the first Europeans to take possession of the land), the groups such as the Germans and Dutch who have been established in Canada for over a hundred years and those who began to arrive only yesterday all have traditions and values that they cherish and that now are part of the cultural riches that Canadians share. The groups vary widely in numbers, geographical location and distribution and degree of social and economic power. The stories of their struggles, failures and triumphs will be told in this series.

As the Royal Commission on Bilingualism and Biculturalism pointed out, this sense of ethnic origin or identity "is much keener in certain individuals than in others."[2] In contemporary Canadian society, with the increasing number of intermarriages across ethnic lines, and hence the growing diversity of peoples ancestors, many are coming to identify themselves as simple Canadian, without reference to their ancestral origins. In focusing on the ethnic dimension of Canadian society, past and present, the series does not assume that everyone should be categorized into one particular group, or that ethnicity is always the most important dimension of people's lives. It is, however, one dimension that needs examination if we are to understand fully the contours and nature of Canadian society and identity.

Professional Canadian historians have in the past emphasized political and economic history, and since the country's economic and political institutions have been controlled largely by people of British and French origin, the role of those of other origins in the development of Canada has been neglected. Also, Canadian historians in the past have been almost exclusively of British and French origin, and have lacked the interest and the linguistic skills necessary to explore the history of other ethnic groups. Indeed, there has rarely ever been an examination of the part played by specifically British – or, better, specifically English, Irish, Scottish and Welsh – traditions and values in Canadian development, because of the lack of recognition of pluralism in the society. The part played by French traditions and values, and particular varieties of French traditions and values, has for a number of reasons been more carefully scrutinized.

This series is an indication of growing interest in Canadian social history, which includes immigration and ethnic history. This may particularly be a reflection of an increasing number of scholars whose origins and ethnic identities are other than British or French. Because such trends are recent, many of the authors of the histories in this series have not had a large body of published writing to work from. It is true that some histories have already been written of particular groups other than the British and French; but these have often been characterized by filio pietism, a narrow perspective and a dearth of scholarly analysis.

Despite the scarcity of secondary sources, the authors have been asked to be as comprehensive as possible, and to give balanced coverage to a number of themes: historical background, settlement patterns, ethnic identity and assimilation, ethnic associations, population trends, religion, values, occupations and social class, the family, the ethnic press, language patterns, political behaviour, education, inter-ethnic relations, the arts and recreation. They have also been asked to give a sense of the way the group differs in various parts of the country. Finally, they have been asked to give, as much as possible, an insider's view of what the immigrant and ethnic experiences were like at different periods of time, but yet at the same time to be as objective as possible, and not simply to present the group as it sees itself, or as it would like to be seen.

The authors have thus been faced with a herculean task. To the extent that they have succeeded, they provide us with new glimpses into many aspects of Canadian society of the past and the present. To the extent that they have fallen short of their goal, they challenge other historians, sociologists and social anthropologists to continue the work begun here.

Jean Burnet
Howard Palmer

[1] *Report of the Royal Commission on Bilingualism and Biculturalism.*
[2] Ibid. Paragraph 8.

Introduction

Almost a century ago, amid the numerous immigrants then pouring into Canada, a 19-year-old youth landed in Montreal. It was 1882 and Abraham Bounadere from Zahle, a small village in The Lebanon overlooking the fertile Beka' valley, had become Canada's first Arab immigrant.[1] By 1901 there were some 2,000 others of Arab origin in Canada, by 1941 this number had grown to 11,857 persons, and today it is estimated that there are between 70,000 and 80,000 Canadians of Arab origin.

What characterizes these immigrants who came to Canada from a culture so dramatically different in language, polity, customs, food, climate and many aspects of religion? What attractions did Canada hold that their home countries did not? What promises were fulfilled and what dreams went unrealized for these Arab immigrants, their children and their children's children?

The Arab Canadians are one facet of the Canadian mosaic. This facet encompasses recent immigrants who are attempting to learn Canada's languages, as well as third-generation Canadians who have never learned their grandparents' mother tongue. It encompasses people whose formative years were spent outside of Canada as well as people who have never been away from Canada's shores. This subgroup of Canadians represents a diverse span of ages, experiences and backgrounds, yet shares a common ethnic designation. This study focuses on the Arab Canadians and their part in Canada's ethnic kaleidoscope.

The immigrant experience is familiar to many Canadians. Fifteen per cent of the population of Canada in 1971 was born outside of this country. However, through the experiences of close relatives, many more Canadians are directly linked to the immigrant reality, and in many ways Canada can be said to be a nation of immigrants and children of immigrants. People from a multiplicity of nations now call Canada home and this diversity has occasionally led to strains. Each wave of immigrants, in Canada's history, has experienced the successive problems

1

of being strangers, adjusting to the society, and eventually themselves becoming the established Canadians *vis-à-vis* still more recent immigrants. Each era has had its characteristic immigration patterns.

Arab immigration began in the latter part of the nineteenth century but the numbers were small. Between 1882, when Abraham Bounadere first arrived, and World War II, virtually all Arab immigrants to Canada came from Syria and what is now known as Lebanon. Changes on the world scene and in Canadian immigration policy resulted in an almost complete halt to Arab immigration between World War I and World War II. During the post-war years, however, there was a change, not only in the volume of immigration but also in the characteristics of Arab immigrants; more of these post-war Arab immigrants were from Egypt than from any other Arab state. The remainder originated from Lebanon, and to a lesser degree, Morocco, Syria, Jordan, Tunisia and other countries.

The educational and occupational qualifications of these later immigrants were not only diverse, but for the first time also exceeded the Canadian average. There was also a shift in religious characteristics. Some 30% of the post-war immigrants were Muslim, whereas the early Arab immigrants were nearly all Christians. As a consequence of these differing waves of immigration, the Arab Canadians today stand as a large and complex ethnic group. They encompass wide internal differences in education, occupation and economic background, as well as differences in religious affiliation, political attitudes, length of residence in Canada, generation and country of origin. These differences are a product of many interacting conditions, both historical and contemporary.

THE RELEVANCE OF THE STUDY

The effects of demographic and socio-cultural factors on the attitudes and behaviour of Arab Canadians have not been studied previously. Also, insufficient attention has been given to the development of the Arab-Canadian ethnic group or to its role and contributions in Canadian society. The bibliographies of research on Canadian ethnic groups of the Department of Citizenship and Immigration, covering the period from 1920 to 1964, list only one two-page article on the Syrians in Western Canada.[2] A few studies on Arab Canadians have appeared in the past 10 years, but their focus has been somewhat narrow.[3] Hence, we have little knowledge about the integration of this group into the Canadian society.

There are several other reasons which suggest the timeliness of this investigation. The Arab-Canadian group offers an interesting opportunity to explore some of the configurations possible in the immigrant context. Notwithstanding the fact that large numbers of immigrants have come to Canada from many differing parts of the world, the dominant and most firmly established traditions and ethos of this country are European, and more specifically, British, in origin. The ease with which a new im-

2

migrant adapts depends on his linguistic, cultural and religious affinity with the new country. Accordingly, one may assume that British immigrants would tend to feel more at home in Canada than Western European immigrants other than British, while the latter would tend to feel more at home here than their central or southern European counterparts. Arab immigrants, on several important variables such as language, culture and religion, bear little resemblance to the Canadian archetype. The contrasts between the Canadian cultural and linguistic heritage and that of the Arab world raise some important questions concerning the social forces which impinge on the socio-economic adjustment, acculturation and assimilation of Arab immigrants into Canadian society. It also suggests possible parallel developments for more recent immigrant groups which are distinctly outside the mainstream of Canadian life.

Another factor in the special situation of the Arab-Canadian minority is the prominent news coverage given in recent years to events in the Middle East. This coverage both in its amount and its content has had considerable influence on the cohesion and adjustment of Arab-Canadian communities across the country. This is partly because of the recency of Arab immigration into Canada and the large number of foreign-born persons in this group, and partly because the media coverage of events in the Arab world influences the structuring and the quality of relationships between Arab Canadians and the larger society. This study addresses aspects of these relationships and some of the unique dilemmas faced by Arab Canadians.

Arab Canadians face still another unusual, if not unique, situation, involving a new kind of enticement towards circular (return) migration. Many of the turn-of-the-century Arab immigrants to Canada anticipated that their presence in the new land would be of short duration and that after a few years of adventure in the new land they would return to their ancestral home. The strength of filial ties acted as a particularly powerful magnet. In addition to such descent ties, however, post-war Arab immigrants to Canada experience new pressures towards return. Some are now being called upon, directly and indirectly, to assist in the process of development in the Arab world. The high level of educational training and the skills of many of the post-war Arab immigrants are often needed for Near Eastern development projects. Capital is only one element in the formula of economic development. A second important element is the availability of a trained labour force at all levels of the occupational hierarchy. Given this need, the Arab states consider Arab *emigrés* to North America a potential source of high-level manpower whose return to the homeland would be of benefit. What is unique today is that many Arab states can recompense returnees at exceptionally high rates from burgeoning oil revenues. Thus the Arab-Canadian community, more than any other in Canada, presents new research opportunities for investigating phenomena arising from significant shifts in the international economic order. In this age of the career-motivated migrant (or transilient, to use Richmond's term), the impact of economic and manpower shifts will be felt both in the sending and receiving countries.[4] This study examines the attitudes of Arab Canadians towards Canada and the Arab world, and as well their attitudes and plans regarding a return move to the Old Country.

THE RESEARCH METHOD

This study is based on research which incorporated several techniques and methodologies. The data are derived from several sources. These include official Government of Canada statistics; materials from the National Archives; historical documents from private individuals and from organizations in the Arab-Canadian community; interviews, averaging two hours in length, with some 30 leaders of Arab-Canadian voluntary and religious organizations; examination of ethnic press publications, both historical and contemporary; informal interviews with Arab-Canadian senior citizens, who were among the early immigrants; participant observation in the Arab-Canadian community and organizations, and a sample survey of Arab Canadians living in two metropolitan centres, Toronto and Montreal. The first six sources of information will be acknowledged at the appropriate places in the body of the text. The last two sources of information require some explanation.

Participant observation is a research technique which requires the analyst to assume a dual role, that of a participating group member and that of a researcher recording and interpreting relevant group activities. During the past five years, as a member of the Arab-Canadian community, the author has held offices in Arab-Canadian organizations; met with community members representing a cross-section of people from different regions in Canada; and attended annual meetings and conventions of regional organizations and of the Canadian Arab Federation, the national umbrella organization. This role as a participant observer has provided access to a rich fund of information regarding the dynamics of Arab Canadianism.

The final major source of information for this study was a sample survey carried out in the spring and summer of 1974. The survey was focused on Ontario and Quebec because 90% of Arab Canadians live in these two provinces. In each of the areas under investigation, a sample of Arab-Canadian residents was selected, with the intent of obtaining adequate representation by sex, age, birthplace, national origin, educational and occupational characteristics and religious affiliation. Several sources of information were consulted in the selection of the samples, including telephone and/or associational directories, local informants, and the respondents themselves. Of the 349 respondents, 175 were from Toronto and vicinity and 174 were from metropolitan Montreal. An interview schedule (Appendix I) was constructed to yield information on background characteristics, reasons for immigration to Canada, social

4

and economic adjustment, survival of ethnic patterns, and attitudes towards Canada and the homeland. The writer was assisted both in Toronto and Montreal by trained interviewers selected from the local Arab-Canadian communities. Subject to specified guidelines, the interviewers were given some leeway in the selection of respondents. The average length of the interviews was about one hour.

The main characteristics of the total sample may be summarized as follows. About 65% were males. Approximately 21% were born in Canada, 24% in Lebanon or Syria, 28% in Egypt, 16% in Palestine (including a portion of Jordan), and the remainder (11%) were born in other countries, including Algeria and Morocco. The educational background of the respondents was relatively high, with about four out of 10 holding a diploma or university degree (including M.D. or Ph.D.). About 48% of the sample were in business or upper white collar occupations (managerial, professional, and semi-professional), 15% were involved in lower white collar occupations (clerical and sales), 17% held blue collar occupations, and the remainder were students, housewives or else retired. About 70% of the respondents were Christians, and the remainder (30%) were Muslims, including Druses. Finally, 47% of the sample were 30 years of age or younger, 38% were in the 31-50 year age group, and the remainder (18%) were over 50 years of age.

The results of the Toronto-Montreal survey will be used throughout the book. Where necessary, the specific question asked in the interview will be stated in the text or in a footnote in order to enable the reader to evaluate the results in relation to the way in which the question was worded. A good portion of the results will be given in the form of straight tabulations and percentages covering the entire sample or the relevant subsection. At times comparisons will be made between or among subgroups within the sample on the basis of such variables as sex, age, birthplace, national origin, religious affiliation, education and occupation. In a few instances responses to several questions in the survey will be combined to form a composite scale, as in the case of ethnic identity, in order to compare different categories or respondents (for example, those classified as "high" and "low" on a given variable). In each instance, the specific procedures followed and the rationale underlying these procedures will be stated in the text.

THE PLAN OF THE BOOK

Chapters One and Two focus on the meaning of Arab ethnicity, the political, social and economic characteristics of the Arab homelands and the implications of these characteristics for Arab immigrants to Canada. The next chapter considers the settlement patterns of the Arab-Canadian community and the factors contributing to Arab immigration to Canada, while Chapter Four examines the reception which Canada has given the immigrants, as well as Canadian images of Arabs. Chapter Five focuses

5

on the economic adjustment of Arab immigrants, while Chapter Six shows how Arab Eastern religious institutions, ethnic organizations and newspapers came into being in Canada. The characteristic features of Arab-Canadian family life are discussed in Chapter Seven. Chapter Eight explores the linguistic and attitudinal adaptation of Arab Canadians, including naturalization as Canadian citizens, plans for return migration and attitudes towards Canada and the Arab world, while Chapter Nine is devoted to an examination of issues relating to cultural preservation and ethnic identity. The conclusions and research implications are provided in the final chapter.

NOTES

1. Elias Karam, "Syrian Immigration to Canada," in Elias Karam, ed., *The Syrian Canadian National Review* (Ottawa, 1935), p. 19.

2. Gilbert Johnson, "The Syrians in Western Canada," *Saskatchewan History*, 12 (1959), pp. 31-32.

3. See, for example, Harold B. Barclay, "An Arab Community in the Canadian Northwest: A Preliminary Discussion of the Lebanese Community in Lac La Biche, Alberta," *Anthropoligica* N.S., 10 (1968), pp. 143-56; Barclay, "The Perpetuation of Muslim Tradition in the Canadian North," *Muslim World*, 59 (1969), pp. 64-73; Barclay, "The Lebanese Muslim Family," in K. Ishwaran, ed., *The Canadian Family*. Second Edition (Montreal, 1976), pp. 92-104; Peter Baker, *Memoirs of an Arctic Arab* (Yellowknife, N.W.T., 1976), Baha Abu-Laban, "The Arab-Canadian Community," in Elaine C. Hagopian and Ann Paden, eds., *The Arab Americans: Studies in Assimilation* (Wilmette, Ill., 1969), pp. 18-36; Abu-Laban, "The Arab Community in the Canadian Mosaic," *Rikka*, 3 (Fall, 1976), pp. 30-31; Abu-Laban, "Middle East Groups," in *The Canadian Family Tree*. Revised Edition (Ottawa: 1979); Louise E. Sweet, "Reconstituting a Lebanese Village Society in a Canadian City," in Barbara C. Aswad, ed., *Arabic Speaking Communities in American Cities* (New York, 1974), pp. 39-52; Abdelmoneim M. Khattab, "The Assimilation of Arab Muslims in Alberta," M.A. Thesis, Department of Sociology, The University of Alberta, 1969; Janice Monti Belkaoui, "Image Creation in the Prestige Press: A Case Study of Arab and Israeli Images, 1966-1974," M.A. Thesis, Department of Sociology and Anthropology, Carleton University, 1976; and Nadia Hanna Wassef, "The Egyptians in Montreal: A New Colour in the Canadian Ethnic Mosaic," M.A. Thesis, Department of Geography, McGill University, 1977.

4. Anthony H. Richmond, "Sociology of Migration in Industrial and Post-Industrial Societies," in J.A. Jackson, ed., *Migration* (Cambridge, 1969), p. 244. The select nature of post-war immigration to Canada is also discussed in Special Joint Committee, *Immigration Policy: Third Report to Parliament* (Ottawa, 1975), p. 53:13.

ONE

Ancestral Ties:
The Meaning of Arab Ethnicity

What does it mean to be an Arab? To many Westerners, the word Arab conjures up images of a nomadic way of life, parched deserts, swaying camels, tribal sheikhs and quickly folded tents. The word Arab is frequently used synonymously with Muslim. To some, Syrians or Egyptians are considered to be separate and distinct from Arabs. These limited or erroneous conceptions require examination and clarification if what it means to be an Arab Canadian is to be understood.

In general, for all Canadians awareness of ethnicity varies by time, place, generation and external events. Ethnic awareness changes when a person emigrates. Prior to immigration, the behaviour of relatives, friends and fellow citizens is defined as human. A sense of ethnicity only takes shape with the awareness of differences. To leave one's land of birth and to travel brings ethnicity into focus. For the immigrant a sense of group membership and conception of personal ethnicity may run head on into the face of the receiving group's conceptions or misconceptions. For second and third generation offspring of the immigrant, ethnicity may have an altogether different meaning. Their knowledge of family history, the demands made on them as a result of their ethnic heritage, their sense of oneness with their immigrating forebears, may at times conflict with their feelings of being Canadian. They are Canadian born and educated and exposed to the broader cultural messages regarding their ancestors' origin, worth and contributions. They may find themselves, unwillingly at times, being labelled as members of a particular ethno cultural group of which they have dim awareness or towards which they feel ambivalent.

These generational differences are important and reflect the difference in exposure to media messages, as well as other differential experiences. Arab-Canadian ethnicity can only be understood in the Arab as well as the Canadian context. This chapter examines the history of the Arab people, their contributions to world civilization, some of the triumphs and some of the anguish of their history, and the meaning of Arab ethnicity in Canada.

ARAB LIFESTYLES: AN OVERVIEW

There was a time in history when the word Arab referred to a well-defined human community which was relatively homogeneous, both physically and culturally. The best contemporary representatives of this community are probably the nomadic Arabs of the Arabian Near Eastern deserts and the North African Sahara.[1] But, in fact, nomads now account for no more than five to eight per cent of the total Arab population. The Western mass media have tended to emphasize, romanticize, and sometimes belittle the nomad, and often to generalize the nomadic conception of Arab ethnicity to the remaining 95% of the population for whom the term Arab carries, among other things, a concrete cultural designation.

In its significant and most common usage today the designation Arab refers to the peoples who inhabit the Arab world and identify themselves as Arabs. The territory of the Arab world extends from the Arabian Gulf in the east through North Africa to the shores of the Atlantic Ocean in the west. It covers an area of about five million square miles and has a population of about 150,000,000. The countries in the League of Arab States which was founded in 1945 include Algeria, Bahrain, Democratic Yemen, Djibouti, Egypt, Iraq, Jordan, Kuwait, Lebanon, Libyan Arab Republic, Mauritania, Morocco, Oman, Qatar, Saudi Arabia, Somalia, Sudan, Syrian Arab Republic, Tunisia, United Arab Emirates, and Yemen. The twenty-second member of the League of Arab States is Palestine.

The Arab world is a vast region of considerable diversity in physical geography, climate and natural resources. The areas most hospitable to man include strips of varying widths along the Mediterranean coast and the valleys of rivers, the major ones being the Nile (in Sudan and Egypt) and the Tigris and Euphrates (mostly in Iraq). Rainfall is not uniform in the region, averaging about 70 centimetres per year along the coastlines and only about 15 centimetres inland. The Arabian and Near Eastern deserts and the North African Sahara are arid lands with burning heat in the summer and temperatures which often reach 45 °C. in the shade. Nature is at its best in the summer months in the mountainous regions of Lebanon, the long favoured summer resort of the Middle East, where temperatures remain pleasantly cool. Not only are water and farmland unevenly distributed throughout the region, but also oil, a new economic resource, is abundant in only a few areas and absent in most others. Although the density of the population is highest in the fertile areas of the Arab world, people can be found wherever habitation is possible.

The social and cultural conditions of the Arab people have been influenced, if not totally determined, by natural resources and climate. Human communities, to survive, try to adapt as well as possible to the environment. In the process of such adaptions, the Arab people have developed different forms of social organization and lifestyles. At one extreme, there is the nomadic or Bedouin lifestyle, the base from which Arab culture has evolved into its present form. At the other extreme is the urban, commercial-industrial lifestyle of Arab cities. Between these two extremes, there are the semi-nomadic, agricultural, and semi-urban lifestyles. The large majority of the Arab population is engaged in agriculture; however, the urban segment of the population is socially, economically and politically dominant.

Notwithstanding the diversity of lifestyles in the Arab world, there is a rich interweaving of customs and values throughout the entire region. This is an important factor in explaining the sense of community among its inhabitants. From Morocco in the west to Iraq in the east, and from Syria in the north to Aden in the south, basic social and cultural complexes bear remarkable similarities. "The more one considers the natural obstacles in communication (and, of course, to settlement) in the Middle East, the more one must acknowledge the accomplishments of past ages in both spreading and holding together a culture whose underlying oneness is no less remarkable than its vigorous variety."[2] Hence, in order to understand how the inhabitants of these diverse areas have come to share cultural commonalities, traditions and, above all, the Arabic language, one needs to appreciate the major historical developments which led to the formation of the Arab world and its peoples.

THE ANCIENT NEAR EAST

The recorded history of the Near East, spanning a period of 5,000 years, is a fascinating tale of interethnic and intercultural contacts between migrants from the Arabian peninsula and ethno cultural groups that came from the north. Large-scale migrations from the Arabian peninsula occurred in successive waves, often under the pressure of acute droughts. All of the immigrant groups whose ancestors once lived in Arabia share a common Semitic descent.[3]

In the third millennium B.C., the Babylonians, the Assyrians, and later the Chaldaeans settled in the country now known as Iraq; after the year 2500 B.C., the Amorites, Canaanites and Phoenicians settled in Syria and Lebanon; and about the year 1500 B.C. the Hebrews and Aramaeans settled in Palestine and Syria.[4] Arab tribes migrated from the peninsula in the first millennium B.C. and established kingdoms in different parts of the Near East.[5] In Syria the Aribi kingdom, with its capital in Jawf, was flourishing in the eighth century B.C. The Nabatean kingdom, with its capital in Petra (modern Jordan), sprang up in the sixth century B.C. The Palmyrene kingdom, with its capital in Palmyra (Syria) was flourishing in the third century A.D. In the sixth century of our era, the Ghassanid and Lakhmid Arab kingdoms flourished in Syria and Iraq, respectively. The Ghassanids were vassals of Byzantium and the Lakhmids were vassals of Persia.

During the long span of history the different peoples that settled the

9

Near East intermingled amid an endless stream of advancing and retreating armies of tribes and empires. If a tribe or a state was not able to establish hegemony over a given area, or was not strong enough even to maintain full independence, it soon was conquered or reduced to the status of a vassal of a stronger state. The competition among different states for the control of trade routes and natural resources was acute, often resulting in the formation of alignments to enhance state interests. Apart from the obvious reciprocal cultural and biological influences which different Near Eastern peoples had on each other, at one time or another they all came under the influence and control of the Persians, the Greeks, the Romans and their successors the Byzantines.

THE ANCIENT AND PRE-ISLAMIC ARABIAN PENINSULA

The Arabian peninsula was not isolated from various Near Eastern cultures and peoples. In the ancient era, as in modern times, it influenced and was in turn influenced by existing world civilizations. Arab tradition divides the peninsula into two regions, the northern and the southern, each of which has experienced unique contacts with the outside and unique internal development.[6] In the south of Arabia, a prosperous agricultural economy existed long before the Christian era. The Minaeans, a southern Arabian tribe, were in control of the region in the second millennium B.C. They were succeeded by the Sabaeans, under whom a kingdom was established about the tenth century B.C. Under one of the Sabaean kings, the famous Ma'rib dam was build around the year 750 B.C. to regulate irrigation and agricultural activity. As sedentary people, the Sabaeans achieved a high level of development which enabled them to extend their contacts and influence to the eastern coastline and possibly the interior of Africa.

Several religions existed side by side in southern Arabia, often in an uneasy truce, but by far the major religion in the region was polytheistic. The generosity of pre-Islamic southern Arabia to the deities was well reflected in the good condition of the temples and the priests' comfortable position. About one-third of the sacred spice crop was appropriated to the gods, and this represented an important source of revenue for the priests.[7] Before the fall of the kingdom in the sixth century A.D., Judaism and, to a lesser degree, Christianity, with their monotheistic messages, were gaining converts.

During the Hellenistic era, or about the end of the fifth century A.D., the prosperity of southern Arabia declined under the Himyarites, mainly because it lost part of its Indian trade to Egypt. Meanwhile, Byzantium began to show a strong interest in southern Arabia not only for religious but also for strategic reasons. The strategic reasons were two: the geographical location of southern Arabia as a link with India, and its potential for checking the Persian Empire from the south. Thus, in 525 A.D. the Abyssinian ruler, under inducement from Byzantium, con-

10

quered southern Arabia. Shortly thereafter (575 A.D.), the Persians captured the region and retained it as a Persian province until the Islamic conquest.

The north of Arabia (the northern boundary of which may be defined by an imaginary line running from the head of the Gulf of Aqaba to the head of the Arabian Gulf in the east) lacked the agricultural civilization which developed in the southern region. To be sure, there were a few agricultural communities scattered throughout northern Arabia, but on the whole, water was scarce and vegetation was sparse. Here the nomadic way of life was the rule rather than the exception. The family, clan (made up of several related familes) and tribe (made up of several clans) dominated the life of the Bedouin. All members of a tribe usually claimed descent from a single ancestor, real or fictitious. Blood relations were of primary importance and the tribe constituted the largest organization of kin.[8] Mutual support of relatives, particularly against strangers, was a duty of all tribe members. An old Arab saying reflects this line of familial obligation, "brothers align together against a cousin, and cousins align together against a stranger."

The political organization of the tribe was simple and democratic. The leader was selected on the basis of achievement and merit. Although a son could inherit his father's position of leadership, he had to have the qualifications necessary for the position and to receive acceptance by the members of the tribe. The tribe protected its interests and those of its members by preventing others from encroaching upon its property or traditional grazing grounds. Intertribal blood feuds were not uncommon and a tribe would stand as one in the face of opposition from the outside. On occasion, conflicts between tribes were arbitrated by an outside party selected by the feuding tribes, but the decision of such a person was not binding. Conflicts within the tribe or clan were resolved in daily assemblies.[9]

The Bedouins who established agricultural communities or settled in cities retained essentially the same tribal system and moral precepts, except that authority tended to be more centralized in these settlements. Among the major cities of northern Arabia was Mecca – a revered city which has survived to the present time in modern Saudi Arabia.

As in southern Arabia, the dominant religion in pre-Islamic northern Arabia was polytheistic. Bernard Lewis describes it:

> The religion of the nomads was a form of polydaemonism related to the paganism of the ancient Semites. The beings it adored were in origin the inhabitants and patrons of single places, living in trees, fountains, and especially in sacred stones. There were some gods in the true sense, transcending in their authority the boundaries of purely tribal cults. The three most important were Manat, 'Uzza, Allat, the last of whom was mentioned by Herodotus. These three were themselves subordinate to a higher deity, usually called Allah. The religion of the tribes had no real priesthood; the migratory

11

nomads carried their gods with them in a red tent forming a kind of ark of the covenant, which accompanied them to battle. Their religion was not personal but communal. The tribal faith centred around the tribal god symbolised usually by a stone, sometimes by some other object. It was guarded by the Sheikhly house, which thus gained some religious prestige. God and cult were the badge of tribal identity and the sole ideological expression of the sense of unit and cohesion of the tribe. Conformity to the tribal cult expressed political loyalty. Apostasy was the equivalent of treason.[10]

Some Christian and Jewish communities, made up mainly of Arab converts, were in existence throughout the land. The influence of the Near Eastern cultures and peoples on the Arabian peninsula occurred through the border states, caravan trade, and religious conversion into Christianity and, more commonly, into Judaism.

In addition to being a centre for the caravan trade, being about mid-way between Syria and Yemen, Mecca was an important religious centre even before Islam. Arabian tribes from all corners of the peninsula suspended disagreements to make their annual pilgrimage to Mecca to worship in the Ka'ba – a square, stone-walled temple – and to "celebrate the holy armistice."[11] Not too far from Mecca, there was a famous market called Okaz, unique in many respects, which served as a festival centre for Bedouins from the whole of Arabia. The most common of all celebrations at Okaz was the recitation of poetry and rhetorical diction, which was one of the most important activities in the Arabian peninsula. Many of the classical Arab poets, whose magnificient poetry has immort-alized their names, lived in the pre-Islamic era. The role of poetry and the Arabic language in uniting the Arabian nomads cannot be over-emphasized. According to Brockelmann, "the Arabs owed their awareness of constituting a people, in spite of all tribal contradictions, principally to their most important common possession, poetry, which to a certain extent evolved and expanded under the auspices of religion."[12]

THE RISE OF ISLAM

In this setting, Muhammad, the Prophet of Islam, was born in Mecca about the year 570. He belonged to a clan, *banu* Hashim, which was part of the tribe of Quraysh. He was an orphan, raised by his grandfather. Through his youth, Muhammad increasingly felt polytheism to be empty, and his belief in God (Allah) became a dominant force. On Mt. Hira, near Mecca, at the age of 40 he received the call to religious work. His wife and a few close friends, several of whom were from influential Mecca families, were among the first believers in the new religion of Islam. The chief elements of the Prophet's teaching in Mecca at that time were the "unity of God, the wickedness of idolatry and the imminence of the divine judgment."[13]

Initially the people of Mecca paid scant attention to Muhammad's preaching. But as his preaching became more intense and followers grew in number, the elites of Mecca were threatened. They turned against Muhammad and his followers and made Mecca unsafe for converts to the new religion. As a consequence, Prophet Muhammad and his supporters migrated to Medina (then called Yathrib), less than 300 miles to the north of Mecca, in 622. This year of *Hijra*, that is, migration, marked the start of the Muslim lunar calendar. Within 10 years from the date of migration, the whole of Arabia was converted to Islam, and Muhammad and his followers were able to return to Mecca for pilgrimage in 632.

The main pillars or precepts of Islam are simple and direct. They include belief in the oneness of God and in Muhammad as His Prophet; prayer five times a day; fasting from sunrise to sunset during *Ramadan*, the ninth month of the Muslim calendar; *zakat*, or the giving of alms to the poor; and pilgrimage to Mecca during one's lifetime, if feasible.

Islam recognizes the divine origin of both Christianity and Judaism, but holds that God's final revelations were transmitted through Muhammad, the "seal" of all prophets. The basic source of Islamic law is the Koran, the Muslims' Holy Book. Next comes the *Shari'a* which includes details, based on the Prophet's words and example, developed and elaborated by jurists. Christianity, Judaism and Islam, the three great monotheistic religions, have many elements in common, an important one of which is the worship of the same God. In this connection, Atiyah states that "The God of the Muslims is the same as the God of the Jews and the Christians, but without the racial exclusiveness attributed to him by the former, or the intricate metaphysical theology woven about him by the latter."[14] However, Islam differs from the other two religions by being at once a religion and a system of organized social, economic, and political relations. The early caliphate manifested a pure expression of Islam as a religion and a political system: the caliph (literally meaning successor) was simultaneously the religious leader and head of state. Thus, to Muslims, religion combines spiritual and secular elements, thereby diminishing the difference between "church" and "state." Perhaps because of this Islam lacks the ministerial bureaucracy which is often both prevalent and elaborate in Christianity.

The first major constitutional crisis encountered by Islam occurred at the time of the death of Muhammad in 632. Prior to his death, Muhammad did not establish a line of succession, and it remained for his survivors to settle this issue. The death of Muhammad was, of course, a stunning blow to his followers who would hardly believe that he died. At that crucial time, Abu Bakr, an old friend of Muhammad's and one of the first believers, announced to the people: "Whoso worshippeth Mohammad, let him know that Mohammad is dead; but whoso worshippeth God, let him know that God liveth and dieth not."[15]

The first four caliphs who succeeded Muhammad constitute an important chapter in Arab history. Abu Bakr was the first caliph to be elected after the death of Muhammad. Upon election, he moved quickly to reconsolidate the Islamic community of Arabia and expand its horizons to the world beyond. It took him only a year to reestablish firm control over the whole of Arabia and ensure the commitment of its inhabitants to Islam. With reference to this feat, Atiyah, among others, notes:

> This rapid recovery of Islam and the tremendous consequences that followed it have been interpreted as meaning that Mohammed did not so much create a new movement as stimulate and redirect the latent forces of an Arab national revival and expansion already present when he appeared – an urge among the Arabs towards unity and an aspiration to a higher religious ideal than the primitive polytheism and animism of the older order.[16]

THE RISE OF THE ARAB EMPIRE

At the time of Muhammad's death, a Muslim expedition was being organized against the Byzantine border states to avenge the death of co-religionists in previous clashes. The first caliph, Abu Bakr, honoured the Prophet's earlier command and ordered the expedition to proceed, despite advice that the campaign was untimely in view of the fragility of the infant Muslim community after the death of the Prophet. The success of the expedition exceeded the Arabs' fondest expectations, and with this the Arab-Islamic conquests of the seventh century A.D. began.

Within the span of four years, 633-637, the Muslim Arabs conquered Syria and Iraq. The decisive Battle of Yarmuk (636) resulted in the defeat of the Byzantine troops in Syria and the ascendancy of the Arabs and the new religion of Islam. The Near Eastern campaign was followed by the conquest of Egypt which was completed in three years, 639-42, with assistance from the Coptic Christians who were in opposition to Byzantium. Further Arab advances to the west of Egypt and to the north and east of the Fertile Crescent were slow in coming. However, following the death of the fourth caliph, Ali, in 661, and the establishment of the Umayyad dynasty in Damascus (661-750), the borders and influence of the Arab Empire grew steadily. The former residents of Arabia, first by conquest and later by peaceful settlement, went as far as central Asia to the east, and through North Africa to the shores of the Atlantic in the west. The highest point of the Umayyad rule occurred in the first 15 years of the eighth century which witnessed further expansion of the Arab Empire in Asia and, following a landing in Spain in 710, the occupation of the Iberian peninsula.

From its inception and for a long time thereafter, the migration of Muslim Arabs from the Arabian peninsula continued without interruption. The long duration of this movement, which lasted for several centuries, is one of its most distinctive features, setting it apart from all the

14

previous migrations of Semitic tribes from the peninsula. It also proved to be of pervasive and lasting effect on the region.

Two additional features of this wave of migration are worthy of note. First, the victorious Muslim Arabs effected a fundamental transformation of the social, cultural, religious, linguistic and ethnic fabric of all hitherto existing societies in the region.[17] To be sure, the Arabs were influenced by the ancient civilizations of Mesopotamia, of the eastern shores of the Mediterranean and of Egypt, and also by the Greco-Roman civilization. However, they were successful in creating a new synthesis of pre-existing cultures which had a distinctive Arab stamp. This distinctiveness is a product of two processes which were at work simultaneously: Islamisation and Arabisation. A proper understanding of the relationship between the twin processes of Islamisation and Arabisation is essential for understanding Arab identity in the Arab world and Arab ethnicity in the Canadian setting.

In the early days of preaching the new religion, Prophet Muhammad's efforts were confined to the Arabs and the Arabian peninsula. As a consequence, Arabism and Islam were at first coterminous. However, following the Islamic conquests of the seventh century, the relationship between Arabism and Islam became more subtle and more complex. Arabisation and Islamisation tended to go hand in hand, but they did not always do so. Where one process succeeded, the second did not automatically follow. Nor are the two processes identical. Whereas Arabisation involved socio-cultural and linguistic conversion, Islamisation involved religious conversion. George Antonius clarifies the relationship between these two processes:

> The two processes, islamisation and arabisation, were not at work together, but, although intimately interconnected, were by no means identical. Nor did they halt at the same frontiers. Islamisation, essentially a spiritual force, progressed much further afield and was able to sweep barriers which arabisation, involving material displacement, could not always overstep. Broadly speaking, every country which became permanently arabised became also permanently islamised. But the converse is not true. . . .
>
> Thus two worlds, one considerably more extensive than the other, were created: the Moslem world and the Arab world, of which the first contained the second. In course of time, the world of Islam reached out to India, China and the westernmost recesses of Africa; whereas the Arab world remained confined to those countries in which the process of arabisation had progressed so far and so deep as to have achieved three lasting results: the enthronement of Arabic as the national language, the introduction of Arab manners and ways of thought and the implantation of an appreciable Arab stock in the racial soil.[18]

As a general characterization of the situation, the above quotation is accurate. Such countries as Iran and Afghanistan offer notable examples

15

of regions which are Islamised but not Arabised. In neither of these countries has Arabic become the national language, and in neither of them do the people regard themselves nor are they regarded by others as Arabs. But the above quotation requires an important clarification. Although Antonious says that "every country which became permanently arabised became also permanently islamised," it should be pointed out that the process of Arabisation did not mean inevitable conversion of the total population to Islam. For amidst the predominantly Muslim population of the Fertile Crescent and North Africa, there were and still are large numbers of Christians and Jews who preserved their religious traditions. These Christian and Jewish natives of the region were Arabised but not Islamised. In fact, native Christians and Jews made significant and creative contributions to the development of Arab civilization.

The second most distinctive and unique feature of the Arab Muslim migration from the peninsula is the extent and permanence of its effects. For the first time in history, the Arabs united "the vast territories stretching from the borders of India and China to the approaches of Greece, Italy and France."[19] This was accomplished for a while by their military and political power, but "for much longer by their language and faith."[20] Today, after the elapse of more than 13 centuries, the vast region known as the Arab world continues to exhibit the essential features of Arab culture and civilization. The noted historian, Philip Hitti, states: "The Babylonians, the Assyrians, the Chaldaeans, the Aramaeans, the Phoenicians – all of whose ancestors were nurtured in the Arabian peninsula – were, but are no more. The Arabs were and remain."[21]

One of the most important effects of the Arabisation of the peoples of the Near East and North Africa was the homogenization of the region socially and culturally. With reference to this process, Bernard Lewis says:

> It was the Arabisation of the conquered provinces rather than their military conquest that is the true wonder of the Arab expansion. By the eleventh century Arabic had become not only the chief idiom of everyday use from Persia to the Pyrenees, but also the chief instrument of culture, superseding old culture languages like Coptic, Aramaic, Greek and Latin. As the Arabic language spread, the distinction between Arab conqueror and Arabised conquered faded into relative insignificance. . . .
>
> Even beyond the vast areas that were permanently Arabised, Arabic exercised a tremendous influence on other Muslim languages. Muslim Persian and Turkish, and later also Urdu, Malay and Swahili, are new languages written in the Arabic script and including an enormous Arabic vocabulary, as great as the Greek and Latin elements in English, and covering the whole world of concepts and ideas.

The survival and expansion of Arabic involved more than the language itself – more, for example, than the continued use of Latin in the medieval West. With the language came Arab taste and tradition in the choice and treatment of themes.[22]

An important concomitant of the twin processes of Arabisation and Islamisation was the process of amalgamation. The contemporary inhabitants of the Arab world are the resultant amalgam, or "demographic compound," to use Sayegh's phrase, of centuries of intermarriage between the Muslim Arabs and "the earlier populations – who were already an amalgam of aboriginal Near Eastern peoples, immigrants from the north and east, residues of imperial settlers, and, above all, diverse Semitic (including Arab) groups."[23] The racial purity of the different peoples that settled the Arab world melted away in the process of mutual physical and cultural absorption. Currently, it is impossible to determine the degree of Arab stock implanted in a given Arab country, much less in a given Arab individual. Thus when we think of Arabs today, we think not of a pure race but of a racially mixed group displaying a wide range of biological variability and all shades of skin colour, hair colour and eye colour.

THE POLITICAL ABYSS

The Arab or Muslim Empire was in existence for about nine hundred years. Following a relatively short period of strong, centralized authority after the Muslim-Arab conquests of the seventh century, independent dynasties emerged in different regions of the Near East and North Africa. As a consequence of this, the centre of gravity of the empire shifted among such capital cities as Damascus, Baghdad, and Cairo. The shifts which occurred in capital cities manifested the rise or fall, as the case may have been, of a particular caliphate or dynasty. For example, the Umayyads, with their capital in Damascus, were succeeded in 750 by the Abbasids who moved the capital to Baghdad. The Arab dynasty in Spain, being Umayyad, became independent in 756. By the end of the eighth century, independent dynasties were to be found in Morocco and Tunisia. The Fatimid Caliphate was established in North Africa in 910 and this was followed by the Fatimid conquest of Egypt and the founding of Cairo in 969. Significantly, by the eleventh century the economic, political and military structure of the world of Islam was both weak and vulnerable.

Because of dissension and internal political disunity, the empire became an easy target for attacks from the outside. In the second half of the eleventh century, Christian forces achieved major territorial gains in Spain and Sicily. These developments were only a prelude to the total eclipse of the Arabs in that region of Europe and the arrival of the Crusaders in the Near East at the end of the century. The most severe attacks and savage destruction, however, were inflicted by the Mongols in the thirteenth and fourteenth centuries. The Mongols were merciless: in the thirteenth century they massacred tens of thousands of people, razed flourishing cities, monuments and orchards to the ground, and left behind "a bleeding remnant and charred wilderness."[24] Again, at the end of the fourteenth century Syria was ravaged by the Tartar tribe under the leadership of Timur. Then the Ottoman Turks arrived in the closing years of the fifteenth century to finish what the Mongols had started. The empire, or what was left of it, was now in a state of manifest decay.

The Ottoman Turks occupied Syria and Egypt in 1517 and found little resistance to their eventual conquest of the entire Near East and North Africa. They became the uncontested masters of the Arabs until the demise of the Ottoman Empire at the end of World War I. It has often been noted that the advent of the Ottoman colonial rule at the beginning of the sixteenth century led the Arabs to fall into slumber. Brockelmann observes that through persistent maladministration, lasting for several centuries, the Turks "inflicted the worst damage on the once so flourishing civilization of Iran and Mesopotamia."[25] In a similar vein, Landau writes:

> Though the Ottomans were converts to Islam, they were by race, historical background, temperament and language very different from the Arabs. But it was they who became the masters, and, often, brutally uncompromising masters, of the Middle East and most of North Africa, the Arabs, henceforth, being reduced to the status of a colonized people. The man in power, the man in government, the man in command of the army, the man at court, in the mosque and the university, was a Turk who despised the Arab as one by nature inferior.[26]

Despite the downfall of the Arab Empire in the sixteenth century, four hundred years of Ottoman colonial rule, and Western imperial rule after World War I, the Arabism of the inhabitants of the region has survived to the present day.

ARAB CIVILIZATION AND CULTURE

The Arab ethnic character is a product of the past achievements of Arab civilization and of present circumstance. One of the forces contributing to the feeling of collective identity among the Arab peoples today is the widespread awareness of a brilliant past, an Arab civilization that made major contributions to the advancement and well-being of mankind. During the Dark Ages, that period between the fall of the Roman Empire and the Renaissance, it was the Arabs who succeeded in preserving and advancing civilization. As Landau notes, "the Arab contribution was twofold. First, they were the transmitters of the legacy of Greece. Next, their enrichment of this inheritance, the fruit of their own endeavors, laid the foundations of western culture. . . . As other civilizations perished, the Arabian flourished."[27]

Islam and Arabism, each in its own way, left an indelible mark on the advancement of civilization. The Islamic faith provided both a spiritual force and an ethos promoting intellectual and scholarly development. Arabism, on the other hand, through the vehicle of the Arabic language, provided an indispensable mechanism for unifying and consolidating what might otherwise have been disparate achievements in different fields. The richness, flexibility and assimilative capacity of the Arabic language contributed immeasurably to the development of an enduring civilization.

A few examples should be sufficient to indicate the magnitude of Arab contributions to civilization.[28] The world is indebted to the Arabs for the creation of modern algebra (an Arabic word), the decimal system, the zero (cipher), and for brilliant work in trigonometry. In philosophy, Arab scholars translated and extended the works of Aristotle and other Greek philosophers. Such medieval scholastics as Roger Bacon, Albertus Magnus, Johannes duns Scotus and, later, Copernicus, profited from and explicitly acknowledged their indebtedness to their Arab predecessors, although later generations of European philosophers did not give credit to Arab philosophy. In medicine, the Arabs made great advances in diagnosis, drug treatment and surgery (particulary that of the eye). In astronomy and chemistry, Europe's indebtedness to the Arabs is indicated by the adoption of many Arabic words, such as zenith, azimuth, nadir, alkali, antimony, and realgar, i.e., red sulphide arsenic. The works of Arab geographers and cartographers, together with the writings of such travellers as Ibn Battuta, were main sources of knowledge, particularly of Africa, for many centuries. Finally, Arab art, music, architecture, calligraphy, textiles, ceramics and glassware, among many other things, have left their mark on the West.

Although the average westerner may not be aware of these contributions, Arabs, in their homelands as well as in their adopted lands, reflect on these contributions with pride. In Canada, for example, two members of the Arab-Canadian community published a book in 1973 which identified Arabic words adopted by the English language.[29] In the Foreword, James Peters, one of the authors, notes:

> We hope our little lexicon will serve as a gentle corrective to the mistaken stereotype of the Arabs as a nomadic, desert-based people, living in barren land and in a barren culture. This stereotype is neither valid for the past nor for the present. To paraphrase Donne, no culture is an island unto itself. Our present collection, we trust, will indicate some measure of the impact of Arabs within the human family.[30]

Although the Arab Empire and associated civilization has passed, the Arabic language and culture as a system of normative values and an adaptive mechanism and design for living have survived. Certainly, the culture has changed in response to internal and external pressures and is different today from what it was in centuries past. The advancement of Western culture and civilization has been a particularly significant source of change, for the Arab world as for the world at large. But the prevailing system of normative values, which penetrated very deeply into all major institutional areas, has retained its Arab stamp.

ARAB ETHNICITY IN CANADA

Official Designations of Arabs in Canada

The pioneer immigrants from the Arab Near East originated from Syria, and when they arrived in Canada in the latter part of the nineteenth and early twentieth centuries they were officially classified as Syrians. The 1901 Canadian Census combined them with Turks ("Syrians and Turks") because at that time Syria was under Turkish control. In the five subsequent decennial censuses (1911-1951), the Syrians were grouped under a separate category ("Syrians"). The designation Syrian was practical and useful, for the large majority of Arabic-speaking people in Canada came from Syria. For their part, the immigrants themselves accepted it as an appropriate label, until the emergence of modern Syria and Lebanon as separate political entities. At this point, the Arab Canadians began to identify specifically with either Syria or Lebanon, depending on the location of their ancestral village or community of origin. Thus, in the 1961 Canadian Census the designation was slightly modified to read "Syrian-Lebanese," presumably in response to the political realities of the region as well as the dual identifications of Arab Canadians.

In the 1960s and 1970s, increasing numbers of Arab immigrants came to Canada from countries other than Syria and Lebanon. Since 1962, official Canadian immigration statistics have grouped all the new arrivals, Arab or otherwise, under the country of last permanent residence. The entries for immigrants from the Arab world include, in addition to Syria and Lebanon, Egypt, Morocco, Jordan, Tunisia, Algeria and Iraq, as well as other Arab states. All of these entries represent politically independent states whose inhabitants, while not sharing a common citizenship, do share a common national origin. In general, they are conscious of their Arab identity which manifests itself in the Arabic language and cultural traditions.

Unfortunately, the 1971 Canadian Census excluded the Arabs (and thus the Syrian-Lebanese) from the list of ethnic groups who were considered for detailed demographic analysis. However, a limited amount of information is provided in this census regarding the number and geographical distribution of Canadians for whom Arabic is the mother tongue. The use of mother tongue for defining ethnicity underestimates the size of the Arab-Canadian community.

The main conclusion to be drawn from this is that the criteria which were used in the past to classify Arab immigrants, or Arab Canadians, are no longer appropriate for determining the boundaries of this ethnic group. For example, given the admission into Canada of a large number of post-war immigrants from different Arab states, the designation Syrian, or Syrian-Lebanese, becomes too restrictive. Also, the criterion utilized at present in official immigration statistics, that of country of last permanent residence, is inadequate because the resulting data will include non-Arabs originating from Arab countries and exclude Arab nationals originating from non-Arab countries. Finally, statistical data based on Arabic mother tongue will exclude a large number of Canadian-born Arabs for whom English or French is typically the mother tongue. Some of these Arab Canadians may not even know their ancestral language.

Dimensions of Arab Ethnicity

Ethnic groups are usually distinguished on the basis of physical and/or cultural characteristics, including one or more of the following criteria: religion, language and national origin. In addition, an ethnic group may have a shared sense of peoplehood or may be regarded by outsiders as a separate and distinct group or both.[31] These are the traditional criteria which, in varying degrees and combinations, define ethnic groups.

First, it should be emphasized that physical or racial characteristics do not provide a valid basis for determining Arab ethnicity. No grouping of traits can be identified as being uniquely Arabian. This is because the contemporary inhabitants of the Arab world are an amalgam of many centuries of intermarriage among migrants from the Arabian peninsula and the indigenous residents of the Near East and, in addition, Persians, Greeks, Romans, Byzantines, European Crusaders, and Turks. Similarly, in Canada, Arab immigrants and their descendants have intermarried with various ethnic groups and they, as well as their offspring, are physically indistinguishable from other Mediterranean or Caucasian immigrant groups.

Nor is religion an adequate criterion for determining Arab ethnicity. While the popular Western image tends to regard Arabism and Islam as one and the same thing, a Muslim is not necessarily an Arab, nor is an Arab necessarily a Muslim. Although there are interrelationships, Arabism and Islam are different. An Arab may be a Muslim or a Christian. A Muslim, on the other hand, may be an Arab, a Turk, a Russian, an Iranian, a Chinese, an Indian, or a national of some other country. The religious pluralism which exists in the Arab world has been transferred to the Canadian setting and, as a result, the Arab-Canadian community is a religious mosaic within a larger cultural mosaic. In terms of religious faith, the Arabs in Canada include, among others, Maronites, Melkites, Syrian (now Antiochian) Orthodox, Protestants, Druses, Shi'i and Sunni Muslims. Thus, religious identity is a variable aspect of Arab ethnicity – a source of difference rather than similarity or common experience.

21

Despite the above, for specific Arab-speaking groups, notably the Maronites of Lebanon, religion provides, at the social psychological level, the primary basis for group consciousness. Members of this religious group define their ethnicity not in terms of their Arabic language and heritage, but rather in terms of Maronite (Christian) historical and territorial roots. For many centuries, the Maronites inhabited recognized areas in the mountainous regions of Lebanon and, with the advent of the French mandate over Lebanon following World War I, the fate of the Maronites became intertwined with that of the state of Lebanon. As Kayal and Kayal observe, "the 'cause' of one became the 'cause' of the other, making the history of the contemporary Maronites the history of Lebanon as well. . . . Because they are the largest Christian community in Lebanon, the Maronites have a very strong identification with the land and a strong sense of nationalism which they insist on tracing back to the pre-Arab Phoenician presence in that area."[32]

While the Maronite church has been largely confined to Lebanon, other Eastern Christian churches, such as the Melkite and Orthodox, encompass many groups and nationalities and thus are both universal and international.[33] Also, while the Maronites have been susceptible to Latinization and Westernization, other Arab Christians have tended to retain their attachment to the Eastern heritage. Since the end of World War II, there has been a determined effort on the part of early and post-war Maronite immigrants to Canada to avoid being mistaken for Syrians. Lebanese nationalism versus Arab (or Syrian) nationalism often, but not always, reflects the social psychological and structural differences between Christian Maronites and other Arab world Christians and Muslims. Such distinctions are, in actuality, exceedingly complex.[34] Loyalties cross sectarian, religious and national boundaries. This mixture of loyalties can also be found among Canadians of Arab origins. Lebanese or Arab identifications or both are far from simple distinctions between Maronite Christian Lebanese, other Christian Lebanese and Muslim Lebanese – labels which, when known, would presumably inform one of the individual's political or ethnic leanings. Such reliance on religious labels would be overly simplistic and erroneous. The Lebanese situation has been complex historically and continues to be so during the current outbreaks of violent political dissension and civil war in the state of Lebanon.

In general, immigrants from the Arab East, despite their uncertain racial origins, religious diversity and variable citizenships, have projected, both among themselves and onto the Canadian population, the oneness which underlies their origin – the objective criterion on which Arab ethnicity is based. They share the Arabic language, similar myths and folklore, Arabic music, Arabic art forms, Arabic food, and similar customs and cultural ethos.[35] To be sure, there are subcultural differences, both in their ancestral homelands and their adopted lands, but objectively these differences tend to represent subgroup variations in such things as citizenship, dialect, sectarian loyalty, custom and political ideology, rather than departures from the Arab cultural mainstream.

With reference to Arab Canadians, there have been many moves by the immigrant generations to teach the ancestral language to their offspring. The teaching of the Arabic language has often occurred at home, and more formally within the context of religious institutions and voluntary organizations. Some of the children of Arab immigrants have learned Arabic in order to communicate better with their parents or other relatives. Knowledge of reading and writing in Arabic is often more limited than knowledge of spoken Arabic and the further Canadian-born children are from the immigrant generation, the less likely they are to know the Arabic language. For these Arab Canadians, as for the descendants of many other immigrant groups, English or French has become the mother tongue.

The above observations about language also hold for Arab sociocultural influences and ethnic identity. Each of these factors takes the form of a continuum, ranging from very low to very high. When the analyst considers all of these factors simultaneously, it becomes increasingly difficult to determine ethnic group membership. For example, what proportion of Arabian ancestry would qualify a person for membership in the Arab-Canadian ethnic group? Should a person know the Arabic language, or at least have some familiarity with it, in order to be considered an Arab Canadian? And to what degree should a person identify with the Arab-Canadian ethnic group in order to qualify for membership in it? Clearly, these are not easy questions and the answers to them cannot be established without resorting to arbitrary decisions.

For present purposes, the term Arab Canadian will refer to first generation Christian or Muslim immigrants and their offspring who originated, directly or indirectly, from any of the Arab states and whose roots are in the Arabic language and culture. The term will also apply to second and succeeding generation persons of Arab or mixed Arab and Canadian parentage, again regardless of religious affiliation or ancestral country of origin. It is recognized that some members of the second or later generations of Arab Canadians may have a small portion of Arab ancestry, may have English or French as their mother tongue, and may be fully Canadianized – culturally, attitudinally and in terms of world view and outlook on life. Also, they may display varying degrees of attachment to and identification with their Arab ancestry.

This definition of Arab Canadians is broader than the classification systems in the Canadian Census and other Statistics Canada publications. Even if the Canadian Census established a generic category of Arab, it would not be identical to our definition, given the census practice of establishing children's ethnicity in accordance with that of the father. According to this practice, the offspring of a non-Arab man and an Arab woman would not be classified as Arab. The utility of our broad definition of the term Arab Canadian is that it can assist the researcher in capturing a wider range of attitudinal and behavioural variability among Canadians of Arab origins.

To sum up, the Arab-Canadian community is a blend of diverse influences from east to west. Included in this community are persons who came to Canada as immigrants, at different points in time, in search of freedom and economic opportunity, as well as persons who were born and raised in Canada and who know no other land as home. Whether they are Christians or Muslims, Arab Canadians combine in varying ways and degrees a common ancestral heritage within the Canadian cultural heritage. Syria, or Lebanon, or Egypt evokes different meanings to the diversity of Arab Canadians. Likewise, the impact of Eastern religions and Arab socio-cultural traditions on their lives in Canada is prone to variation at the social psychological level. Yet they are bound together by common ancestral roots, linguistic and cultural, and by being a part of the variegated Canadian culture and by sharing a Canadian identity with over 23 million countrymen.

NOTES

1. Edward Atiyah, *The Arabs* (Harmondsworth, Middlesex, 1958), p. 7.
2. G.M. Wickens, "Introduction to the Middle East," in R.M. Savory, ed., *Introduction to Islamic Civilization* (Cambridge, 1976), p. 4.
3. Philip K. Hitti, *History of the Arabs* (London, 1970), p. 3ff. The Semitic groups such as the Jews, Phoenicians and Arabs are supposed to be descended from a single ancestor: Shem, the son of Noah.
4. *Ibid.*, p. 9.
5. *Ibid.*, pp. 67-81; and Carl Brockelmann, trans. Joel Carmichael and Moshe Perlman, *History of the Islamic Peoples* (New York, 1960), pp. 6-8.
6. Bernard Lewis, *The Arabs in History* (Hutchinson University Library, 1964), p. 23.
7. *Ibid.*, p. 25.
8. Brockelmann, *op. cit.*, p. 4.
9. *Ibid.*, p. 5.
10. Lewis, *op. cit.*, p. 30.
11. Atiyah, *op. cit.*, p. 21.
12. Brockelmann, *op. cit.*, p. 11.
13. Lewis, *op. cit.*, p. 39.
14. Atiyah, *op. cit.*, p. 13.
15. *Ibid.*, p. 30.
16. *Ibid.*, pp. 31-32.
17. Cf. Fayez A. Sayegh, *Arab Unity* (New York, 1958), p. 14ff.
18. George Antonious, *The Arab Awakening* (London, 1938), pp. 16-18.
19. Lewis, *op. cit.*, p. 140.

20. *Ibid.*
21. Philip K. Hitti, *The Arabs: A Short History* (London, 1965), p. 1.
22. Lewis, *op. cit.*, pp. 132-33.
23. Sayegh, *op. cit.*, p. 15.
24. Rom Landau, *Arab Contribution to Civilization* (San Francisco, 1958), p. 72.
25. Brockelmann, *op. cit.*, p. 240.
26. Landau, *op. cit.*, p. 72.
27. *Ibid.*, p. 9.
28. For a more detailed account, see *ibid.*; Wickens, *op. cit.*, pp. 1-13.
29. James Peters and Habeeb Salloum, *Arabic Contributions to the English Vocabulary* (Toronto, 1973).
30. *Ibid.*, p. iii.
31. See Milton M. Gordon, *Assimilation in American Life* (New York, 1964), p. 24; and Louis Wirth, "The Problem of Minority Groups," in Ralph Linton, ed., *The Science of Man in the World Crisis* (New York, 1945), p. 35.
32. Philip M. Kayal and Joseph M. Kayal, *The Syrian-Lebanese in America* (Boston, 1975), p. 35.
33. *Ibid.*, p. 41.
34. For example, in a recent study of the Arab American community of Boston, Elaine C. Hagopian notes:

    The Boston community does have a sense of its Middle Eastern identity, but in highly specialized ways. Most of these people have not considered themselves to be Arab, do not want to be called Arab, and yet seem to love everything Arab – especially when it is not called Arab. People often refer to their language as Syrian rather than Arabic, though this practice varies. Most are unaware of the history of the Middle East and how it affected them and their relations with other groups in the area. Many are bitter with memories, passed on from generation to generation in great flourish and detail, of the 1860 massacre of Christians, for which they blame the "real" Arabs, that is, the Muslims. None have any realization of how that massacre came about or who committed it. Even those members of the community who identify themselves as Arabs have a strong residue of bitterness over how they believe Christians were treated by Muslims in the Arab world. It is one of the first questions they raise with visiting Arabs.

    See "The Institutional Development of the Arab-American Community of Boston: A Sketch," in Elaine C. Hagopian and Ann Paden, eds., *The Arab-Americans: Studies in Assimilation* (Wilmette, Ill., 1969), p. 77.
35. The emphasis on language and culture as the primary basis for defining Arab ethnicity is consistent with the views of contemporary writers. For example, Antonius observes that the word "Arab" gradually came to mean a citizen of the extensive Arab world – not any inhabitant of it, but

25

that great majority whose racial descent, even when it was not of pure Arab lineage, had become submerged in the tide of arabisation; whose manners and traditions had been shaped in an Arab mould; and, most decisive of all, whose mother tongue is Arab. The term applies to Christians as well as to Muslims, and to the off-shoots of each of these creeds, the criterion being not islamisation but the degree of arabisation. *Op. cit.*, p. 18.

TWO

The Ancestral Homeland:
Social and Cultural Background

All immigrants to Canada bring with them much more than their physical possessions. Their view of life and the world has been profoundly shaped by the religious, family and socio-political foundations of their past. Language, conceptual frameworks and world views have been shaped by their previous experiences and the life-long echo of ethnic memories. Even second and third generation Canadians may carry the remnants of past civilizations which reappear, in many-sided forms, generation after generation. For Arab Canadians, no less than for other ethno-cultural groups, an understanding of their present and future involves some understanding of their origins.

In an attempt to understand the roots of the Arab-Canadian experience, the present discussion will be organized around five major institutional areas: the familial, religious, political, economic and educational. In each instance, the discussion will focus on main social and cultural themes in the Arab world, as well as major variations around these themes. Similarities and differences found within the Arab-Canadian community are often intimately linked with common and variable socio-cultural elements in the background of Arab immigrants to Canada.

FAMILY AND KINSHIP TIES

The family occupies a focal position in the social organization of the Arab world.[1] While the family is an important institution in Western societies as well, its hold on its members and their activities there is not as great as in the Arab world. The fabric of the Arab family embraces an elaborate system of social controls and mutual obligations to which its members more or less conform. Such obligations permeate a larger kinship group than the nuclear family of husband, wife and children. Many Arabs have experienced, at one point or another in their family cycle, an extended family living arrangement consisting of husband, wife, unmar-

27

ried daughters, unmarried and married sons and their wives and children and, depending on the particular circumstances, perhaps other (particularly female) relatives of the male household head. Even when they are not, in actual fact, living together, the web of family commitments often encompasses a diverse degree of kinship.[2] An example which illustrates the extent of Arab kinship is the case of an Arab emigré who, after living many years in the United States, returned to his village birthplace carrying gifts for some 65 people, all of whom were related to him.[3] The continuing sense of obligation and family commitment tend to remain with Arab immigrants, in spite of the long distances which separate them from their land of birth.[4]

The traditional Arab family is patriarchal and emphasizes sex role differentiation. Women and girls are socialized to be dependent and submissive vis-à-vis male members of the family. The domestic role is stressed for women and, from an early age, young girls are expected to assume responsibilities around the home. In contrast, young boys are given greater freedom from onerous responsibilities in the home and they are also given freedom to explore the larger society.[5] In adult years, this pattern is reflected in a woman's role archetype which focuses primarily on the domestic sphere and a man's role archetype which is "one of concern with matters outside the home."[6] However, it should be noted that the degree of privatization of the adult female role has varied considerably. In particular, among nomadic and village people, many women perform important instrumental or economic tasks outside the home. While there has been a cultural ideal that the women of a family be sheltered and isolated from the larger society, this has been more of an urban than a rural or nomadic phenomenon. Non-urban women played too important an economic role to enforce this ideal. Similarly, the veil, as a symbol of the differentiated status of Muslim women, was confined to urban areas; currently, it is a rapidly disappearing artifact, found only in very traditional pockets of the Arab Near East.

Muslims have allowed the practice of having more than one wife at a time, but it has been limited to a minority of families. Marriage to more than one wife (that is, polygyny) is usually not viable for the majority of people in a society.[7] In the Arab world, the trend is in the direction of an even further reduction in the incidence of this marriage form. Marriage and divorce law reforms in several Arab states reflect this pattern and women's organizations have been active in seeking the legal change necessary to reflect this social change. Monogamy is characteristic, not only of Arab Christian marriages, but also of the overwhelming majority of Arab Muslim marriages, contrary to the stereotypes held by some Westerners.

Most marriages are arranged, particularly among Muslims. The power of the extended family is reflected in this practice. Premarital dating and complete freedom of mate selection are not common. Arranged mar-

28

riages are usually endogamous and a high priority is given to marriage of cousins on the father's side, although this priority is declining in importance. Increasingly, the opinions of the prospective partners are not only given consideration, but may rule the final choice of mate. Even with a degree of increasing individual freedom, however, endogamy remains the prevailing practice, particularly with regard to religious origin.

The prerogatives of patriarchy are reflected in the differential pressures placed on male and female Muslims when they are contemplating a religious intermarriage. Should a Muslim woman wish to marry a non-Muslim, the prospective husband must convert to Islam. In contrast, a Muslim male may marry a non-Muslim woman without the requirement that she convert to his religion. The underlying rationale for this practice is that husbands not only have more power than wives to enforce a particular religious environment within the home, but also, in the event of a divorce, since children traditionally remain with the husband's lineage, the children of a non-Muslim father would be lost to the faith.

The virginity of the unmarried female is highly valued and there are often extreme negative sanctions invoked against women who engage in premarital sexual relations. Negative sanctions regarding extramarital relations are also very strong. The concept of family honour is closely tied to the chastity of its female members. Family honour can be tarnished, not only by verbal or physical attacks from outsiders, but by the unmarried woman's loss of virginity or the married woman's extramarital sexual transgressions. Similar prohibitions do not apply as strongly to the male members of the family. However, males are expected to be the protectors of family honour. In this role, fathers, brothers and husbands are frequently expected both to restrict and to judge the behaviour of daughters, sisters and wives. The concept of family honour, somewhat alien to the Canadian scene, plays an important role in the Arab world, as in many Mediterranean countries.[8] Violence (sometimes against the women in the family) and protracted feuds with outsiders can arise in defence of the family's honour.

Children (particularly sons) are highly valued. The birth of the first son signals a name change for his parents. If, for example, the first son is named Ramsey, the father becomes known as "Abu Ramsey" (the father of Ramsey) and the mother as "Im Ramsey" (the mother of Ramsey). This change in names is important to traditional couples and is generally a cherished transition in adulthood. Similarly, children are often identified by their father's name (for example, as "Ibn Khalid" or the son of Khalid). The high value placed on parenthood, together with the traditional aversion towards contraceptive techniques, means that the average family size in the Arab world is greater than in Canada. However, differences in family size among Arabs are associated with the same factors as in the West. Thus, there is a negative relationship between education and family size and between socio-economic status and family size.

Religion is also related to fertility, with Muslims tending to have more children than Christians.

Thus, the traditional family in the Arab world is male dominant, monogamous, and sexually conservative with particularly heavy restrictions on female conduct. Arabs tend to value children highly and emphasize a broad sense of familism which encompasses obligations, reciprocities and privileges for individual family members. Although precise statistics are lacking, it appears that in the Arab world as elsewhere the functions and obligations of the extended family unit are becoming more circumscribed as the conjugal family unit gains prominence. Further, the self-sufficiency of the larger family system has weakened as it has become more dependent on the larger economy. There have been significant changes in the position of women, in particular in the past three decades as they have had access to formal education.[9] Like other institutions in the Arab world, the family has been experiencing changes, both in its structure and functioning. Familism, however, continues to be a distinctive feature of the region.

RELIGIOUS DIVERSITY

The religious identification of the turn-of-the-century Arab immigrants to Canada was predominantly Christian: Maronite, Melkite, and Orthodox. These three faiths were about equally represented and, together, claimed over 90% of the immigrants. The remainder of the immigrants consisted of other Eastern Christian and Protestant groups, as well as Muslims and Druses. In the post-World War II period, the proportion of Arab Muslim and Druse immigrants increased considerably and, in addition, a new Christian group, the Copts of Egypt, was added. There is today a wide spectrum of religions represented in the Arab-Canadian community and it is estimated that the Christians outnumber the Muslims by a ratio of about three to one.

Social scientists are in agreement that religion provides a strong basis for the development of social identity, as well as ethno centrism. Even more than religion, however, a particular religious sect is often the underlying basis for ingroup formation and community organization. In a recent study of Arabs in the United States, Kayal and Kayal observe that "it is religion as a dynamic social institution which is the key to understanding Arab-American history. It is religion as theology and religion as social interaction which has guided the development of nationalist identities in the Middle East and especially ethnic identities in America."[10] While scholars may debate the degree to which religion has been central to the social adjustment of the Arab people, there is agreement that religion did and does play an important role. The present discussion will focus on the history and traditions of Eastern Christianity and Islam, the two broad religions which supplied the bulk of Arab immigrants to Canada and from which Arab Canadians, differentially, continue to derive their spiritual inspiration.

Arab Christians

Precise figures are not available, but the best estimate is that 6-7%, or about 9,000,000, of the inhabitants of the Arab world are Christians.[11] They live mostly in Egypt, Lebanon, Syria, Iraq, Jordan and the Holy Land (Israeli-occupied territories). Of all the Christian communities in the Arab East, the Copts of Egypt are the largest (about 6-7 million).[12] The Maronites of Lebanon and the Syrian-Antiochian Orthodox are the next largest (about 750,000 each). They are followed by the Melkites (500,000), and the Catholic and Gregorian Armenians (about 400,000).[13] The remainder, a small portion, are made up of Chaldeans, Protestants and Western Christians, among others. The highest proportion of Christians to the total national population is found in Lebanon where there are about equal numbers of Christians and Muslims. Except for the Copts of Egypt and the Maronites of Lebanon who concentrate in their respective countries, Christian communities are dispersed throughout the Fertile Crescent.

The divisions which occurred in the church during the early years of Christianity are reflected in the Eastern Christian churches. To a large degree, they are also reflected in the different types of Christians who emigrated to Canada. The origin of many of these divisions is to be found in the issue of apostolic succession, often taking the form of political rather than theological differences. From among the different bishops that succeeded the apostles as heads of the Christian communities, three stood out as highest in rank. These were the bishops of Rome, Alexandria and Antioch, all of whom claimed apostolic foundation. At the Council of Chalcedon (450 A.D.) two new Great Sees were created: Constantinople and Jerusalem. Because of their recognized authority and jurisdiction, these five bishops were classified as patriarchs. The whole of Christendom was divided among these five self-governing Patriarchates. Eastern Christendom consisted of the Patriarchates of Constantinople, Antioch, Alexandria and Jerusalem, while Western Christendom was under the jurisdiction of the Patriarchate of Rome. The Patriarch of Rome was viewed by Catholics as the head of the Universal Church.

The Eastern Christian churches evolved in interaction with their immediate surroundings. Because of relative social and geographical isolation, different Christian communities came to possess distinctive rituals, traditions and modes of expression.

The geographical domains of the four Eastern patriarchates criss-crossed and overlapped, contributing to religious diversity at the local level. In the context of Eastern Christianity, the word "rite" stands for the total way of life of any given church. It refers, more specifically, to the totality of services provided by the church together with its manifold formal procedures and associated local customs and canon laws. A distinctive liturgical language was also adopted by each church.

Over the years the Eastern churches diverged and converged, exhibiting schisms, the formation of independent churches and some reunions with Rome. The Great Schism between the Patriarchates of Constantinople and Rome, however, occurred in 1054. Eventually this schism came to involve the other Eastern patriarchates (Alexandria, Antioch and Jerusalem) over whom Constantinope had a gread deal of influence. The roots of the separation date back to the nineth century when the Pope supported the "wrong" (i.e., unsuccessful) contender to fill the seat of the Patriarchate of Constantinople.[14] Over the next 200 years, the dispute between Constantinople and Rome was generalized to include differences of rite. Rome's failure to accept certain Byzantine customs was a source of discontent in the Eastern Orthodox Church. The Latin and the Orthodox Churches accused each other of being schismatic, but the fact of separation remains.

Following the occupation of Constantinople by the Ottoman Turks in 1453 and the subsequent creation of the Ottoman Empire, the Patriarch of Constantinople developed a privileged status. "The Turks looked on the Patriarch of Constantinople as the head of all Orthodox Christians in their dominions. The other Patriarchates also within the Ottoman Empire – Alexandria, Antioch, Jerusalem – remained theoretically independent but were in practice subordinate."[15] Despite the Ottomans' sponsorship of the Patriarch of Constantinople, Eastern Christianity did not follow the path of evolution into one monolithic church.

Distinctions within Eastern Christianity were further nourished under the *millet* system of government which was devised by the Turks, whereby non-Muslim sects were recognized as corporate religious communities which had full legal control in matters pertaining to personal status, including marriage, divorce, inheritance and adoption. The Turks relied heavily on the delegation of power and authority in the administration of the empire, resulting in the concentration of power in the hands of a few. As a consequence of this, religious leaders wielded a high degree of power and influence not only in their specialized domain, but also in secular political affairs – a pattern the remnants of which have survived to the present time. In the past, as at the present time, individual and group vested interests have played an important role in perpetuating social distance among different sects and religious groups. Under such circumstances, what is surprising is not the existence of some disharmony, but rather the existence in the vast region of the Arab world of a high degree of harmony in the face of stubborn obstacles to its development.

The Eastern churches are now divided into four major groupings: The Nestorians, the Monophysites, the Eastern Orthodox, and the Uniates.[16] For our purposes, it will be sufficient to comment briefly on the origins of each division in order to place the phenomenon of Arab Christianity in its wider context.

The Nestorian and Monophysite Churches

The Nestorians and Monophysites adhere to antithetical doctrines and both are considered to be heretical groups. They are in communion neither with Rome nor with Constantinople. They separated from the Universal Church in the fifth century partly as a result of theological controversy and partly as a result of regional politics. The former group was named after Nestorius who became Patriarch of Constantinople in 428 and lasted for about three years until he was deposed in 431. Nestorius advocated the doctrine that there were two persons in Christ: Jesus the ordinary man and the "Word of God" that resided in Him. According to this belief, Mary was not the Mother of God. The Monophysites, on the other hand, held that there was one person in Christ – the Divine. Whereas the Nestorians viewed Christ as a human being in whom God resided, the Monophysites discarded Christ's human side and viewed Him solely as a deity. The positions of both of these groups contrasted sharply with that of the Universal Church which "defined the true doctrine to be that Christ was a single person but with two natures, the divine and the human; true God and true man."[17]

Nestorianism was rejected by Byzantium, and it had no chance of survival were it not for its protection by Persia which was the Roman Empire's rival state to the east. Nor were the Nestorians welcome in Egypt because Nestorius had been deposed at the hands of St. Cyril, the Patriarch of Alexandria. Geographically, the Nestorian Church had no place to go but east. By comparison, the Monophysite Church was championed by Dioscor, St. Cyril's successor to the patriarchate seat in Alexandria. Opposition to Monophysitism came chiefly from Constantinople, but this was all the more important for its vigorous growth in Egypt. By accepting Monophysitism, Egypt was manifesting some form of nationalism or resistance to its status as a Byzantine conquered territory.

At the present time, the Nestorians are relatively few in number and they live mostly in Iran, India and parts of China. They are not connected in any significant way to Arab Christianity, except for the small numbers that live in Iraq and Syria, and in Canada they are negligible in number. The Monophysites, on the other hand, form two separate communions. The first communion consists of four groups which are in complete communion with each other. These are the Coptic Orthodox of Egypt, the Abyssinians, the Jacobites of Syria, and a segment of the Malabar Christians. The second separate and independent communion under Monophysitism is made up of the Gregorian Armenian Church. In terms of the Canadian experience, the Egyptian Coptic component of Arab immigration was most pronounced in the 1960s and early 1970s. The Armenians also came in sizable numbers to this country, their immigration antedating that of the Copts.[18]

33

The Orthodox Church

The third major division of Eastern Christianity is that of the Orthodox Church. This church holds essentially the same beliefs as the Catholic Church, except that it rejects the doctrine of immaculate conception and "the doctrine regarding the papacy and the double procession of the Holy Ghost."[19] Orthodoxy insists "that *several* churches have the apostolic succession, and that the Church of Rome is only one of these, no more important spiritually than the others."[20]

While the doctrinal disputes between the Eastern Orthodox and the Catholic Churches are not major, the two churches followed independent courses of development, particularly after the Great Schism of 1054. Differences of rite and liturgical expression have kept the two churches separate and distinct. Also, as noted earlier, under the Ottoman policy of investing special powers in religious leaders, the Patriarch of Constantinople was like a pope in Eastern Christendom. However, following the decline and fall of the Ottoman Empire in this century, the different national Orthodox churches became independent for several reasons. First, the patriarch did not endear himself to the national Orthodox churches by his policy of appointing Greek higher clergy to them with no regard for the mother tongue of the people involved. Second, the wars of political independence were an important factor in the eventual independence of the national churches. Finally, the Patriarch of Constantinople was associated with the Turkish colonial regime, and the colonized peoples' hostilities toward that regime were extended to the patriarch himself.

Presently the Eastern Orthodox Church consists of a score of independent patriarchates that follow the Byzantine rite and are in communion with each other and with the Patriarch of Constantinople, their titular head. The Patriarchates of Antioch and Jerusalem represent mainstream Orthodoxy within Arab Christianity. The Patriarch of Antioch is located in Damascus, Syria. The Syrian Orthodox were among the first Syrians to emigrate to Canada, together with the Melkites and the Maronites who will be discussed next.

The Uniate Churches: Maronites and Melkites

The final grouping within Eastern Christianity consists of the Uniate Churches. These churches are in communion with Rome or form part of the Catholic Church. They regard the Pope as the head of the church and share identical beliefs with Catholicism. But the Uniate Churches are autonomous and they have their own patriachs over whom only the Pope has authority. These Eastern Catholic Churches practise different rites and employ different liturgical languages. In analysing Arab Christianity, these factors need to be considered.

The Maronites and the Melkites are two major communities of Christians in the Arab East, accounting for more than one-half of the early Arab immigrants to Canada. Despite the fact that they are in communion with Rome, the Maronites and the Melkites carry significantly different attitudes toward various issues. The differences between the two groups may be traced to their distinctive historical experiences in the Near East.[21]

In brief, the Maronites were named after the patron saint of the church, Maroun (d. ca. 410), an ascetic monk and a member of the Church of Syria which followed the Antiochian rite and used Syriac in its liturgy. About the middle of the seventh century, under the leadership of Yuhanna Maroun (d. ca. 707) who founded the church in Lebanon, the Maronite peasants settled in the northern part of that country. The Maronites originated as a Monothelite Christian sect, holding the unorthodox doctrine that Christ had one will. But the Monothelite doctrine was repudiated in the twelfth century, due to contacts with the Crusaders and French missionaries, and the Maronite church came to accept papal authority. The relationship between the Maronite church and Rome was strengthened in the eighteenth century, when the union with Rome was sealed, and more recently in 1964 when the Maronite patriarch was made a cardinal. The Maronite church has retained Syriac in its liturgy and, following the union with Rome, "adopted the Roman catechism, introduced the name of the Pope into the mass, limited clergy marriage to the lower degrees, prohibited the habitation of monks and nuns in the same premises and allowed the reception of the host by the clergy, but not the laymen, in both kinds."[22]

The Melkites were an Antiochian community of Christians that accepted the decree of the fourth General Council (451) against the Monophysites and the Nestorians. From the seventh century, successive military assaults on Antioch forced the Melkites to seek the protection of the Byzantine emperor, and it was only a matter of time before they came under the complete jurisdiction of the Patriarch of Constantinople. Thus their former contacts with Rome were disrupted, particularly after the Great Schism of 1054. But the Melkite Christian community had the seeds of its own division. In the seventeenth century, through the influence of Jesuit missionaries in Syria, a number of Melkite bishops separated from the parent Orthodox church and entered into communion with Rome. Naturally, the resulting tension between this splinter group and the larger Syrian Orthodox community was severe, and it was carried into the eighteenth century and beyond. "Most hostilities between the Melkites and their Syrian Orthodox brothers, which flare up even today, can be traced back to this basic jurisdictional quarrel."[23]

Both the Melkites and the Syrian Orthodox follow the Byzantine rite and use the Greek language in their liturgy. In spite of these similarities, both groups have developed distinctive social identities and, since separation, they have maintained some degree of social distance from each other not only in the Arab East but also in North America.

Doctrinal and socio-historical differences among the Maronites, the Melkites and the Syrian Orthodox are associated with different modes of adaptation. In the United States, for example, the Maronites, compared to the other two groups, have exhibited greater readiness to relinquish their Eastern heritage, merge with the Latin Church, and assimilate into American life.[24] Contrariwise, the Melkites and the Syrian Orthodox have tended to maintain a higher degree of attachment to their Eastern religious traditions and Arab cultural heritage. The results of this study suggest that the adaptive experience of these three groups, respectively, is the same in Canada as in the United States.

Arab Muslims

The second main religion relevant to the study of Arab Canadians is Islam. Not many Muslim Arabs came to Canada at the turn of this century. However, the proportion of Muslim Arab immigrants to this country increased considerably after World War II, although Arab Christians continue to outnumber Arab Muslims, both as immigrants and as Canadian residents.

Like the Christian faith, the Islamic faith also faced splintering. The first major schism in Islam centered around the issue of succession after the death of the Prophet Muhammad. A segment of the Muslim community at that time wanted the successor to be Ali, Muhammad's cousin and son-in-law, while the larger portion of the community wanted to settle the issue by acclamation. The former group has come to be known as the Shi'ites, meaning partisans, and the latter has come to be known as the Sunnis (Orthodox). The Shi'i sect is very large in Iraq and is well represented in Lebanon. The Sunni sect, on the other hand, is the predominant division of Islam throughout the Arab world. In terms of the Canadian experience, the Sunni component of Arab immigration has been by far the larger of the two.

Over the years Islam witnessed additional controversies regarding belief, resulting in the formation of several sects or splinter groups such as Imami, Ismaili, and Zaidi (all subsects of Shi'i), as well as Alawi (Nusayri), Baha'i, Yazidi and Druse.[25] The Druses are probably better represented in Canada than any of the other sects. Indeed, some of the early Arab immigrants were Druses, but most of the Arab-Druse immigrants came to this country after World War II. It will be worthwhile to comment briefly on this sect.

The formation of the Druse sect dates back to the eleventh century when the Fatimid Caliph al-Hakim abu Ali al-Mansour (996-1020) claimed his own divinity. Following al-Hakim's death, Muhammad ibn-Ismail ad-Darazi, after whom the sect was named, and his successor Hamzah ibn-Ahmad al-Hadi preached the cult of al-Hakim among the Isma'ilites (a Shi'ite group) of Syria.[26] The members of the Druse sect are divided into two categories: the initiates and the uninitiates. The sect operates in secrecy. Its rituals and beliefs are concealed from its uninitiated members, and more so from strangers or researchers. At the present time, the Druses are concentrated in Lebanon and Syria.

The main conclusion to be drawn from the preceding discussion concerns the fusion of secular and political elements in the structuring of religious beliefs. At first glance, it may appear that the widest gap in the Arab world is between the Christian and Islamic faiths. While this division is basic, sectarian divisions within each religion are very, perhaps no less, important and need to be considered. While religious or sectarian separateness and distinctiveness are basic considerations, sectarian jealousies, bitterness and feuds in the Arab East often revolve around political rather than purely religious issues. In this context, the recent civil war in Lebanon can be better understood not as a religious war, but rather as a socio-economic and political struggle among diverse Lebanese groups. To be sure, religion or sect did play a role in initiating and sustaining the conflict, but the substantial amount of crossing of religious and sectarians lines in this conflict needs to be recognized and explained.[27]

POLITICAL CONDITIONS

With the advent of Ottoman colonial rule at the beginning of the sixteenth century, the Arabs resigned themselves to an inferior political status and almost static social and economic conditions. Either directly or indirectly, the Turks controlled virtually all of the Arab world, together with parts of the non-Arab Middle East as well as parts of Europe. The Turks were the uncontested masters of the region, feared not only by their subjects within the empire, but also by European nation states. For over two centuries, the Ottoman soldier or military machine was fierce, superior to any other in existence anywhere in Europe at that time.

But that was soon to change. While post-Renaissance Europe was making significant technological and military advances, the Ottoman Empire was beginning to crumble under its own weight. As Europe entered the take-off stage of social and economic development, the Ottoman Empire was entering a cycle of decline as a result of complacency and of inflexibility and inefficiency in its military and bureaucratic machines. The competition between the European nation states and the Ottoman Empire, and among the European powers themselves, for the control of strategic areas and trade routes with India, were important factors in Europe's colonial ambitions in Arab lands. The competition between France and Britain in Europe had repercussions in the Middle East. The more distant the provinces were from Constantinople the more vulnerable they were to the onslaughts of European colonizers.

Napoleon Bonaparte's conquest of Egypt, 1798-1801, was the first major European expedition to the region since the Crusades. The French occupation of Egypt, though short-lived, was an important event in more than one respect. First, it demonstrated to France and other European powers that the notion of invincibility of the Islamic world was a myth.

37

Second, Napoleon brought with him to Egypt an Arabic press which he used for propaganda purposes, and the impact of this press on the intellectual life of Egypt and neighbouring Arab provinces was far-reaching. Third, the French conquest of Egypt awakened the Arab people from their deep slumber and sharpened their curiosity about the West and interest in modernization. Muhammad Ali, the emergent political leader of Egypt at that time, attempted to modernize and industrialize Egypt. He initiated ambitious educational and economic programmes and sent student missions to Europe in order to strengthen the intellectual ties with the West. Many of the educational contacts were established with France. As a result, Egypt produced some of the greatest nineteenth century Arab reformers, and a good portion of the contemporary educated elite in Egypt is still oriented, both linguistically and intellectually, towards France. This explains why many Egyptian immigrants to Canada chose Montreal as their destination.

The forced evacuation of French troops from Egypt at the hands of Muhammad Ali, at the beginning of the nineteenth century, did not completely end France's colonial role in North Africa. The French troops invaded Algeria in 1830, occupied Tunisia in 1881, and instituted a "protectorate" system over Morocco in 1912. All three of these North African territories remained under French control until after World War II when they achieved political independence. The French orientation of these Arab North African states is rooted in their colonial past. In varying degrees, the political and intellectual elites of these countries were and still are familiar with the French language and elements of the French culture. However, the situation was problematic in Algeria which the French regarded as an integral part of France. Here the indigenous language and culture were severely disrupted. As a result, since independence in 1962, the Algerian government has been involved in massive Arabisation programmes in an attempt to restore the integrity of Arab culture and language. Again, Canada-bound immigrants from these three Arab states have tended to gravitate towards Montreal and the Province of Quebec.

Britain's colonial ambitions in the Arab world were no less grand than those of France. The British, in their turn, occupied Aden on the southwestern tip of the Arabian peninsula in 1839 and Egypt in 1882. Next, the British began to extend their sphere of influence in southern Arabia and the Gulf. Except for Egypt, where both the English and French streams of education have been available, the areas which came under British control have tended to teach English, while French-dominated areas have tended to teach French.

The final colonial bid in North Africa came at the hands of Italy, which seized Libya in 1911-12. Libya remained under foreign control until her independence in 1951.

Thus, before the outbreak of World War I, all of North Africa and large portions of the Arabian peninsula and the Gulf were under European control. The remainder of the Arab world was firmly in the hands of the Turks.

The Arab National Movement

The Arab national movement had its beginnings around the middle of the nineteenth century. According to Antonius, "The story of the Arab national movement opens in Syria in 1847, with the foundation in Beirut of a modest literary society under American patronage."[28] The Arab national movement was and still is a secular movement, drawing support not only from Arab Muslims but also Arab Christians. Indeed, Arab Christians were among its first exponents, and at present "they provide many of the most passionate Arab nationalists."[29] The Syrian Protestant College (founded in 1866), later to become the American University of Beirut, was the meeting ground for budding Arab nationalists. In both Syria and Egypt, the leaders of the Arab national movement were inspired by the achievements of Western civilization, including the political system which existed in Europe. The principles of constitutionalism, justice and freedom, the cornerstones of the European system, were missing in the Arab world. These were singled out for special commendation.[30] In the early phase of its development, the Arab national movement underlined the need for reform in all major areas of social life, as well as the need to abolish foreign rule and domination. By the turn of the twentieth century, the Arab national movement had gained enough momentum and popular support to pose a threat to the Turkish rulers.

At the outbreak of World War I, Greater Syria was placed under Turkish military rule.[31] The military governor, Jamal Pasha, attempted to purge Arab nationalists but succeeded only in strengthening Arab desire for independence. This had led the Arabs to turn to the European powers for support of their national aspirations for political independence. Reciprocal support of the Arabs and the Western Allies in World War I was premised on the fulfillment of these aspirations. The letters exchanged between one influential Arab leader, Sharif Husain of Mecca, and the British government reflected these aspirations and extracted a British promise to support independence for the Arabs. Hence, Husain revolted against the Turks in 1916 and declared himself King of the Arab countries. Husain's son, Faysal, was also actively involved in the fight. He led the military campaign against the Turks through Palestine and Jordan and his forces entered Damascus and established an Arab government on October 1, 1918. On that same day, an Arab government was established in Lebanon and the Sharifian flag was raised over public buildings.

However, France and Great Britain frustrated Arab moves for immediate independence, for they had other plans for the Fertile Crescent. Under a 1916 secret agreement (the Sykes-Picot Agreement), France and Great Britain divided the area between themselves. France was particularly interested in Syria and Lebanon, while Great Britain was interested in Palestine and Iraq. The French Army occupied Beirut in October, 1918, as a first step towards fulfilling the terms of the secret agreement and the British Army eventually withdrew to its corresponding domain of interest. The hold which the French and the British had over the area was formalized in the 1920 San Remo (Italy) Conference which entrusted France with the mandate over Syria and Lebanon, and gave the mandate over Palestine and Iraq to Great Britain.

Meanwhile, Faysal, already declared King by the Syrian Congress which met earlier in Damascus, was in a difficult position *vis-à-vis* the French who, from the beginning, were hostile towards Arab nationalism. The French mandatory regime faced heaviest resistance in Syria, but with a superior army the French swiftly occupied Damascus in July, 1920, and, later in the same month, Faysal was forced to leave Syria. These events marked the successful implementation of European colonialism in the Near East.

According to the League of Nations, the purpose of the French and British mandates was to prepare the Arabs for self-rule. However, the two mandates were received with great suspicion and outright violence. The Arabs were eager to achieve political independence and any disagreements that existed among them revolved around the question of how it was to be achieved. In Syria and Palestine, for example, there was a strong desire for a united Arab state under a constitutional monarch. In Lebanon, on the other hand, the population was divided: a segment, best represented by the Maronites, advocated the establishment of a separate and independent republic, while another segment, best represented by the Muslims, as well as the Syrian Orthodox and Protestants, were supporters of the United Arab state concept.

Political Independence

While Arab resistance to colonialism was directed towards the Turks in the first two decades of this century, after World War I it was transferred onto the French and British who supplanted the Turks. Between 1920 and 1950, the Arab people devoted a considerable amount of resources and energy to the fight against European colonialism. The struggle for independence was intense and costly, both in life and material possessions. The mounting national pressure against colonialism led to the termination of the British mandate in Iraq in 1932, and the recognition of an independent Egypt under the terms of the 1936 Anglo-Egyptian treaty. Shortly thereafter, the French mandate in Syria and Lebanon was terminated (1941), followed by the termination of the British mandate in Palestine (1948). The list of newly-independent Arab countries expanded to include Transjordan (1946), Libya (1951), Morocco, Sudan and Tunisia (all three becoming independent in 1956). In 1961 and 1962, Kuwait and Algeria, respectively, became independent. Between 1963 and 1978, the remaining Arab states declared their independence.

The Arab national movement, in general, succeeded in removing the European colonial system and in liberating Arab lands, except for Palestine. The termination of the British mandate in Palestine in 1948 was simultaneously accompanied by Israel's declaration of statehood. From the Arab viewpoint, Israel constitutes both a physical and psychological discontinuity in the Arab national movement. As a result of the creation of the state of Israel, about 1.5 million Palestinian Arabs have been dispossessed, their lands taken away by force, and their status reduced to that of refugees. After four Arab-Israeli wars (1948, 1956, 1967 and 1973) and much violence throughout and even after the signing of a peace treaty between Egypt and Israel on March 26, 1979, the question of Palestine and the more general issue of the Arab-Israeli conflict remain. The tension in the Middle East has been broadened to encompass the international arena, presenting a threat of nuclear confrontation among the superpowers.

In the post-independence Arab world, the political climate has been far from stable. The political systems of the Arab states have varied considerably, ranging from absolute monarchies to constitutional republics, from Western-type capitalist political economies to planned socialist economies, and from pan-Arab orientations to strictly local or even religious orientations. The contradictions are not only between but also within the Arab states. In any given Arab country, different social structures, orientations and ideologies are in almost constant confrontation, and different segments of the populations often exhibit correspondingly differing degrees of loyalty to the existing regime. Political events in the past quarter century have brought these contradictions to the fore and it is unlikely that they will disappear in the foreseeable future.

The main conclusion to be drawn from the preceding discussion is that while the Arab people have in common the experience of a colonial past, there are temporal and regional differences in the details of this experience, and these may influence the adjustment and behaviour of Arab immigrants to Canada. For example, more recent generations of Arab immigrants to Canada have experienced the fight against European (French and British), not Turkish, colonialism. Compared to the turn-of-the-century Syrian immigrants, post-war Arab immigrants have celebrated political independence in their country of origin and experienced the ups and downs of the post-independence Arab world. Above all, many of the recent Arab immigrants carry strong attitudes regarding the Arab-Israeli conflict as they have been directly influenced by it.

Also, immigrants from regions previously colonized by France seem to gravitate towards French Canada, whereas those previously colonized by Britain seem to prefer English Canada. The correlation between region of origin and destination in Canada is not overwhelming, but it is strong. Finally, the attitudes of Arab immigrants towards Canada and the Arab world seem to be associated with political events and perception of instability in the country of origin. Egypt provides an example. Most post-war Egyptian immigrants to Canada were disaffected by the nationalization measures implemented by the late President Nasser in the early 1960s. These same immigrants seem to have more positive attitudes toward Egypt today as a result of President Anwar Sadat's reorientation of internal and foreign policy.

To sum up, some of the differences and contradictions in existence in the Arab world today are reflected in the Arab-Canadian community. To understand differences in the political orientations of Arab Canadians, one must understand not only Arab politics, but also the complex relationship between loyalty to the adopted land and loyalty to the Arab ethnic group.

SOCIO-ECONOMIC CONDITIONS

As in the case of political conditions, knowledge of economic conditions in the Arab world will enhance our understanding of the Arab-Canadian ethnic group. This is so partly because economic conditions in the Arab world have played an important role in Arab immigration to Canada. This is as much true of poor peasant immigrants as of more advantaged professional immigrants. In addition, the economic background of Arab immigrants is related to their mode of adaptation to the new environment. Finally, knowledge of the economic conditions of the Arab world will enhance our understanding of the economic relations between Canada and that part of the world. Undoubtedly, the attitudes of Arab Canadians towards their country of origin and the adopted land are influenced, at least in part, by these economic relationships. Also, following the world energy crisis of the early 1970s, trade and economic exchanges between Canada and several Arab states have become increasingly significant.

The Arab world is part of what is known as the Third World. Like other Third World countries, the countries of the Arab world in general are predominantly agricultural. Longrigg states that about 60-80% of the inhabitants of the Middle East derive their livelihood directly from the land.[32] In comparison, only seven per cent of the Canadian labour force was involved in agriculture in 1971. Also, judging from such indices of human resources as school enrolment ratios or scientists, doctors and engineers per 10,000 population, the Arab world today suffers from underemployment of its human resources and low per capita Gross National Product, except in the rich, oil-producing countries such as Kuwait, the United Arab Emirates and Saudi Arabia. Poverty remains a major social problem in many parts of the Arab world. In view of the unprecedented inflow of "petrodollars" into the region in the past five years, the Arab press has popularized the phrase "rich countries of poor people."

It would be misleading to give the reader the impression of static social and economic conditions in the Arab world. The Arab world is radically different from and more developed than what it was when the pioneer Arab immigrants arrived in Canada in the latter part of the nineteenth and early twentieth centuries. At that time, agricultural productivity in the region was very low, and industry was largely of the handicraft variety with distribution limited to local markets. Many of the early immigrants were poor peasants repelled by adverse economic conditions in their village communities.

Both nature and social conditions help explain the low standard of living which was and, to a large extent, still is prevalent in the region. Only 10% of the land surface is cultivable, and despite the ingenious methods utilised (e.g., terracing of mountain slopes), the vagaries of rainfall and the inferior organic content of the soil and its tendency to salinate as a result of regular irrigation are main factors in low agricultural productivity. With reference to the scarcity of water resources, Arabs jokingly tell stories of desert Bedouins diligently digging wells for water and to their chagrin discovering oil! On the social side, among the major drawbacks are the land-tenure system which has land fragmentation as one of its consequences, lack of capital investment in agriculture, and continued dependence on traditional methods rather than modern agricultural technology.[33] To these serious drawbacks must be added the colonial systems which had adverse economic effects because of their predominant concern with the economic needs of the parent countries.

Various attempts at social and economic development of the Arab world were started during the inter-war period, but the process did not accelerate until after World War II. In the past quarter century, newly-independent Arab states have not only encouraged but also participated directly in industrial development projects. In certain countries, notably Nasser's Egypt, Algeria, Iraq and Syria, socialist ideology has guided the developmental process. Regardless of the prevailing ideology, however, many of today's Arab capital cities have grown beyond the recognition of the preceding generations. In terms of their high-rise apartment buildings, complex communications networks, powerful financial institutions and elaborate commercial activities, large Arab cities are scarcely different from their European or Canadian counterparts. Moreover, there has been steady industrial and agricultural development, manifested by the construction of several major dams and increasing dependence on modern technology. Although the recent changes in the material aspects of Arab culture, relative to the past, have been no less than revolutionary, the gap between the Arab world and the industrialized West remains wide. More importantly, the aspirations of the Arab people for a higher standard of living have not yet been realized. There is considerable public pressure for further development.

The hopes of the Arab people for speedy economic development have been raised immensely in the last five to ten years. The revenues of oil-producing countries have multiplied manifold from this natural resource, and development plans drawn by Arab governments are astounding by any standards. The example of Saudi Arabia is perhaps as extreme as it is illustrative. Recently the Saudi government allocated no less than $142 billion for a five-year national development plan. Similarly, high-level spending on development projects is to be found in all the Arab states of the Gulf, as well as Iraq, Libya and Algeria. The economic benefits of these development projects will penetrate other Arab and foreign (mainly Western) countries, but the main beneficiaries of these programmes are the oil-producing states themselves. It would appear that Arab hopes for speedy social and economic development are not unrealistic.

While economic want in its pure sense was an important factor in early Arab immigration to Canada, the situation of post-war Arab immigrants to this country is much more complex. Many of today's Arab immigrants are attracted to Canada more for political, educational, cultural and career considerations than for economic need. This is reflected in their adjustment in the new environment.

At a different level of analysis, the economic links between Canada and the Arab world have been strengthening, partly as a result of a conscious policy on the part of the Canadian government and partly as a result of new realities affecting the Arab world. For example, Canadian exports to the Arab world increased from about $26 million in 1969 to $341 million in 1975. Canadian imports from Arab states also increased, from about $51 million in 1969 to $1,359 million in 1975. Canadian exports to the Arab world include agricultural products and, increasingly, manufactured goods and technical services (engineering, industrial and construction design), while the main Canadian import from the Arab world is crude oil. Thus, the total volume of trade between Canada and the Arab world increased from $77 million in 1969 to a high of $1,700 million in 1975.[34]

Another important aspect of the developing economic bond between Canada and the Arab world involves the repatriation of "petrodollars." Because of large capital surpluses in oil-producing Arab states, investment abroad has increased markedly. "Canadian public and private institutions have not been slow to avail themselves of these sources of investment capital."[35] Although precise figures on Arab investment in Canada are not available, indications are that the magnitudes involved are very large. For example, a 1975 issue of *Maclean's* states:

> The word in the investment and banking communities is that Arab oil money is very much a factor in the Canadian economy. More than $1.5 billion has been invested here during the past 18 months and investment bankers are hoping for at least that much again in the next 12 months.[36]
>
> Other reports indicate that provincial public utilities alone sold more than $500 million worth of bonds in the Arabian peninsula in 1974-75.[37]

In the past, the main economic interlock between Canada and the Arab world took the form of remittances sent by Arab Canadians to village communities and relatives left behind. Such remittances are not uncommon even today. But the new economic interlock at the national level, between Canada and the Arab world, is of a large order. And what is more, its potential to expand is such that Canadian exports to the Arab world could average about $1 billion a year for the next 10 years.[38] In national and regional conferences of Arab-Canadian organizations, spokesmen for the Arab ethnic group have been urging the Canadian government and public to strengthen mutually beneficial trade relations with the Arab world.[39] The reasons underlying this call for stronger economic relations are multiple and complex, but they undoubtedly embody the assumption that stronger economic relations would lead to better and friendlier relations between the Canadian and Arab peoples.

Economic development and education are interrelated processes. In the next section we will discuss educational development in the Arab world, again with a view to enhancing our understanding of that part of the world and the Arab immigrant population in Canadian society.[40]

EDUCATIONAL DEVELOPMENT

Prior to World War I, education of Arab youth was left largely to local communities and individuals. The dominant educational institution was the Islamic *kuttab*, which stressed religious instruction and tradition. Manned by local religious leaders, the *kuttab* followed a relatively simple form of instruction and extended the benefits of literacy to only a fraction of the young. High schools, except in certain limited regions, were practically unknown.

In addition to the *kuttab*, there were two less prevalent but nonetheless socially significant types of schools. These were the national sectarian schools and the missionary schools. The national sectarian schools are the older of the two, dating back to the fifteenth century. They were established by Western-educated (e.g., French- and Italian-educated) clergymen returning from abroad to educate their own religious communities. The missionary schools, on the other hand, were started by foreigners – mostly French, British and American missionaries. A large number of missionary schools were established in the nineteenth century. The national sectarian and missionary schools represent the earliest Western (European and American) influences on the development of education in the Arab world. The missionary schools were in existence not only in the regions directly controlled by the European powers, but also in the Fertile Crescent which was under direct Turkish control.

Following World War II, the newly independent Arab states attempted to focus national efforts on social and economic development. The most feasible first steps towards modernization were in the area of education. Hence, in the past three decades most Arab states have widened their

45

educational bases and have moved towards formalization, universalization and secularization of their educational systems. These developments
brought about the demise of the *kuttab*.

There is little doubt that Western ideology was influential in at least
three respects in the development of Arab aspirations for education.
First, the above-noted missionary schools were based on Western techniques and forms of organization. They were more numerous and perhaps
more influential than the national sectarian schools in that their student
populations were of mixed religious origins. These schools are still in existence in many parts of the Arab world, but in several cases they have
lost their missionary zeal, if not their European or American orientation.
Second, nineteenth century Arab intellectuals and social reformers (as
distinct from clerics), many of whom had studied or travelled in Europe,
agitated for the development of a modern educational system similar
to the one which they had observed in Europe. Third, following World
War I the mandatory powers, in response to Arab agitation, assisted in
developing modern public schools. The relative importance of each of
these conditions varied from one country to another, and in certain Arab
countries formal education was not an integral part of the culture until
recently.

A second main factor in educational growth in the Arab world has
been social and economic development. This process has led to bureaucratic growth, both in the public and private sectors of the economy.
Social and economic development and bureaucratic expansion, resulting
in a more complex occupational structure with increased rank differentiation, create a greater demand for trained personnel. The agency that
can cope with these demands most effectively is a modern system of
education. Hence, education has come to be associated with economic
development.

Economic development appears to have stimulated educational
growth in yet another way. There is little doubt that economic development has been an important factor in stimulating urbanization and rural-
urban migration. For example, in a recent study of industrialization in
Alexandria, about one-third of the workers interviewed came from rural
areas.[41] Similarly, Cairo has attracted a large number of rural migrants.
Janet Abu-Lughod notes that throughout this century over one-third of
Cairo's population has been of rural origin.[42] The growth in urbanization
has been accompanied by an increased popular demand for a host of
public services including education. The response of many Arab governments has been favourable for many reasons, among them the fact that
educational costs are relatively lower in urban (heavily populated) areas
than in rural ones; thus, educational facilities in urban areas continue to
be better and more numerous than those in rural areas.

The magnitude of expansion of educational systems in the countries of
the Arab world is well reflected by such indicators as expenditures on

education, numbers of schools, numbers of teachers, and enrollments.[43] There has been a steady increase in the proportion of students enrolled to the total population of the appropriate age-group, at all three levels of education. In certain Arab states, there is near universal coverage of the school age population at both the elementary and the secondary levels. Generally, however, secondary schools and, to a greater degree, universities in the Arab countries continue to be highly selective.

With reference to sex differences in education, enrollment statistics show that the educational opportunities available for females in the Arab countries have improved substantially in recent years, although, in comparison with males, Arab females are still less represented than males at all levels of education. Female enrollments account for about 40% of the total enrollments at the elementary level, 30% of the total enrollments at the secondary level, and about 20% of the total enrollments at the university level. These statistics underline important qualitative changes in the traditional female role, more so perhaps in some Middle Eastern countries than in others.

. Educational development represents a major structural change in society. While it is a product of a multiplicity of internal and external conditions, it acts also as an independent variable and a prime mover in furthering change and development. Perhaps the most important consequence of the Arab educational renaissance is its impact on the occupational structure. There is increasing demand at the present time for professional and technical personnel, as well as for skilled labour. Relevant to this, the educational institution serves two important functions. First, by responding to the demands of industrial development it contributes to the development of native talent. Second, it equips students with the resources necessary for upward social mobility. In combination, these two functions influence the structure of society by contributing to the expansion of the middle classes and the upgrading of the labour force.

Available evidence indicates that formal education is a decisive factor in political socialization and mobilization. Almost invariably educational development and its usual concomitants, urbanization and industrialization, tend to create a new political role for the urban workers and middle class segments of the population. Grass roots participation becomes a reality, and traditional bonds of political integration tend to give way to "modern" orientations and attitudes. Enhanced political involvement tends, on the one hand, to cause the political elite to respond to the demands of the growing mass of enfranchised citizens and, on the other hand, to divide political orientations along class lines. These structural changes and accompanying political orientations help explain important aspects of the recent civil war in Lebanon.

Of particular relevance to an understanding of the Arab-Canadian community is, again, the variable educational experiences of different waves of Arab immigrants. On the average, the post-war Arab immigrant to Canada has had more formal education in his country of origin than his earlier counterpart. More important than this quantitative difference is the qualitative difference in the educational experience of these immigrants. Typically, more recent Arab immigrants to Canada have had direct or indirect experience with Arab national systems of education. Like other national systems of education, the Arabs give their students ethnically-relevant interpretations of history, world events, and national aspirations. They also tend to homogenize the population in subtle ways and, at times, in ways that are not so subtle. Because of temporal differences in national experience, contemporary Arab youth, compared to earlier generations, carry their own world views and political orientations. They are also probably more secular, more activist and more nationalistic.

There is another notable side to education in the Arab world which may help explain political and attitudinal differences not only in the Arab population in general but also within its educated segments. According to Kahlil Gibran (famous author of *The Prophet*), foreign missionary schools (including the French, English, American, Italian, German and Russian) in the Arab East have been no less divisive than beneficial:

> Education has come to us from the West in the form of charity. We have devoured the foodstuff of this charity; we are a hungry people. This foodstuff has revitalized us, but in so doing it has deprived us of life. On the one hand, it has awakened our mental faculties and sharpened our minds. On the other hand, it has divided our minds, weakened our unity, severed our connective tissue, and disunited our sects. Our homeland has become an abode for small disparate colonies, each different from the others in its attitudes and tastes, and each, connected by a cord to a patron Western country, raises the flag of its patron country and extolls that country's virtues and glorious traditions.[44]

The focus of the above discussion has been the modernization of educational systems in the Arab world. By modernization we mean formalization, universalization and secularization. In the past 30 years, the Arab countries appear to have gone a long way towards modernizing education. Judging from UNESCO publications, this trend will continue.

When the pioneer Arab immigrants arrived in Canada in the nineteenth and early twentieth centuries, the Arab national systems of education were still in their embryonic stage. Still a colonized minority, these early immigrants, compared to their more recent counterparts, were not moulded by an Arab national system of education or by developments resulting from such a system. Part of the attitudinal and behavioural differences within the Arab-Canadian ethnic group are attributable to the varied educational experiences in the country of origin of successive generations of Arab immigrants.

SUMMARY

Arab immigrants to Canada bring with them a cultural heritage which is significantly different from that which characterizes Canadian society. With regard to the family, for example, the normative attitudes of the Arab people emphasize sex role separation, patriarchy, and filial obligations. Although it is undergoing change, particularly in urban areas, the family continues to be a focal point of social organization in the Arab East. Also, within the context of Eastern Christianity and Islam, the normative attitude of Arab society has been shaped by the fusion of spiritual and socio-political elements, and by the long history of uneasy religious pluralism. Loyalty not only to one's religion, but even to one's sect, may be viewed as an extension of loyalty and obligations to the family. This aspect of Arab culture has practically no parallel in Canadian society.

The Arab ethnic character has also been moulded by the unique political, economic, and educational conditions in the Arab world. Until recently, the Arab experience was grounded in the oppressive Turkish and European colonial systems. In the aftermath of World War II, the general decolonization of the Arab world brought about a revolutionary situation in virtually all aspects of social life. It can all be summed up in one word: *change*. While the process of social change is occurring in many different parts of the world, including Canada, the experiences of the contemporary inhabitants of the Arab world are qualitatively different from those of Western Europe or North America. For the Arab East is in the take-off stage in the process of social and economic development. In terms of normative values and lifelong experiences, this sets Arab immigrants to Canada apart from the host population.

Because of the acceleration of the process of social and economic development in the Arab world in the past quarter century, the normative attitudes of the earlier and the more recent generations of Arab immigrants to Canada have been shaped by different experiences in the homeland. Their patterns of ethnic and social concerns are not the same.

Finally, the sociological unity of the Arab world is one of the region's most remarkable features. This unity has persisted despite pluralism and the fragmentation of the region into a score of politically independent Arab states. It should be recognized, however, that there are subcultural variations both within and between different Arab states. Due to these variations, as well as unique personal experiences in the country of origin, Arab immigrants to Canada have encompassed wide differences in attitudes, values, world views and aspirations.

NOTES

1. For an overview of the Arab family, see William J. Goode, *World Revolution and Family Patterns* (New York, 1963), pp. 123-139, and Ed-

win Terry Prothro and Lutfy Najib Diab, *Changing Family Patterns in the Arab East* (Beirut, 1974).

2. Among Bedouins, both nomadic and settled, even larger kinship structures are found with the tribe being the largest organization of kin. All members of a tribe usually claim descent from a single ancestor, either real or fictive. In a sense, therefore, a tribal chief is the head of a very large family. He is the functional equivalent of the patriarch in a large extended family.

3. Abdulla M. Lutfiyya, *Baytin: A Jordanian Village* (The Hague, 1966), p. 57.

4. Cf. Philip K. Hitti, *The Syrians in America* (New York, 1924), p. 87.

5. Muwaffak Al-Hamdani and Baha Abu-Laban, "Game Involvement and Sex-Role Socialization in Arab Children," *International Journal of Comparative Sociology*, 12 (1971), p. 188.

6. E.T. Prothro, *Child Rearing in The Lebanon* (Cambridge, 1961), p. 129.

7. Given that the sex ratio in adulthood is around 100 and given the economic issues relating to the practice of polygyny, generally in so-called "polygynous societies," polygyny actually "tends to be practised only by a small segment of the population." See G. Leslie, *The Family in Social Context* (New York, 1976), p. 35.

8. See, for example, J.G. Peristiany, ed., *Honour and Shame: The Values of Mediterranean Society* (London, 1965).

9. It should be noted that the Muslim faith, in is early stages, made significant contributions towards the improvement of the status of women. Polygynous marriage was practised before the advent of Islam; however, Islam set restrictions both on the number of wives and on the behaviour of the polygynous husband. Further, the Koran specified women's property rights, marriage rights and right to property settlements in the case of divorce.

10. Philip M. Kayal and Joseph M. Kayal, *The Syrian-Lebanese in America* (Boston, 1975), p. 20.

11. The above figure is the same as the one provided by Kayal and Kayal, although the Kayals give a five to seven per cent range on the proportion of Christians in the Arab Near East. *Ibid.*, pp. 23 and 52-53. The total figure is larger than the one which may be derived from *Middle East and North Africa*, 21st Edition (Europa Publications, 1974-75), as presented in L.M. Kenny, "The Modern Arab World," in R.M. Savory, ed., *Introduction to Islamic Civilization* (Cambridge, 1976), p. 152. The reason for this difference is mainly due to the fact that the latter publication underestimates the number of Coptic Christians in Egypt.

12. Cf. Edward Wakin, *A Lonely Minority; the Modern Story of Egypt's Copts* (New York, 1963), pp. 24-25. According to Wakin, there were 4,000,000 Copts in Egypt in 1960, representing 14.8% of the total population. There were an estimated 40,000,000 people in Egypt in 1975, which suggests that the Coptic component was no less than 6,000,000 in 1975.

13. According to the best available evidence, Syria and Lebanon account for the large majority of Armenians in the Arab East. These two countries, combined, have an estimated 300-350,000 Armenians.
14. See W.L. Scott, "The Eastern Christian Churches," in Elias Karam, ed., *The Syrian Canadian National Review* (Ottawa, 1935), pp. 50-51.
15. Timothy Ware, *The Orthodox Church* (Harmondsworth, Middlesex, 1963), p. 100, as quoted in Millett, "The Orthodox Church: Ukrainian, Greek and Syrian," in Jean Leonard Elliott, ed., *Immigrant Groups* (Scarborough, 1971), p. 63.
16. These groupings follow the ones discussed in Scott, *op. cit.*, pp. 42-54.
17. *Ibid.*, p. 49.
18. For a brief discussion of the history of Armenians in Canada, see *The Canadian Family Tree* (Ottawa, 1967), pp. 29-34.
19. Scott, *op. cit.*, p. 52.
20. David Millett, *op. cit.*, p. 52.
21. For a recent account of these two sects, see Kayal and Kayal, *op. cit.*, pp. 23-59.
22. Philip K. Hitti, *Lebanon in History, from the Earliest Times to the Present*. Third Edition (London, 1967), p. 406.
23. Kayal and Kayal, *op. cit.*, p. 34.
24. *Ibid.*, p. 30ff.
25. Tareq Y. Ismael, *Government and Politics of the Contemporary Middle East* (Homewood, Ill., 1970), pp. 12-23.
26. Cf. Carl Brockelmann, *History of the Islamic Peoples* (New York, 1939), p. 161ff.
27. For a recent analysis of the civil war in Lebanon, see Leila Meo and Edward Said, *Lebanon: Two Perspectives* (Detroit, 1975); and Fouad Moughrabi and Naseer Aruri, eds., *Lebanon: Crisis and Challenge in the Arab World* (Detroit, 1977).
28. George Antonious, *The Arab Awakening* (London, 1938), p. 13.
29. G.M. Wickens, "Introduction to the Middle East," in R.M. Savory, ed., *Introduction to Islamic Civilization, op. cit.*, p. 5.
30. Irbrahim Abu-Lughod, *Arab Rediscovery of Europe* (Princeton, N.J., 1963), p. 157ff.
31. The term Greater Syria refers to a geographical entity which includes, at a minimum, those countries which after World War I came to be known as Syria, Lebanon, Palestine and Transjordan.
32. Stephen H. Longrigg, *The Middle East* (Chicago, 1963), p. 233.
33. *Ibid.*
34. See L.A. Devoie, "Growth in Economic Relations of Canada and the Arab World," *International Perspectives* (November/December, 1976), pp. 31-32.
35. *Ibid.*, p. 32.
36. As quoted in *Ibid.*
37. *Ibid.*
38. *Ibid.*, p. 33.

39. An Arab-Canadian economist has written several articles on this subject. See Ibrahim Hayani, "Saudi Arabia – the Land of Oil and Money," *Canadian Business* (November, 1975), pp. 28-29; Hayani, "Investment Opportunities in Iraq," *Canadian Business* (September, 1975), pp. 34-38; and Hayani, "The Petrodollar Problem," *Canadian Business* (March, 1975).

40. The discussion of educational development draws heavily on Baha Abu-Laban and Sharon Abu-Laban, "Education and Development in the Arab World," *Journal of Developing Areas*, 10 (1976), pp. 285-394; and Abu-Laban and Abu-Laban, "Educational Development," in Abdeen Jabara and Janice Terry, eds., *The Arab World: from Nationalism to Revolution* (Wilmette, Ill., 1971), pp. 32-54.

41. Hassan Saati and G.K. Hirabayashi, *Industrialization in Alexandria: Some Social and Ecological Aspects* (Cairo, 1959).

42. See Janet Abu-Lughod, "Cairo: Perspective and Prospectus," in L. Carl Brown, ed., *From Madina to Metropolis: Heritage and Change in the Near Eastern City* (Princeton, N.J., 1973), pp. 95-113. For a more complete history of the City of Cairo, see Abu-Lughod's *Cairo: Thousand and One Years of the City Victorious* (Princeton, N.J., 1971).

43. Cf. Abu-Laban and Abu-Laban, "Education and Development in the Arab World," *op. cit.*, p. 288ff.

44. G. Kahlil Gibran, *Collection of Complete Works*, Vol. 3 (Beirut, 1955), p. 243. (Arabic) The above quotation was translated from Arabic by the present author.

THREE

The Chosen Land:
Arrival and Settlement

One day in the summer of 1883, a Syrian youth named Joseph Jebawy
was strolling the main streets of Montreal admiring the sights which
would catch the eyes of an immigrant from the Near East. Nothing
looked familiar. The layout of the city, the buildings, the people, the
languages spoken, the culture – all these and more were radically different from Syria, the country from which he had emigrated with his
father. He continued walking until he came to the vicinity of Notre Dame
Cathedral, across from the famous Place d'Armes square. There, amid
all the unfamiliar sights which surrounded him, he glimpsed a face which
did not look so strange. The young man with the familiar appearance
was selling artifacts on the street. Jebawy's suspicions were confirmed
when he discovered that Peter Tady, the peddler, was a Syrian, like
himself, who had emigrated to the New World. The news of Jebawy's
discovery soon reached his father and Abraham Bounadere, yet another
youthful Syrian, who had arrived in Montreal a year earlier. On the evening of that same day, the four Syrian men had a joyous social gathering
in Bounadere's residence, a simple room located at the corner of
Laguachetière and St. André Streets. These men were the first four
Arabic-speaking immigrants to set foot on Canadian soil.[1]
   The beginning of Syrian immigration to Canada coincided with a
period during which increasing numbers of immigrants were gravitating
toward this country. For example, in 1882 Canada admitted a total of
112,458 immigrants, compared to only 47,991 immigrants admitted in
the year preceding. Also, between 1881 and 1890 Canada admitted a
total of 886,177 immigrants, compared to only 342,675 admissions during the 10-year period immediately preceding. More importantly, in the
last two decades of the past century, an increasing number of immigrants
to Canada came from outside the United States and Western Europe.
During this period, the proportions of immigrants from eastern, central
and southern Europe were increasing.[2] Thus Canada's ethnic

kaleidoscope began to take a more variegated form and the admission of Arab immigrants added a new dimension to it.

This chapter will discuss the evolution and main characteristics of the Arab-Canadian community from the early days of immigration to the present time, settlement patterns, age-sex composition and causes of immigration.

INFLOW OF ARAB IMMIGRANTS

The Early Period (1882-1945)

According to the best available evidence, the number of Syrian residents in Canada increased from four in 1883, to 10 in 1885, and to 50 in 1890.[3] The formative period for the Arab-Canadian community was between 1891 and 1901, during which time increasing numbers of Syrian immigrants were joining their kindred in Montreal and elsewhere in Canada. On the average, about 150 such immigrants arrived in Canada annually during this period. The data suggest that the Arab ethnic group had established firm roots in Canadian soil by 1901 when an estimated total of about 2,000 people of Syrian origin made their domicile in Canada.

Immigration statistics show that a substantial number of Syrians crossed the Atlantic in the first decade of this century. The rise in the numbers of Syrian immigrants to Canada at this time coincided with one of the heaviest immigrations in Canadian history. Syrian immigration in the first 12 years of this century has been recorded as follows:[4]

1900-1901	464
1901-1902	1,066
1902-1903	847
1903-1904	369
1904-1905	630
1905-1906	336
9 months ended	
March 31, 1907	227
1907-1908	738
1908-1909	189
1909-1910	195
1910-1911	184
1911-1912	144

In 1911, there were an estimated 7,000 people of Arab origin in Canada.

There was a sudden and significant decline in the number of Syrian immigrants to Canada after 1908. During the period 1900-1908, an average of over 600 Syrian immigrants were admitted annually. Between 1909 and 1912, the average number of annual admissions fell to 177. After 1912, Syrian immigration to Canada was reduced to a trickle.

From the 1880s on, the steady increase in the number of immigrants from countries other than the United States and those of Western Europe was met with a rising tide of public opposition. Immigrants from Asia, in particular, were among the first to be viewed as undesirable. Due to heavy pressure from British Columbia, the Dominion government moved to restrict the entry of these immigrants. Thus, in 1885 a head tax of $50 was imposed on Chinese immigrants and, in 1903, this was raised to $500.[5] Japanese immigration to Canada was held in check by the Japanese government itself, as a result of the 1907 Gentleman's Agreement between Canada and Japan.[6] In addition, two restrictive Orders-in-Council came in 1908, also in response to British Columbia's agitation against the admission of immigrants from the Orient. The first order in council excluded immigrants "who did not come to Canada by *direct continuous journey* from their homeland."[7] The second Order in Council, P.C. 926, imposed a stiff $200 landing fee requirement on immigrants from Asia other than Japan and China. Although P.C. 926 was aimed at immigrants from India, British Columbia's major concern, the Superintendent of Immigration in Ottawa interpreted it to include Syrians, among other Asiatic groups.[8] This measure effectively restricted Syrian immigration to Canada.

During World War I, the Depression of the 1930s, and World War II, the Canadian government moved to limit the volume of total immigration, and this resulted in further restrictions on immigration from countries other than Britain and the United States. In the intervening years, the restrictions on Asian, hence Syrian, immigration remained unaltered, except for minor revisions. For example, in 1923 the Canadian government regarded the following classes of Asian immigrants as admissible: wives and minor children of Canadian residents, farmers, farm workers, and female domestic servants, "subject to a $250 landing money requirement and there being no contrary legislation (i.e. Chinese) or agreement (i.e. Japanese)."[9] Syrians, compared to other ethnic groups, did not engage appreciably in agricultural or domestic service occupations, hence these categories did not serve them well.[10] At any rate, the government moved to delete these occupational classes in 1931, and ruled that only full Canadian citizens, not residents, could bring their wives and minor children to Canada.

In view of the above, the rate of growth of the Arab-Canadian community, from 1911 to 1951, was very slow, and based largely on natural increase, that is, surplus of births over deaths. Table 1 shows the number of Syrian-born Arabs in Canada for the period 1911-1941. It will be observed that between 1911 and 1921, the Syrian-born Arabs increased by 972 persons, or from 2,907 in the former year to 3,879 in the latter year.[11] Between 1921 and 1931, only 74 persons of Arab origin were ad-

TABLE 1

Syrian-Born Arabs In Canada By Sex,
1911-1941

Year	Total	Male	Female
1911	2,907	1,885	1,022
1921	3,879	2,395	1,484
1931	3,953	2,305	1,648
1941	3,577	2,057	1,520

Sources: *Census of Canada*, 1931, Vol. I, Table 24, and
1941, Vol. IV, Table 18.

mitted to Canada; and between 1931 and 1941, with immigration all but discontinued and some first-generation Arabs passing away, the Syrian-born population decreased by 376 (from 3,953 in 1931 to 3,577 in 1941). Part of the decline in the number of Syrian-born immigrants may be due to return migration, but we do not have information on this process. Practically no Arab immigrants came to Canada between 1941 and 1945.

The above discussion has been confined to first-generation Arab Canadians, which is only a portion of the ethnic community. Table 2 shows the growth of this community by sex, for the period 1921-1971. The effects of restrictive immigration on the size of the Arab-Canadian population are clearly reflected in this table. The figures contained in Table 2 show that between 1921 and 1951 the growth rate of the Arab ethno-cultural group was small. This ethnic community increased by 22% between 1921 and 1931, 9% between 1931 and 1941, and only 4% between 1941 and 1951.

The Post-war Period

Since the end of World War II, the Canadian government has been under pressure from different sources, including ethnic groups, to liberalize its immigration policy. The government's response was slow in coming, but gradually more permissive immigration regulations were passed, the net effect of which was to allow admission of more immigrants from countries other than the United States and Western Europe. Specifically, shortly after the war, the Chinese Immigration Act was repealed and the continuous journey regulation pertaining to Asians was rescinded. Also, residents of Canada were allowed to sponsor different classes of relatives, but the policy allowed more degrees of sponsorable relatives for citizens of European than Asiatic countries. Significantly, however, "the citizens of most Middle Eastern countries came to be treated as Europeans rather than Asians for the purposes of sponsorship."[12]

Further regulations designed to reduce discrimination on the basis of race or national origin were passed in 1962 and 1967. Collectively, these regulations allowed citizens of Asian and African countries, among

TABLE 2

The Arab Population of Canada, By Sex, 1921-71

Year	Total	Male	Female
1921	8,282	4,595	3,687
1931*	10,753	5,796	4,957
1941	11,857	6,288	5,569
1951	12,301	6,469	5,832
1961	19,374	10,112	9,262
1971**	28,550	16,135	12,415

Sources: *Census of Canada, 1921*, Vol. I, Tables 22 and 25; *1941*, Vol. IV, Table 1; *1951*, Vol. I, Table 32; *1961*, Vol. 1.2, Table 35: *1971*, Bulletin 1.3-4, Table 18; and W. Burton Hurd, *Ethnic Origin and Nativity of the Canadian People* (Ottawa: Dominion Bureau of Statistics, 1941), p. 193, Table 2.

*The total for 1931 is obtained from Hurd (cited above). The corresponding sex distribution is determined on the basis of 116.9 males per 100 females, which is four points higher than the comparable 1941 sex ratio. See Hurd, p. 75, Table XXXIV.

**The 1971 figures are based on "mother tongue" rather than "ethnic origin." As such, they are an underestimate of the Arab-origin population of Canada.

others, to sponsor more degrees of relatives and provided nationals of these countries with more access as independent immigrants.

The liberalization of Canadian immigration policy brought nearly 4,000,000 immigrants in the period 1946-1975. More than one out of every 100 of these immigrants came from the Arab world, the exact total being 48,619 persons. Table 3 shows the number of Arab-origin immigrants admitted annually during this period. It will be seen that the heaviest influx of immigrants from Arab countries was in the second half of this period, during which the average number of persons admitted annually reached about 3,000 persons.

The period following World War II, particularly the decade of the 1960s, has witnessed not only a substantial growth in Arab immigration to Canada, but also significant changes in the characteristics and national origins of Arab immigrants. Prior to 1945, virtually all of the Arab immigrants to Canada came from Syria and Lebanon. In the post-war years, however, the national origins of Arab immigrants became more diversified, though Lebanon and, to a lesser degree, Syria have continued to send substantial numbers of immigrants to Canada. As Table 4 shows, between 1946 and 1975, the largest number of immigrants from the Arab world came from Egypt, followed by immigrants from Lebanon, Morocco, Syria, Jordan and Tunisia. In addition, a total of 1,904 immigrants originated from other Arab countries. Included among

TABLE 3

Arab Immigrants to Canada, 1946-1975

Year of Arrival	Number	Year of Arrival	Number
1946-1955*	1,491	1966	3,114
1956**	571	1967	3,608
1957**	563	1968	5,437
1958**	353	1969	3,256
1959**	404	1970	2,641
1960**	337	1971	1,967
1961**	301	1972	2,123
1962	1,912	1973	3,595
1963	2,281	1974	4,533
1964	3,379	1975	3,839
1965	2,914		
Total (1946-1975)	48,619		

Sources: Department of Manpower and Immigration, *Immigration Statistics, 1956; 1957; 1958; 1959; 1960; 1961; 1962; 1963; 1964; 1965; 1966*, Table 2; *1967; 1968; 1969; 1970; 1971; 1972; 1973; 1974*, Table 3; and *1975, Fourth Quarterly Report*, Table 1.

*The figure for the period 1946-1955 is taken from *Immigration Statistics, 1970*, Table 13.

**For the period 1956-1961, the figures are based on "ethnic origin." For the preceding and following years, the figures are based on "country of former or last permanent residence."

them were immigrants from Algeria (391), Saudi Arabia (301), Kuwait (285), Iraq (187), Libya (87), Sudan (55), Bahrain (45), Qatar (45), United Arab Emirates (U.A.E.) (23), Somalia (13), Mauretania (12), Yemen (12) and Oman (7).

Turning now to the total Arab-Canadian community in the post-war period, Table 2 shows that it rose from 12,301 persons in 1951, to 19,374 in 1961, and to 28,550 in 1971. In relative terms, the size of this ethnic community increased by 57% between 1951 and 1961, and 47% between 1961 and 1971.

The figure of 28,550 persons for 1971 is based on the number of Arab Canadians claiming Arabic as their mother tongue. This figure is a substantial underestimate of the actual size of the Arab-Canadian group because it does not include those Arab Canadians whose mother tongue is not Arabic (and there are many of those) or is not reported as Arabic. Technically, the 1971 figure is not comparable to the figures given for the preceding decennial years. Since the 1971 Canadian Census does not record a total for the Arab-Canadian community, as distinct from

TABLE 4

National Origins of Post-War Arab
Immigrants to Canada, 1946-75

Country of Last Permanent Residence	Number of Immigrants	Percentage
Egypt	18,115	37.3
Lebanon	16,333	33.6
Morocco	7,234	14.9
Syria	3,713	7.6
Jordan	737	1.5
Tunisia	583	1.2
Other*	1,904	3.9
Total	48,619	100.0%

Sources: See Table 3.

*The category of "other" includes 441 Arab immigrants officially classified as "Arabian" for whom no country of origin is specified.

mother tongue affiliation, we were forced to rely on estimates. Judging from the inflow of Arab immigrants to Canada, and allowing for natural increase, there were an estimated 50-60,000 people of Arab origin in Canada in 1971; and 70-80,000 at the end of 1975. Thus, a more realistic growth rate for the Arab-Canadian community, between 1961 and 1971, would be 30%.

Because of the shift from "ethnic origin" to "country of last permanent residence" in the data reported in *Immigration Statistics*, it is not easy to determine the precise origins of Arab Canadians. Judging from the statistical data presented, we can estimate that about one-half of the people in the Arab-Canadian community are of Syrian-Lebanese origin, one-fourth are of Egyptian origin, and the remainder are from other Arab States.[13]

To sum up, the two significant periods of growth in the history of the Arab-Canadian community are the formative period, 1891-1911, and the post-war period, starting in 1951. Both net migration and natural increase have played a significant role in the demographic evolution of the Arab ethno cultural group, but net migration has been the more important of the two.

GEOGRAPHICAL DISTRIBUTION

Immigrant groups have followed different settlement patterns in Canada. Some groups such as the Jews are largely urban, others like the Hutterites are rural, and still others like the Ukrainians are mixed. Some

59

groups such as the Irish are spread across the country, while others like the Doukhobors concentrate in one province or region. In cities as well as rural areas, some ethnic groups, like the Chinese or Italians in certain cities and Hutterites in rural areas, are identified with a physically separate neighbourhood or district, while others today like the Scottish are not so segregated. Apart from their sheer information value, these differing settlement patterns are significant because some of them facilitate while others hinder contacts with other Canadians. Hence the acculturative change of immigrant groups is influenced to a large degree by their geographical distribution. This section will focus on formation and geographical distribution of Arab settlements in Canada.

The Early Period

Historically, the Arab immigrants' first major destination in Canada was Montreal. Upon arrival in Montreal, many started as peddlers, ditch diggers, factory workers, or unskilled workers in a variety of service jobs. Of all the occupations in which Syrian immigrants were involved, peddling was to have the most profound effect not only on their economic well being, but also on their geographical distribution. At first, peddlers confined their activities to Montreal and its environs. They were supported in their endeavours by a yet more enterprising group of Syrian immigrants – those who opened wholesale stores to replenish the peddlers' merchandise. The Montreal experience was very encouraging and the energetic Syrian entrepreneurs, driven by a dream of success, began to move to other cities and provinces in the late 1880's and 1890's.

Accounts of geographical mobility of early Syrian peddlers and entrepreneurs show that they were prepared to go wherever business opportunities presented themselves. In the final decade of the last century, they penetrated the Quebec-Ontario countryside and, in addition, established businesses in Three Rivers, Ottawa, Toronto, London, Windsor (Leamington), Sault Ste. Marie and North Bay. At one point or another, Syrian business ventures, of shorter or longer duration, were also extended to such northern communities as Cobalt, Cochrane, Cowganda, Elk Lake, Matheson and New Liskeard.[14]

Syrian immigrants did not settle permanently in every community in which business was established. At that time they were geographically mobile, moving elsewhere when their business outgrew a given community. While some Syrian-origin Canadians lived permanently in smaller towns throughout the region, it was in larger cities, such as Montreal, Toronto and Ottawa, that the more enduring settlements were established. Business and job opportunities were abundant in these cities and Syrian immigrants were prone to follow in each other's footsteps. The coming together of relatively large numbers of Syrian immigrants in these cities was an important factor in the development of ethnic institutions, both religious and social. The new settlements became independent of the one in Montreal, attracting new arrivals from the Arab East and evolving in interaction with their immediate environment.

The next phase of settlement formation occurred in the first decade of this century when Syrian immigrants carried their business to the Maritime Provinces and to Western Canada. In the former region, the largest Syrian settlement was established in Halifax and the Sydney/Glace Bay region (Nova Scotia), followed by those in Saint John (New Brunswick), Charlottetown (Prince Edward Island) and St. John's (Newfoundland), in that order. Formation of Arab settlements in Western Canada occurred in Winnipeg and Edmonton and, to a lesser degree, Saskatoon, Calgary and Vancouver – again, in the larger cities. A few Syrian Arab families went into farming, homesteading mainly in Saskatchewan (around Saskatoon and Swift Current), but also in Manitoba and southern Alberta. Some Syrian immigrants settled in smaller centres throughout the region. As a general rule, supportive ethnic institutions were founded only in the larger urban settlements. The only exception to the rule concerns the small northern Alberta town of Lac La Biche which received its first Arab immigrant, Ali Abu Shehadi, in 1904.[15] In Lac La Biche, an identifiable Arab Muslim community evolved with a mosque and other distinctive ethnic organizations. The crystallization of an Arab ethnic community in Lac La Biche, despite the small number of Arab residents in that locality (about 100), was a postwar development, due largely to its members' ethnic loyalty and success as fur traders, mink ranchers and shopkeepers.

It is clear that the pioneer Syrian immigrants settled predominantly in Canadian cities. Well-informed Canadian officials were aware of this pattern of urban settlement among Syrians as early as 1913.[16] In the latest year for which relevant information is available (1941), prior to the influx of post-war Arab immigrants 86% of Syrian-born immigrants were classified as "urban."[17] The percentages varied by province: 89% in Prince Edward Island, 87% in Nova Scotia, 77% in New Brunswick, 94% in Quebec, 87% in Ontario, 64% in Manitoba, 49% in Saskatchewan, 66% in Alberta and 78% in British Columbia.[18] Another indication of the urban residence of Syrian immigrants is that in 1941, eighty-three per cent of them lived in places of 1,000 population and over, and 52% lived in cities of 30,000 and over.[19]

The earliest available statistics on the geographical distribution of this immigrant group are for the year 1911. Table 5 shows the numbers of Syrian-born immigrants and their percentage to the Canadian population, for Canada and the provinces, 1911-1941. It will be observed that first generation Arab Canadians, relative to the host Canadian population, were fairly evenly distributed throughout Canada. This is as true of 1911 as the three succeeding decennial census years (1921, 1931 and 1941). The provinces which attracted the largest numbers of Syrian-born immigrants were Quebec and Ontario and, to a lesser degree, Nova

TABLE 5

Percentage of Syrian-Born Immigrants to the Canadian Population, and Number,* for Canada and the Provinces, 1911-1941

	Canada	P.E.I.	Nova Scotia	N.B.	Quebec	Ontario	Manitoba	Saskatchewan	Alberta	British Columbia
1911	0.04	0.01	0.07	0.04	0.04	0.04	0.03	0.04	0.02	0.03
	(2,836)	(9)	(345)	(141)	(802)	(1,011)	(138)	(197)	(75)	(118)
1921	0.04	0.03	0.08	0.06	0.06	0.05	0.02	0.03	0.02	0.02
	(4,134)	(27)	(419)	(233)	(1,416)	(1,467)	(122)	(227)	(118)	(105)
1931	0.04	0.05	0.07	0.04	0.05	0.04	0.02	0.03	0.02	0.02
	(4,078)	(44)	(359)	(163)	(1,437)	(1,373)	(140)	(277)	(146)	(139)
1941	0.03	0.05	0.06	0.03	0.04	0.03	0.02	0.02	0.02	0.01
	(3,567)	(48)	(347)	(137)	(1,333)	(1,136)	(146)	(179)	(159)	(82)

Source: W. Burton Hurd, *Ethnic Origin and Nativity of the Canadian People* (Ottawa, 1941), Table 5, pp. 196-197.

*The n's are not included in the original source. They are computed on the basis of the percentages given relative to the appropriate provincial populations. The total n's for Canada are the summations of the provincial figures. The summated n's are within the acceptable range of rounding error for the corresponding percentage, except for the 1921 figure of 4,134 which represents 0.047 of the total Canadian population. Presumably this is due to rounding errors in the reported provincial percentages.

Scotia: throughout the period, approximately eight out of 10 Syrian-born immigrants lived in those three provinces. The remainder were distributed in the other six provinces.

In more concrete terms, the Syrian Canadians' relatively even spread, in relation to the inhabited areas of Canada, may be shown for 1941. On an index of segregation ranging from a low of 56 (for United States-born immigrants) to a high of 156 (for Icelanders), Syrian-born Canadians scored 80.[20] On this index, an immigrant group that was average on segregation would score 100. Comparison with other foreign-born immigrant groups shows that in 1941 the Syrians were eighth out of 36, preceded by the American, Scottish, French, Welsh, Irish, Danish and Swiss immigrants. No comparable indices are available for other census years, but according to the best available judgment Arab immigrants to Canada are among the least residentially segregated ethnic groups.

Another main characteristic of the early Syrian immigrants' residential distribution was the absence of separate neighbourhoods in which they and their institutions concentrated. In Toronto and Montreal, for example, the pattern followed was to locate at first in rooming houses in the inner city, but to disperse within a relatively short period of time.[21] The case records of the Arab Community Centre in Toronto reveal many inquiries from post-war Arab immigrants about the location of Toronto's Arab community. The Centre's uniform response is that the Arab community is scattered: the churches, mosques, businesses, restaurants, and residences of Arab Canadians are all dispersed. The Arab-Canadian community in Toronto and elsewhere in Canada is more of a mental than physical construct. It is, above all, a community of interest, a community of social and kinship networks that transcend neighbourhood and municipal boundaries.

The Post-war Period

The geographical distribution of the Arab-origin population of Canada for the years 1941-1971 is shown in Table 6. Although the 1971 figures, which are based on mother tongue rather than ethnic background, underrepresent the actual size of the Arab-Canadian community, they seem accurately to portray the geographical distribution of Canadians of Arab origin (judging from data on the destination of post-war Arab immigrants to Canada).

In 1941 Quebec and Ontario accounted for about two-thirds of the Arab population of Canada, with Quebec having an Arab community slightly larger than that of Ontario. Nova Scotia ranked third, followed by New Brunswick, Manitoba, Saskatchewan and Alberta. The two provinces with the smallest Arab-Canadian population in 1941 were British Columbia and Prince Edward Island.

In 1951 there was a slight change in the geographical distribution of the Arab population. While Quebec and Ontario continued to account for about two-thirds of the total number, Ontario's Arab community ex-

63

TABLE 6

The Arab Population of Canada, by Sex, for Provinces, 1941-1971

	Canada	New-foundland	P.E.I.	Nova Scotia	N.B.	Quebec	Ontario	Manitoba	Saskat-chewan	Alberta	British Columbia
1941											
Total	11,857	—	182	1,469	573	4,002	3,810	445	681	428	262
Male	6,288	—	98	786	303	2,135	1,985	242	352	251	131
Female	5,569	—	84	683	270	1,867	1,825	203	329	177	131
1951											
Total	12,301	277	208	1,397	392	3,622	4,578	455	466	504	393
Male	6,469	138	120	746	214	1,916	2,358	250	237	281	204
Female	5,832	139	88	651	178	1,706	2,220	205	229	223	189
1961											
Total	19,374	417	240	2,153	984	5,302	7,137	590	678	1,327	530
Male	10,112	213	129	1,157	505	2,817	3,632	304	354	720	270
Female	9,262	204	111	996	479	2,485	3,505	286	324	607	260
1971*											
Total	28,550	35	105	675	185	7,540	16,835	345	240	1,965	620
Male	16,135	20	50	375	100	4,215	9,510	210	130	1,115	400
Female	12,415	15	55	300	80	3,320	7,325	140	110	845	220

Sources: *Census of Canada, 1941*, Vol. IV, Table 1. The Territories had a total of 5 males. *Census of Canada, 1951*, Vol. I, Table 32. The Territories had a total of 9, of whom 4 were women. *Census of Canada, 1961*, Vol. I, Part: 2, Table 35. The Territories had a total of 16, of whom 5 were women. *Census of Canada, 1971*, Bulletin 1.3-4, Table 18. The Territories had a total of 10.

*The figures for 1971 are based on "mother tongue" rather than "ethnic origin."

ceeded that of Quebec by almost 1,000. Nova Scotia continued to have the third largest group in Canada, but it was smaller in 1951 than in 1941. Quebec and Saskatchewan also experienced a decline in the size of their Arab ethnic communities between 1941 and 1951. The data for 1961 reflect essentially the same pattern of distribution as for 1951, except that the size of the Arab communities in almost all the provinces increased considerably.

Between 1961 and 1971, three significant changes seem to have occurred in the geographical distribution of the Arab-Canadian community. The data for 1971 (Table 6) give an indication of these changes. First, the size of the Arab community in Ontario has greatly surpassed that of Quebec. Second, Alberta has the third largest Arab community in Canada. The Arab community of Nova Scotia now trails behind that of Alberta. Third, in 1971 Arab Canadians are more concentrated than in earlier years. About 92% of those claiming Arabic as mother tongue live in Quebec, Ontario and Alberta. In contrast, in 1961 the first three provinces accounted for only 75% of all Canadians of Arab origin.

Further insight into the current settlement patterns of Arab Canadians may be derived from *Immigration Statistics* which reports, annually, the intended destinations of immigrants from abroad. As immigrants enter Canada, each immigrant is questioned by an immigration officer about his (her) ethnic (racial) identity, citizenship, country of former residence, mode of arrival, destination in Canada, and intended occupation, among other things. Much of this information is summarized and published in statistical form.

An undetermined number of immigrants do not necessarily go to the province or city they report at the time of the interview, or if they go do not settle permanently there. However, for post-war Arab immigrants our sampling survey lends a considerable degree of validity to the measure of reported destinations. Specifically, the following question was asked of all first generation Arab Canadians: "To which city or town did you go when you first came to Canada?" The results show that about 75% of the respondents still live in the city to which they went when they first arrived in Canada, another 15% live in a different city in the same province, and only 10% live in a different city and province. A separate survey of Arab residents in Toronto further confirms that Arab-origin immigrants to Canada are not, geographically, a highly mobile group.[22]

Table 7 shows the origin and destination of post-war Arab immigrants. It is noteworthy that 58% reported Quebec as their destination, 32% reported Ontario as their destination, and five per cent selected Alberta. Thus, between 1946 and 1974, Quebec was mentioned as a point of destination about twice as frequently as Ontario, and about twelve times as frequently as Alberta. These three provinces, combined, accounted for about 95% of all post-war Arab immigrants.

The fact that a large proportion of the post-war wave of Arab im-

65

TABLE 7

Origin and Destination of Arab Immigrants to Canada, 1956-74

	Canada	New-found-land	P.E.I.	Nova Scotia	N.B.	Quebec	Ontario	Manitoba	Saskat-chewan	Alberta	British Columbia	NWT & Yukon
Egypt	17,156	21	4	87	105	11,827	4,209	196	112	366	229	—
Lebanon	14,493	8	46	543	113	5,385	6,444	78	117	1,507	244	8
Morocco	6,689	—	—	—	4	5,344	1,272	40	2	2	23	2
Syria	2,391	1	6	27	7	1,300	883	12	23	75	57	—
Jordan	521	2	—	8	1	49	366	24	2	33	36	—
Tunisia	468	—	—	1	1	382	74	2	—	6	2	—
Other	1,573	4	3	20	19	611	700	19	17	119	61	—
TOTAL	43,291	36	59	686	250	24,898	13,948	371	273	2,108	652	10

Sources: See Table 3.

66

migrants were from North Africa (57%), hence French-oriented, is a strong factor in their attraction to Quebec. On the average, about seven out of 10 immigrants from Egypt, Tunisia, Algeria and Morocco indicated preference for Quebec as a destination at the time of entry into Canada. In contrast, only four out of 10 Syrian-Lebanese immigrants registered a similar preference. Although the relative proportion of Quebec-bound Syrian-Lebanese immigrants is not as high as that of immigrants from North African Arab states, it has nevertheless yielded a large absolute number of immigrants selecting Quebec as an intended place of residence.

The drawing power of Quebec as a destination for Arab-origin immigrants, which is prominently reflected in Table 7, is hardly noticeable in Table 6. This is probably due to the fact that Canada-bound immigrants from Morocco were overwhelmingly Jewish and thus were not included in the "Arab-speaking" group shown in Table 6. Also, an undetermined number of immigrants from Egypt, together with their children, apparently did not report Arabic as their mother tongue. This is understandable since some of these immigrants were of a different ethnic origin, e.g., Armenians. Finally, the statistical data provided in Tables 6 and 7 are clearly not identical, and the discrepant totals shown in the two tables are based on different definitions and assumptions.

The post-war Arab immigrants have been no less urban oriented than their earlier counterparts. Canadian cities, with their established Arab communities, have been magnets for these immigrants. Also, in terms of their educational and occupational qualifications, the post-war Arab immigrants have been better suited for the urban than the rural labour force. Indeed, post-war immigrants to Canada, including those from Arab states, would have found it difficult to go into farming even if they were so inclined, due to diminishing opportunities for land settlement and mounting economic pressures on rural residents to migrate to urban areas. Thus, the urban focus of the early Arab-Canadian community has been reinforced by the recent arrivals.

Likewise, post-war Arab immigrants have reinforced the residential desegregation which characterized their predecessors. In a recent study of Toronto's Arab community, Reed concluded that "geographically there does not appear . . . to be a closely knit residential Arab community."[23] According to Reed, the pattern for new Arab immigrants was to locate, first, in the inner city of Toronto, and then move outward into mixed neighbourhoods.[24] Toronto is typical of the dispersed residential location of Arab Canadians today.

In the survey of Arabs in Toronto and Montreal, the following question was asked of all the foreign-born respondents: "Why did you go to (name of city or town of destination) when you first came to Canada?" The responses centred around five main categories: "relatives" (45%), "friends" (9%), "university" (7%), "orientation of the city of destination (whether English or French)" (16%), and "perceived prosperity of

67

that city," that is, abundance of work opportunities (12%). The balance of the responses, or 11%, referred to such varied reasons as "church," "only place I know of," and "recommended by the Immigration Officer." Clearly, "family" and "friends" were important factors in the Arab immigrants' selection of a destination in Canada. It is noteworthy that Arab immigrants to Canada made no explicit reference to the "Arab community" and its related institutions as factors in the selection of a destination. These are probably relevant, but only to the extent that they are comprehended by the prior factors of "family" and "friends." The findings suggest that for new Arab immigrants to Canada, ethnicity *per se* was not a crucial factor in geographical location; hence the even geographical spread of this ethnic group.

While "family" and "friends" accounted for the majority of responses regarding the selection of a destination in Canada, they were of minor importance in local residential choice. Reeds's study of Arab residents in Toronto lists the following reasons for the respondents' locating in their present residences: "convenience to work, school, shopping" (36%), "close to friends or relatives" (11%), "cost of dwelling was adequate (condominium or home)" (16%), "cost of rent was reasonable" (9%), and "good transportation" (16%). The balance of the responses listed the following reasons once or twice each: "residential area," "only dwelling available," "larger premises," "close to church," "out of way of noise," and "home purchased by parent."[25] On the basis of these findings, it might be observed that despite strong descent ties, there were no clear incentives for Arab Canadians to establish their own "Arabvilles" in Canada. Dispersion of Arab-Canadians' residences in Canadian cities remains the rule rather than the exception.

AGE-SEX COMPOSITION

Patterns of Change: Early and Later Years
Descriptive accounts of early Syrian immigrants to Canada characterize them as mostly male, relatively young, and largely unattached. This characterization emerges not only from Karam's study of Syrian immigrants, but also from official statistics and reminiscences of older respondents with whom I came in contact during this study. The Syrian immigrants' age-sex composition was certainly different from that of Canada as a whole, although relevant statistics on Syrians are not available for all census years.

It seems that in the first few years of Syrian immigration to Canada, women were almost totally absent because of cultural restrictions on their independent movement. However, in the late 1880s couples, some with children, as well as unattached women began to arrive.[26] Also, as men became more established socially and economically, women came to reunite with their husbands, or to get married if their suitor was unable to go to the "Old Country" to fetch his bride to Canada. The unattached women immigrants in general did not come to Canada as independent persons, but rather as relatives or persons sponsored by Syrians already resident in this country. This is consistent with the Arab cultural tradition of female dependency and emphasis on the nurturant role. The presence of Syrian women provided not only a secure and stable home environment in a strange land, but also a complementary economic role to that of the husband or guardian.

The sex composition of a given group of people is often depicted in the form of a "sex ratio" or "masculinity ratio," usually expressed as the number of males per 100 females. For Arab Canadians, as for other ethnic groups, two sets of sex ratios are available. The first set of sex ratios is for foreign-born Arab Canadians, that is, immigrants, and the second for Canadians of Arab origin regardless of whether they were born overseas or in Canada. Table 8 shows some basic facts about the sex composition of Arab immigrants and Arab-origin Canadians for the period 1911-1971.

Several important facts may be derived from Table 8. First, for any given year, the sex ratio is higher among immigrants than Canadians of Arab origin. Second, between 1911 and 1971 there was a steady decline in the percentage of men to women for both immigrants from the Arab world and the Arab-Canadian ethnic group, with only one exception. The exception concerns the increase in the percentage of males to females among Arab-origin Canadians from 109 in 1961 to 112 in 1971. This increase was due not only to the obvious over-representation of male immigrants from Arab states during the 1962-71 period, but also to the large number of such immigrants (30,512) which dwarfed the Arab-Canadian community of 1961 (19,374; sex ratio: 109).

The trend towards a steady decline in the percentage of males to females may be explained in large measure by marital status, a factor which equally influences the immigrant population and the resident ethnic group. Marriage and parenthood have a decisive balancing effect on the sex distribution of a given group of people, immigrant or otherwise. The evidence points to the presence of an increasing number of married couples with children among Arab immigrants in recent years, and to the eventual marriage of those who landed in Canada as unattached immigrants. The consistently lower proportion of males to females in the Arab-Canadian ethnic group, in comparison with the Arab immigrant population, is due primarily to the higher proportion of married adults in this group and, secondarily, to the return of some immigrants, inevitably most male, to their country of origin.

Differences Within the Post-war Arab Immigrant Group
As indicated earlier, the national origins of Arab immigrants to Canada have become more diversified in the past 20 years. While the sex ratio for

TABLE 8

Percentage of Males to Females for Arab Immigrants and Arab-Origin Canadians, 1911-71

	Males as Percentage of Females	
Year	Arab Immigrants	Arab-Origin Canadians
1911	184	—
1921	161	125
1931	140	117
1941	135	113
1951	—	111
1961	127*	109
1971	115	112**

Sources: See Tables 1 and 2 which give the numbers of males and females for the 1911-1941 immigrant groups and for the Arab-Canadian community (1921-1961); and Department of Manpower and Immigration, *Immigration Statistics, 1956; 1957*, Table 7; *1958; 1959; 1960; 1961; 1962; 1963; 1964; 1965*, Table 8; *1966; 1967; 1968; 1969; 1970; 1971*, Table 9.

*This percentage is based on the sex distribution of the 1956-1961 immigrant groups.

**This percentage is an estimate, representing the mid-point of the figures given for the Arab-Canadian community for 1961 (109) and Arab immigrants for 1971 (115).

Arab immigrants to Canada has been declining, there are noteworthy differences within the group. Table 9 shows the sex ratios for post-war national immigrant groups from different parts of the Arab world for the period 1956-74. It will be observed that the percentages of males to females ranged from a high of 232 for immigrants from Tunisia to a low of 99 for immigrants from Morocco. Only immigrants from Syria came close to the average of 121; the immigrants from Egypt and Morocco, who constitute a substantial portion of all Arab immigrants, were considerably below it. The Lebanese immigrants, the only remaining numerically significant group, were characterized by a relatively high sex ratio (141).

A fuller understanding of the demographic characteristics of Arab immigrants to Canada may be gained by considering age along with sex distribution. Among other things, this will assist in identifying the age groups in which the surplus of males is highest. Because of lack of information about the age and sex distribution of early Syrian immigrants, the present discussion will be limited to post-war Arab immigrants (1956-74). The age and sex distribution for Canada will serve as a standard for com-

TABLE 9

**Masculinity Ratios for Post-War Immigrants
From Selected Arab States**

Country	Number of Males per 100 Females
Tunisia	232
Algeria	184
Iraq	156
Jordan	148
Kuwait	148
Lebanon	141
Saudi Arabia	139
Syria	118
Egypt	110
Morocco	99
Total Post-war Arab Immigrants	121

parison. The population pyramid in Figure 1 shows the age-sex composition for Canada (1971), while Figure 2 shows the comparable distribution for post-war immigrants from the Arab world (1956-74).

Examination of Figures 1 and 2 shows that the Arab immigrant population is more youthful than the Canadian host population. Thirty-one per cent of the Canadian population are less than 20 years of age. The most outstanding difference betwen the two populations centres around the middle age group: 48% of the Arab immigrant population, as compared to 28% of the host population, are young adults (20-39 years of age). The position of the two populations is reversed in relation to the age group 40 years of age and over; 33% of the Canadian population and only 20% of Canada's Arab immigrants belong to this age group.

The second important fact shown in Figures 1 and 2 concerns the significantly higher proportion of males among the Arab immigrant population than in the Canadian population. Whereas the Canadian population at large is about evenly divided between the sexes, there is a clear surplus of males among Arab immigrants. Again, the greatest difference between the two groups is to be observed in the percentages of males to females in the middle (20-39) age group: 102 for the Canadian population, compared to 149 for the Arab immigrants. The younger and older age groups in both populations are almost evenly divided between the sexes. Thus the traditional image of immigrants from overseas, as being mostly male, young and unattached, still applies to Arab immigrants, but perhaps to a lesser degree today than at the turn of the century.

71

FIGURE 1
Age and Sex Distribution Canada: 1971

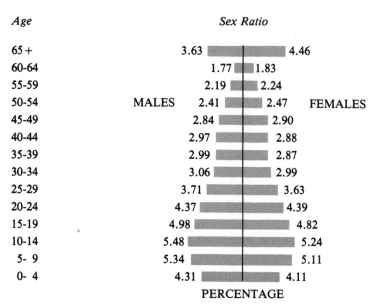

Age   *Sex Ratio*

Source: Population Research Laboratory, University of Alberta.

FACTORS IN MIGRATION

The Early Syrian Immigrants

The Arabs who migrated to Canada in the latter part of the nineteenth and the first few decades of the twentieth centuries were mostly Syrians and Christians. Estimates of the proportion of Christians among early Syrian immigrants to North America have ranged between 90% and 97%. The 1931 Census of Canada records only 645 Muslims in the country, out of a total of 10,070 Arab-origin Canadians. Why did emigration occur mostly from Syria? Why were Christians more inclined than other religious groups to migrate? And what were the intentions of early Syrian

72

FIGURE 2
Age and Sex Distribution Total Arab Immigrants: 1956 to 1974

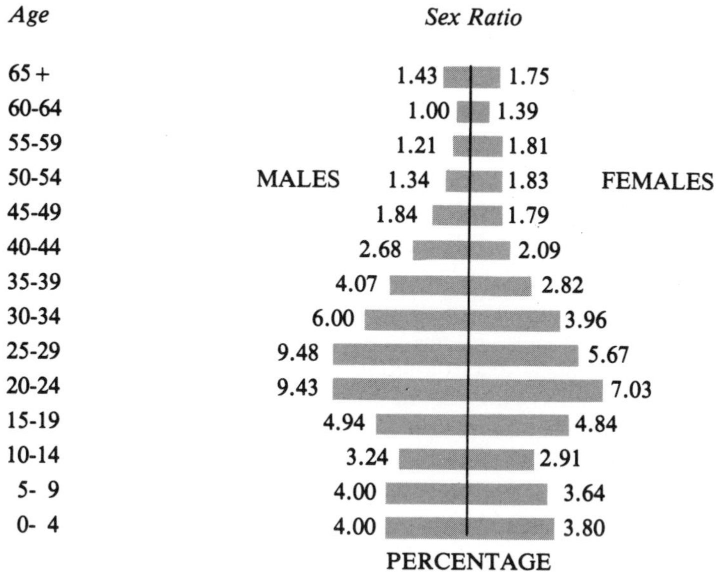

Age   *Sex Ratio*

Age	Males		Females
65+	1.43		1.75
60-64	1.00		1.39
55-59	1.21		1.81
50-54	MALES 1.34		1.83 FEMALES
45-49	1.84		1.79
40-44	2.68		2.09
35-39	4.07		2.82
30-34	6.00		3.96
25-29	9.48		5.67
20-24	9.43		7.03
15-19	4.94		4.84
10-14	3.24		2.91
5- 9	4.00		3.64
0- 4	4.00		3.80

PERCENTAGE

Source: Population Research Laboratory, University of Alberta.

immigrants? Answers to these questions will help identify causal factors in early Syrian immigration to Canada.

Awareness of the existence of large numbers of Christians in Syria provides a useful background, but does not constitute an adequate answer. For one thing, the Copts of Egypt, who outnumbered the Christian population of Syria, did not show a similar inclination to migrate. Also, the Christians of Syria were a numerical minority and they could not have swelled the ranks of emigrants by chance. To answer the above questions and thereby gain insight into the reasons underlying the migration of Christian Syrians, it is necessary to consider various aspects of Syrian society at that time and probe the motivational structure of the migrants themselves.

73

To begin with, the larger portion of the Arab world was under Turkish control until the end of World War I. Syria had the misfortune of being geographically very close to the Sublime Porte (the Ottoman Turkish court and government in Constantinople) and thus was subject to firmer control than other dominions of the Ottoman Empire. As a colonized people, Muslim and Christian Syrians were socially and politically oppressed under the Turkish rule – more so, for example, than the geographically more distant inhabitants of Arabia. But Syrian Muslim oppression was mitigated by their religious affinity with the colonial administration. No such mitigating circumstance existed for Syrian Christians. The Syrian Christians, in general, felt greater pressure from the Turkish rulers than their Muslim compatriots.

The aversion of Canada's early Syrian immigrants to the Turkish rule was well expressed by the Very Reverend Michael Zarbatany, parish priest of St. Nicholas Cathedral of the Syrian Eastern Orthodox Church, Montreal, who migrated to Canada in 1902:

> Syrian Christians were, therefore, living under the shadow of oppression, with the massacre of the 60s [1860s] still fresh in their memories, never knowing what fatal surprises the morrow held for them, and constantly discriminated against in their contacts with constituted authority. In view of all this and of their natural bent towards trade, and fondness for travel, is it to be wondered at that they should finally have found in emigration to America 'the Land of Freedom,' relief from all their fears and worries?[27]

In a similar vein, a Syrian-Canadian writer attributed the migration of Christian Syrians "to the pressure of the Turkish rule and the well known discrimination of that vindictive power against the Christian elements of its empire. . . ."[28]

One important aspect of the Turkish government's misrule concerns the *millet* system of administration which gave non-Muslim sects full legal control over matters pertaining to personal status, including marriage, divorce, adoption and inheritance. While non-Muslim religious leaders welcomed this autonomy, the *millet* system was used insidiously to divide the population, heighten the visibility of Christian sects and thus aid the government in having a stronger hold over them. Although religious separateness was not new to the region, the *millet* system exacerbated the situation by strengthening social and friendship relations within each sect and weakening them among sects. Because of increased social isolation from each other, sects tended to harbour feelings of jealousy, rivalry and suspicion towards each other. The Turkish rulers, in turn, paid scant attention to potentially explosive situations confronting different sects and tended to encourage conflict between sects. A notable example of this is the fierce Druse-Maronite conflict of 1860 which claimed the lives of over 11,000 Christians. The dislocations resulting from that conflict were felt for many decades and were an important factor in the migration of Syrian nationals.[29]

Another important element in the structure of Syrian society, relevant to the migration of Syrian Christians to the New World, was the presence of a large number of European (and, later, American) nationals in the region. European traders and missionaries were allowed as early as the seventeenth century under agreements between certain European powers and the Sublime Porte. According to these agreements, European nationals were to be under the direct protection of their respective consulates, subject only to the laws of their own countries regardless of where they lived in the Turkish dominion. Largely because of the presence in large numbers of these European nationals, the process of Westernization went farther in that region than anywhere else in the Arab world. Lebanon, in particular, is frequently identified as the most modern and most Westernized among the Arab states. The role of the missionaries was (and still is) particularly important, for in addition to their religious function they opened Western-type schools and established strong social relations with the local residents. The French missionaries worked closely with the Maronites, while the British missionaries established strong relations with the Druse and the Greek Orthodox sects. Typically, it was the Syrian Christians, not the Muslims, who acquired a Western orientation.

In addition to all the above, the economic conditions of the Syrian masses were miserable. The economy of The Lebanon, that is, the mountainous region of modern Lebanon, in particular, was hard hit by the decline of the silk industry, low agricultural productivity and increasing population pressure. The mountain peasants, many of whom were Christians, were searching for the slightest hint of possible relief. For many of these Syrian-Lebanese migrants, economic necessity played a major role in the desire to move. As we shall note in a subsequent chapter, Canada-bound Syrian immigrants came with little education and hardly any capital, but with a strong determination to work hard and succeed. The goal frequently expressed by these immigrants was to live in Canada for a short period and then return to Syria with enough money to guarantee their economic security there.

Beyond those conditions which pushed the Syrian migrants away from their homeland, there were conditions in Canada which pulled them to the adopted land. Canada was seen as a land of freedom and economic opportunities. This pull factor was revitalized constantly in Syrian villages and towns by remittances received from relatives abroad and by success stories of Syrians in the New World. Immigrants who returned to Syria, either permanently or for a short visit, provided concrete evidence of the promise which Canada held for immigrants.

Once the Syrian community was established in Canada, about the turn of the century, increasing numbers of Syrians looked to that community as to its counterparts elsewhere in the Americas with hope. On its part, the community did not disappoint. Syrian immigrants already established in Canada were receptive to and supportive of their kindred who wanted to join them in the New World. There was room, plenty of room, for newcomers from the Near East in the Syrian-Canadian community's expanding business and trade. Thus, relatives, friends and former neighbours were assisted in making the move to Canada. Naturally, the newcomers reinforced the early Arab immigrants' Christian and Syrian characteristics.

The Post-war Arab Immigrants

Canada's post-war immigrants from the Arab world were more heterogeneous than their earlier counterparts. More recent migrants included a larger proportion of non-Christians, they came from more diverse Arab countries, they represented a wider range of educational and occupational backgrounds, and they carried varying political ideologies and orientations. The reasons underlying their migration were both similar to and different from those characterizing the earlier wave of Arab immigrants. Social, economic and political factors in the Arab world were still primary reasons for the emigration of many Arab nationals, but the substance of these factors today is different from that of 70 or 80 years ago. A most important difference in the socio-political context of the earlier and more recent waves of Arab immigrants to Canada was the termination of Turkish colonial rule at the end of World War I and the eventual political independence of most Arab states in the post-World War II period.

The results of my survey of Canadians of Arab origin provide insights into the reasons underlying their immigration. The following question was asked of all foreign-born respondents: "For what reason(s) did you come to Canada? (List as many as may apply)." Table 10 provides a statistical summary of the responses to this question.

From this table, it will be observed that a large plurality of the responses centred around inducements in Canadian society. Included in these inducements are job and economic opportunities, educational opportunities, better future, and better standard of living. Clearly, the Canadian dream seems to have weighed heavily on the motivational structure of recent Arab immigrants. Also, judging from the evidence provided, recently the balance was more in favour of "pull" factors in the chosen land than "push" factors in the land of birth.

While both early and recent Arab immigrants were attracted by social and economic opportunities in Canada, there are important differences between the two groups. The former group consisted of a large number of mountain villagers and destitute individuals for whom emigration was an economic necessity. In contrast, post-war Arab immigrants included a large number of professionals and highly skilled individuals for whom emigration was rather an avenue for the fulfillment of high career and

TABLE 10

Factors in Arab Immigration to Canada		
1. Social and Career Advancement		*45%*
a. job and economic opportunities	23%	
b. educational opportunities	12	
c. better future	6	
d. better standard of living	4	
2. Kin and Friends		*21*
a. to join family and relatives	13	
b. for the sake of my children	4	
c. accompanied my family	3	
d. to join friends	1	
3. Political Considerations		*12*
a. political alienation from the home country	9	
b. to be free – democracy	2	
c. lost my country – cannot go home	1	
4. Spirit of Adventure		*9*
a. wish for adventure and change	5	
b. came to visit & travel and then stayed	4	
5. Miscellaneous Reasons		*13*
Total %		100
Number of Responses		(454)

professional aspirations. Moreover, many of the occupationally well-placed among recent immigrants referred to the goal of a higher education as a primary reason for coming to Canada. Some of these respondents entered the country as students and later decided to seek permanent residence. The goal of higher education was almost totally absent among the pioneer Arab immigrants.

Kin-related considerations constitute the second most important factor in post-war Arab immigration to Canada. About 21% of the responses given referred to family reunions, maintaining an intact family unit, and aspirations for children. In a few cases, friendship considerations played a role in the motivational structure of immigrants. The results further show that female respondents, as well as respondents with lower educational qualifications, tended to refer to family reasons more frequently than their male counterparts.

The third most important contribution to post-war emigration from the Arab world is the factor of political estrangement. The specifics of this factor varied, of course, from one respondent to another and from

77

one Arab country to another. Such terms as political instability, insecurity, loss (or fear of loss) of freedom, political repression, discriminatory treatment, and government policy (e.g., socialism) illustrate the nature of push factors involved. Respondents from Palestine added another element to the issue of political instability, and that is expulsion from and inability to return to the homeland.

The effects of political instability could be random, in the sense that they would prompt disparate individuals at different levels of the occupational hierarchy to migrate, or nonrandom, in the sense that they would prompt certain occupational groups or categories of people to migrate. Both types of effects were observed among our respondents. The first type of situation is exemplified by an immigrant from Lebanon who gave, as reasons for immigration, "political instability at home, democracy in Canada, and wish to join relatives." Reflecting further on the situation in Lebanon, he said: "The government is unjust. Each regime prefers its people and its own group and pays no attention to the needs of the masses." It is not easy to determine, in this case (or in other similar cases), whether political instability was a primary or a secondary reason for emigration.

The second type of situation involved instances in which the incidence of political estrangement or instability was not randomly distributed throughout the population. Leaving aside the issue of Palestinian refugees, these were typically associated with a fundamental restructuring of the political economy of a given country. A prime example is the Egyptian government's adoption of a socialist path under the late President Gamral Abdel Nasser. Not surprisingly, the political-economic reconstruction of Egypt led to the alienation of many people whose property, work, or means of livelihood were threatened by the socialistic measures of the early 1960s. At that time, the Egyptian government additionally imposed severe restrictions on imports, luxury goods, foreign travel, and export of Egyptian currency. As a consequence, the disaffection in Egypt spread to include such occupational groups as industrialists, entrepreneurs, financiers, businessmen, large landowners, professionals, and some white-collar workers in the tertiary sector of industry. These are upper-level occupational categories, which helps explain the select nature of Canada's immigrants from Egypt, educationally and occupationally. There was a heavy representation of Eastern Christians in these occupations. Since 1961, increasing numbers of alienated Egyptian nationals have been emigrating to different parts of the world, and a significant number of them have been Coptic and descendants of Lebanese-origin Maronites.

The results of my survey indicate that immigrants from Egypt tended to verbalize political disaffection and hopes for a higher standard of living and better future more frequently, and family reasons less frequently, than immigrants from other Arab states. In some cases, respondents attributed their migration, and that of their compatriots, partly to what they considered to be discriminatory treatment of non-Muslims in Egypt, and partly to lack of opportunities for advancement. The infrequent reference to family as an underlying reason for immigration is due to the short history of this stream of immigration to Canada, as well as the tendency among immigrants from Egypt to come as family units.

Table 10 shows that about nine per cent of the responses to the question on reasons for immigration to Canada refer to search for adventure, change, and travel followed by a decision to stay permanently. This composite factor is certainly not unique to Arab immigrants, but its presence as a motivating element in this group should be acknowledged. Although this factor ranks fourth on the list, it accounts for a good portion of the responses.

It is clear that the causes of Arab immigration to Canada are multiple. Like many other immigrant groups, Arab immigrants hoped for freedom and prosperity in the new land. Post-war Arab immigrants were influenced by factors similar to those which prompted the Syrian pioneers to come to this country. Yet there are important sources of differences between the two groups, the two most important being the differing political contexts which earlier and more recent Arab immigrants left behind, and the differing goals which each group set out to accomplish.

SUMMARY

The two main waves of Arab immigration to Canada occurred around the turn of the century and in the post-World War II period, particularly the 1960's. The latter is by far the larger of the two waves, hence the current numerical dominance of the foreign-born. Regardless of the wave in which they came, Arab immigrants have sought economic opportunities and freedom. Urban Canada has been their haven and, despite common ties to Arabic language and culture, they have spread rather evenly through the inhabited areas of the country, with no signs of neighbourhood concentrations. This settlement pattern makes ethnic integration problematic.

The changing character of Arab-Canadian immigration, in terms of evolutionary changes which have occurred both in the sending countries and in Canada, together with the wide time gap separating the two major waves of immigrants, has contributed to diversity within this ethnic group. Whereas the turn-of-the-century immigrants were overwhelmingly Christians from Syria and Lebanon, the post-war immigrants included both Christians and substantial numbers of Muslims from different Arab states, notably Egypt. A microcosm of the Arab world, this ethnic group encompasses a wide range of social and political orientations and varied adaptive experiences in the adopted land. It is a mosaic within the larger Canadian mosaic.

NOTES

1. Elias Karam, "Syrian Immigration to Canada," in Elias Karam, ed., *The Syrian Canadian National Review* (Ottawa, 1935), p. 19.
2. For a relevant discussion of immigration during this period, see Norman MacDonald, *Canada: Immigration and Colonization, 1841-1903* (Toronto, 1965).
3. Karam, *op. cit.*, pp. 19, 21 and 23.
4. Recorded by the Superintendent of Immigration, Ottawa, in a January 16, 1913, letter to Hon. Dr. Roche. See *Records of the Immigration Branch*, RG76, Vol. 431, File No. 622436: "Immigration from Syria and Lebanon, 1905-1910, 1913."
5. Department of Manpower and Immigration, 2. *The Immigration Program* (Ottawa, 1974), pp. 5 and 7.
6. Donald Avery, "Canadian Immigration Policy and the 'Foreign' Navy," in Jay Atherton *et. al.*, *Historical Papers 1972* (Montreal, 1972), p. 140.
7. Manpower and Immigration, 2. *The Immigration Program.* p. 9. (Emphasis in original)
8. See the Superintendent's letter to the Hon. Dr. Roche (Footnote 4).
9. 2. *The Immigration Program*, p. 13.
10. The majority of Syrian immigrants preferred self-employment as peddlers or shopkeepers, but some of them had to work as unskilled industrial labourers in urban centres. Although Canadian immigration policy, during the period 1896-1914, sought not to swell the urban population, there were no laws prohibiting the admission of city workers if they could make their way to Canada. See 2. *The Immigration Program*, p. 7.
11. There is a large discrepancy between these figures and the ones recorded by the Superintendent of Immigration, Ottawa, in 1913 (Footnote 4). The analyst will frequently encounter inconsistencies in statistical data arising from changes in definitions and procedures, as well as other factors. Judging from immigration statistics, the data reported in Table 1 appear to underestimate the numbers of Syrian-born Canadians.
12. 2. *The Immigration Program*, p. 22.
13. It is believed that the overwhelming majority of immigrants from Morocco were of Jewish background. There was no attempt to collect detailed information on this group, mainly because many of its members were being integrated into Montreal's Jewish community.
14. For further details, see Karam, *op. cit.*, p. 25ff.
15. A.M. Khattab, "The Assimilation of Arab Muslims in Alberta," M.A. Thesis, Department of Sociology, The University of Alberta, 1969, p. 23.
16. See footnote 4. The pattern of urban settlement among Syrians, or more generally Arab Canadians, has continued from the early times to the present. For information on pre-war Syrian immigrants, see W. Burton Hurd, *Ethnic Origin and Nativity of the Canadian People* (Ottawa, 1941), Table XXV, p. 62; Table 11A, p. 206; and Table 16, p. 209.

17. *Ibid.*, Table 11, p. 205.
18. *Ibid.*
19. *Ibid.*, Table 11A, p. 206; and Table 16, p. 209.
20. For a fuller discussion, see *ibid.*, pp. 88-92.
21. Karam, *op. cit.*, pp. 21-22.
22. Denys R. Reed, "The Arab Community in Toronto," unpublished manuscript, 1973.
23. *Ibid.*, p. 10.
24. *Ibid.*, p. 11.
25. *Ibid.*, p. 15.
26. Cf. Karam, p. 21.
27. Michael Zarbatany, "A Short History of Syria," in Karam, *op. cit.*, p. 17.
28. Karam, *op. cit.*, p. 25. Similar attitudes were expressed by Syrian immigrants to the United States. Cf. Philip M. Kayal and Joseph M. Kayal, *The Syrian-Lebanese in America* (Boston, 1975), p. 66.
29. Some non-Christians, adversely affected by the civil war, were also prompted to migrate. In his biography, an early Druse immigrant to Canada, for example, relates his father's experience. See Sheikh Muhammad Said Massoud, *I Fought As I Believed* (Montreal 1976), p. 5ff.

FOUR

Canada's Reception: Images of the Arabs

Towards the turn of the century, there was a dramatic change in the character of Canadian immigration. The dominant Anglo-Saxon group witnessed a heavy inflow of immigrants from eastern and southern Europe and Asia.[1] This change occasioned heated public debates focusing on two major issues: the first concerned the impact of immigration on Canadian culture and the second concerned the desirability of different types of immigrant groups.

Critics of the new immigration argued that Canada was and should remain Anglo-Saxon.[2] Although immigrants from northwestern Europe (the British Isles, the Scandinavian peninsula, Germany or France) were seen as presenting little or no threat to dominant traditions and institutions, the new immigrants of Latin, Slavic, Semitic and Oriental extractions were seen as distinct dangers.[3] Surfacing in some quarters of Canadian society, this view bifurcated the world into the familiar and hence superior and the unfamiliar and hence inferior.

As an extension of the above, there were assessments of the potential assimilability of different national groups. Popular images and stereotypes were further developed and elaborated, affecting virtually all immigrant groups. While there was recognition of the need for a larger Canadian population, some immigrants were more favourably regarded than others. The result was what might be termed a continuum of tolerability. At one extreme, there were those groups which, in the public mind, were seen as possessing such positive qualities as strength, initiative and self-reliance; at the other extreme, there were those groups that were seen as possessing such undesirable qualities as illiteracy, destitution and inability to conform to majority group standards. While there were parallels between this view and the bifurcated view of superior versus inferior civilizations, it differed in that it involved predictions regarding the assimilability and future development of specific immigrant groups on Canadian soil. Although there was no complete agreement among government officials and social critics, these predictions

82

reflected clear patterns. For example, whereas Oriental immigrants were judged to be unassimilable and thus undesirable, Slavic immigrants were judged to be potentially educable and assimilable, and hence tolerable.[4]

STEREOTYPES OF EARLY SYRIAN IMMIGRANTS

Like other immigrant groups, new Canadians of Arab or Syrian origins were, and still are, objects of comparative evaluation and stereotyping. As a consequence of this, certain perceived qualities of the Arabs have been accentuated and elaborated in the public consciousness. The picture is not altogether complimentary. While the content of the stereotype has changed over time, both in popular and serious discussions of the Arabs, stereotyped thinking has remained.

In one of the early studies of immigration to Canada, published in 1909, J.S. Woodsworth, then Superintendent of All Peoples' Mission in Winnipeg, quotes two negative assessments of Syrian immigrants. The first assessment, attributed to James D. Whelpley, author of *The Problem of the Immigrant*, says of the Syrians and Armenians:

In the country of their adoption they usually become itinerant merchants or factory hands. They are generally of a most undesirable class; and, while not vicious, their intellectual level is low. There are exceptions to this rule, but not in sufficient numbers to remove from this immigration movement the bad reputation it has attained among those brought into contact with it. The most dangerous feature is the general prevalence of contagious and loathsome diseases, some of which are difficult of detection, any one of which constitutes a serious threat to foreign communities into which these aliens are absorbed.[5]

The second negative assessment is attributed to Dr. Allan McLaughlin, of the U.S. Marine Hospital Service. Between 1903 and 1905, McLaughlin wrote a series of articles on "Immigration" for the *Popular Science Monthly*. In one of these articles, he was emphatic in his disapproval of the Syrian immigrants:

The mental processes of these people have an Oriental subtlety. Centuries of subjection, where existence was only possible through intrigue, deceit, and servility, have left their mark, and, through force of habit, they lie most naturally and by preference, and only tell the truth when it will serve their purpose best. Their wits are sharpened by generations of commercial dealing, and their business acumen is marvellous. With all due admiration for the mental qualities and trading skill of these parasites from the Near East, it cannot be said that they are anything in the vocations they follow but detrimental and burdensome. These people, in addition, because of their miserable physique and tendency to communicable disease, are a distinct menace, in their crowded, unsanitary quarters, to the health of the community. In their habits of life, their business methods, and their inability to perform labour or become producers, they do not compare favourably even with the Chinese, and the most consoling feature of their coming has been that they form a comparatively small part of our total immigration.[6]

Woodsworth did not examine the assertions of the two authorities critically. Neither did the then-Superintendent of Immigration in Ottawa, W.D. Scott, who regarded the Syrians as an undesirable class of immigrants. In office correspondence, Scott stated that the Syrian peddlers were "more of a nuisance than anything else to the residents of Canada."[7] On a different occasion, Scott said:

It cannot be denied that many of the Syrians who have come to this country have been successful from a financial point of view. Montreal especially furnishes many examples of Syrian merchants who have made large amounts of money not only in their regular capacity as traders but also as dealers in real estate. There is, however, a higher standard of citizenship than the mere ability to acquire dollars and cents, and it is in that broader sense, viz., lack of desire to assimilate, that the Syrians are looked upon by the Department as undesirable immigrants. A large number of Syrians who came to this country also suffer from trachoma and other eye diseases. Generally speaking, Syrians are city dwellers confining their attention largely to peddling or, when their financial position justifies, opening up stores for the sale of goods of Eastern manufacture.[8]

The terms most often applied to early Syrian immigrants may be summarized as follows:

Peddlers, factory workers
Skillful traders
Low intellectual level
Admirable mental qualities
Deceitful, habitual liars
Miserable physique with infectious diseases
Unsanitary, health menace

The image provided covers four major dimensions – occupational characteristics, mental qualities, moral qualities and health characteristics – all of which are couched in negative evaluative terms. The two seemingly positive qualities of Syrians, skill at trade and admirable mental qualities, are mentioned in relation to peddlery which, itself, is viewed as a non-productive and burdensome occupation. There seems to be a contradiction between Whelpley's and McLaughlin's evaluations of Syrians' mental abilities; however, the contradiction is probably more apparent than real because the two writers seem to be addressing different aspects of mental ability.

There are three sets of facts about early Syrian immigrants from which the above stereotype seems to have been manufactured. Although precise statistics are not available, it is true that many of them took to peddling and trade, in the hope that they would improve their economic position rapidly and then return to their homeland. Second, according to informants, the educational qualifications of these immigrants were quite low and many of them were illiterate. Again, precise statistics are not available, but it is relevant that of all the Syrian immigrants arriving at port of New York in 1899, 41% were illiterate; the comparable figure for 1904 was 55%.[9] Finally, upon arrival in Canada many of the early Syrian immigrants, being young and single, roomed together in crowded surroundings for both social and economic reasons. For any given person, this was a temporary accommodation arrangement which ended upon marriage.[10] There is little in these facts, even if augmented by other isolated bits of evidence of an unsystematic nature, to warrant a wholesale condemnation of early Syrian immigrants on occupational, mental, moral or health grounds.

The myths created about Arab immigrants were neither innocent nor unbiased. Whelpley and McLaughlin, together with Woodsworth, were reflecting the beliefs and ideologies of their contemporaries. It is impossible to estimate the difficulties faced by Arab Canadians in the face of these negative stereotypes, but a few assessments can be made.

THE OFFICIAL RESPONSE TO STEREOTYPING

Immigration Restriction

The most immediate and concrete effect of negative stereotyping was the creation of legislative measures to restrict the entry of "less desirable" ethnic groups. In particular, immigrants of Asian origin were singled out for discriminatory treatment. This was accomplished, in part, by Order in Council, P.C. 926 (1908), which required these immigrants to have "in their actual and personal possession and in their own right $200 upon arrival."[11] In view of the destitution which characterized the overwhelming majority of immigrants of Asian origin, the $200 requirement was severe. In practical terms, it meant debarment from entry to Canada. The effect of P.C. 926 on Syrian immigration to this country was substantially to reduce its volume, until the post-World War II period when Canada's immigration policy was liberalized.

Not surprisingly, Syrian Canadians made numerous representations to political leaders, requesting that their ethnic group be exempted from the restrictive Order in Council, P.C. 926. Their arguments centred around three main points: Syrians were Caucasians (white) and, as such should not be debarred from entry to Canada; P.C. 926 was aimed at East Indian (Hindu), not Syrian, immigrants; and following the 1920 San Remo conference, Syrian Canadians further argued that Syrians should be classified as of European rather than of Asiatic origin, because Syria (i.e., the Greater Syria region, including modern Syria and Lebanon, Palestine and Jordan) was under British and French protection.

The politicians to whom such representations were made frequently sent related inquiries to the Superintendent of Immigration in Ottawa, but the latter invariably provided an unfavourable interpretation of P.C. 926. For example, with reference to an inquiry from the Honourable Dr. Roche, on the eve of receiving a delegation of Syrians from Montreal, the Superintendent's January 16, 1913, response read in part as follows:

> The delegation will no doubt represent to you that P.C. 926 was promulgated solely for the purpose of debarring the entry of Hindoos. Such an assertion upon their part, if made, will not be in accordance with the facts of the case. Primarily it was the large influx of Hindoos which directed the attention of the then Government to the question of Asiatic immigration, and when the question was under consideration it was felt that with the possible exception of Russia in Asia that continent did not supply to this country a class of people who would become assimilated and form true Canadians in the best and widest meaning of the term. The regulation above referred to was, therefore, intentionally drafted so that it would include not only the Hindoos but also Arabians, Turks, Syrians and Persians. . . .
>
> I consider it would be a great mistake to so alter P.C. 926 that it would not apply to persons of Syrian origin.[12]

Also, in response to a similar inquiry from one Mr. Clements, the Superintendent of Immigration's March 27, 1913, letter stated, in part:

> I have before me your letter of the 22nd instant, with its enclosure, being a letter addressed to you by certain Syrians now resident at Prince Rupert and district. . . .
>
> . . . In a book called 'Strangers Within our Gates', written by Rev. James S.Woodsworth, Superintendent of All-Peoples' Mission, Winnipeg, some not very complimentary remarks are made with reference to people coming from the Turkish empire. I quote the following. . . .
>
> In view of the above, I am not prepared to recommend any change in the Asiatic Order-in-Council.[13]

The issues of immigration restrictions and racial origin, looming large in the minds of Syrian Canadians, were considered, as late as 1935, in Joseph's Helal's report on the history and accomplishments of the Syrian National Society of Canada:

> Another important matter dealt with by this society was in respect to the interpretation of the Canadian Immigration Act of the racial

origin of Syrians. In (this) case, although the monetary restriction still remains, the Society succeeded in establishing, to the fullest satisfaction of the authorities, the fact that Syrians do not come under any racial category other than that of the white race, so that the Asiatic classification became technical rather than real.[14]

In practice, however, it was not until the 1950's that Arab, including Syrian and Lebanese, immigrants to Canada could sponsor the same classes of relatives as did their European counterparts.

The Issue of Turkish Citizenship
In addition to the above, early Syrian immigrants were adversely influenced by another factor unique to this ethnic group. Though Arab in origin, they were Turkish subjects and in Canada, much to their discomfort, the distinction between Turk and Syrian was often blurred. The fact that official Canadian statistics combined the two categories was disagreeable but not harmful to these immigrants. However, the issue became critical when Turkey became Canada's enemy in World War I. At that time, Syrians were regarded as alien enemies on technical rather than substantive grounds. As late as 1920, a senior Canadian official stated that Syrians were "still regarded as persons who were citizens of Turkey, an alien enemy country, and they would not be given any facilities either by Ottawa, or this office (the London office of the Superintendent of Emigration for Canada), to reach or enter Canada, and if they (were) rejected, they must take their own responsibility."[15]

Clearly, the well-being of Syrian Canadians was being threatened by this attitude. Even before World War I, Syrians attempted to correct Canada's image of them by expressing negative attitudes towards Turkey, the country that controlled their ancestral homeland and oppressed them.[16] At that time, many Syrians acquired Canadian citizenship, in part to avoid further association with Turkey. On the eve of and throughout World War I, their patriotism was singularly towards Canada. A celebrated example of this was the case of a Syrian from Montreal, named Salim Boosamra, who purchased a ring at an auction for the Patriotic Fund, paying $1,000 for it. The full story was carried on the front page of the September 19, 1914, issue of the *Montreal Daily Star*. The report concluded by stating that "Mr. Boosamra told how he had come to Canada from Syria a poor man, and was glad to be able to help the Fund."

The confusion regarding the identity and origin of Syrian Canadians was resolved by a 1937 agreement between France and Turkey allowing these Turkish citizens to opt for Syrian or Lebanese nationality. Appropriate arrangements were made for implementation of the agreement, and declarations of nationality had to be taken on or before May 28, 1938. Persons failing to take a declaration by the set deadline would be considered by the Turkish government as Turkish subjects. Inquiries were made by Syrian Canadians regarding the implications of such declarations to their status in Canada, and the Secretary of State for External Affairs ruled that the taking of such a declaration would not jeopardize their position and responsibilities as naturalized British subjects.[17] With this the blurring of the line between Syrian and Turk came to an unceremonious end.

THE ZIONIST IDEOLOGY: A NEW CHALLENGE FOR ARAB CANADIANS

Negative attitudes towards Arab immigrants during the early part of this century were part of a broader ideological climate which generally dichotomized the world's peoples into the acceptable and the unacceptable. Not only Arabs were subject to invidious comparisons, but also Chinese, Japanese, East Indian and eastern, central and southern European immigrants. It was a climate of relative tolerance laced with the potential for hostility, the legacy of which has been shared by many non-mainstream immigrant groups. However, the Arab Canadians faced an additional problem threatening their acceptance in Canada in the form of Zionism, an international political movement, which had as its goal the establishment of an independent Jewish state in Palestine, then an Arab country occupied by indigenous Christian and Muslim Arabs. By the early 1940s, repercussions from the Zionist movement were making significant impact on the Arab-Canadian community.

The Zionist movement had been established in the latter part of the nineteenth century in response to the oppression of Jewish communities through much of Europe. The movement's founder, Dr. Theodor Herzl, argued that since anti-Semitism was impossible to eradicate the only sure protection for Jews would be through the existence of their own Jewish state. The first Zionist Congress met in Basle, Switzerland, in 1897 and the following programme was formulated: the promotion of Jewish immigration to Palestine; the "organization and binding together of the whole of Jewry" through appropriate means; moves to strengthen and foster Jewish national sentiment and consciousness; and working to gain the approval of major world governments for Zionist objectives.

Through the years the *raison d'être* of the movement was elaborated, as were its strategies. One of the major issues facing the Zionist movement at the beginning was to justify the creation of a Jewish state in Palestine. The justification which was developed and elaborated through a carefully conceived and funded campaign encompassed some uncomplimentary characterizations of Arabs.

For example, in a recently published autobiography, M.S. Massoud has described the period from 1943-48 as a formative one of Arab consciousness in Canada.[18] The development of Arab-Canadian consciousness was, in large measure, a response to the intense propaganda campaign mounted by Zionists working towards the establishment of Israel and United Nations approval (given in 1947) to partition Palestine into Jewish and Arab states. Massoud, a Lebanese Druse who came to Canada as a teenager in 1909, found himself drawn into active defense of the Arab cause during this period. According to his report, his involvement came as a direct result of the following statement by a rabbi which was carried in the August, 1943, issue of the *Montreal Daily Star*: "Arabs are by nature a lazy people. They have dried up the land in Palestine and turned it into a desert. Therefore England should give this land to the Jews. They can make it flourish as it used to in Roman times." [19]

Another prominent Jewish leader, Herbert Mowat, Executive Director of the Canadian-Palestine Committee, in a 1945 letter quoted in the House of Commons, referred to Arabs as "a *primitive* people . . . [who have] profited in gold and various concessions in the past. . . . There is no doubt that a policy on Palestine agreed upon by the United States, Great Britain, and the other united nations will be one to which the Arabs will be *forced* to adjust themselves. . . ." [20]

Literature, speeches and films which argued the Zionist case, in the process argued the unworthiness of Arab identification with Palestine and of Arab protests against its annexation. Arabs were often portrayed as lazy, primitive, fanatical and barbaric. For example, the best-selling pro-Zionist book, *Exodus*, published in the late 1950s and made into an extremely successful, award-winning film, contains many negative characterizations of Arabs which, couched in the seemingly innocuous entertainment medium of the novel have a powerful impact. When the film based on this book was shown in Toronto, groups of Arab Canadians picketed the theatre in protest. One of the picketers was quoted in the press as describing Uris' book as the "embodiment of all that is most reprehensible in Zionist propaganda [because it] assassinates the character of Arabs from beginning to end." [21]

In a sense, Arab Canadians have been doubly jeopardized. On the one hand, they were the objects of negative stereotyping, much the same as other non-mainstream immigrant groups. But unlike these groups, Arab Canadians have also been maligned by the ideology of the Zionist movement which, in the process of justifying the Zionists' claims to Palestine, served to buttress negative stereotypes of the Arab. The following section will document examples of contemporary writing on Arabs, both in the entertainment and educational media, which continues to reflect the influence of the Zionist perspective.

CONTEMPORARY PORTRAYALS OF THE ARABS

For various reasons, social attitudes towards a given ethnic group may change over time and, similarly, stereotypes associated with the group in question may undergo modification and change. In this section, I will identify changes occurring in Canada in the recent past in the portrayals of the Arabs.

89

In a recent study of English- and French-language social studies text-books used in Ontario schools, McDiarmid and Pratt observe that "prejudice still manifests itself in textbooks, but because it has been less respectable it is more subtle. Immigrants may no longer be called 'shiftless and vicious,' but there are still instances where they are referred to as 'a problem' or 'a swarm.' It may be that these terms have a more immediate effect on readers' attitudes than would more obvious discriminatory references."[22] The question of effects aside, the important implication of this is that at the present time, as a general rule, one is not likely to encounter blatantly-worded stereotypes of Arabs. Despite this significant shift in form, available evidence indicates that negative social attitudes towards and stereotyping of Arabs continue to exist.

For example, in a specially designed analysis of 69 history texts approved for use in Ontario schools in Grades 5 to 12, McDiarmid and Pratt have identified the ten evaluative words most frequently applied to each of four groups: Arabs, French Canadians, Indians and Negroes. The results are shown in Table 11. With reference to Arabs, one will encounter such evaluative terms as cruel, feuding, pagan, dictator, fierce and resentful. To be sure, not all the evaluative terms applied to Arabs are negative, but the composite image, in general, is unfavourable. The resulting stereotype of Arabs, as well as that of Indians and Negroes, revealed by McDiarmid and Pratt's study, is prevalent in North America.[23]

Using a continuum ranging from +2 (most favourable) to -2 (most unfavourable), McDiarmid and Pratt were able to identify the relative positions of the four groups considered in Table 11. The results are shown in Figure 3. It is clear from this figure that only French Canadians are treated favourably in the textbooks under study. The Arabs, Negroes, and Indians, in that descending order, are all located on the negative side of the continuum.

In a broader analysis of 143 Canadian textbooks, McDiarmid and Pratt show that the five evaluative terms most often applied to Muslims are: infidels, fanatical, great, devout and tolerant.[24] While the terms Muslim and Arab are not synonymous, the target group, Muslims, is not totally irrelevant to the study of Canadian images of Arabs. In contrast, the evaluative terms most frequently applied to Christians – the control group in the study – include: devoted, zealous, martyr, great and famous.[25] It is doubtful that these evaluative terms would apply equally to Eastern Arab Christians and Western Christians. Canadians, and Westerners in general, tend to associate Christianity and related favourable qualities with Western rather than with Eastern Christians. The core curriculum of the United Church of Canada's Sunday School textbooks does not even acknowledge the existence of Arab Christians.[26] If and when their existence is acknowledged, Eastern Christians do not receive favourable treatment. A recent survey of Ontario school teachers, for example, shows that "the picture given of Eastern Chris-

TABLE 11

Ten Evaluative Terms Most Often Applied to Four Groups
in History Texts Used in Canada

Arabs	French Canadians	Indians	Negroes
great	great	savage	friendly
cruel	brave	friendly	unfriendly
feuding	courageous	massacre	savage
kind	skillful	skillful	faithful
pagan	heroic	hostile	kind
brilliant	determined	fierce	fierce
dictator	proud	great	primitive
fierce	devoted	murder	murder
friendly	famous	unfriendly	violent
resentful	daring	thief	backward

Source: McDiarmid and Pratt, *Teaching Prejudice*, p. 127.

tians was one of rigid dogmatism, deceit, and hypocrisy – in short, of Byzantine deviousness."[27]

In a follow-up study of the treatment of the Middle East in social science textbooks authorized for use in Ontario schools, Kenny confirms that Canadian texts contain biases and factual errors regarding Arabs and Islam. For example, in one textbook the author asserts "that Islam was born among the nomads of Arabia, who were 'wholly illiterate,' and for whom 'caravan-raiding was a cherished pastime.' "[28] Kenny's study also shows that Ontario school teachers reflected the same stereotypes and biases found in social science textbooks. For example, in response to a question about the characteristics most frequently associated with Arabs, teachers noted the following: "wild, uncivilized, nomadic, backward, disorganized, and militant against Israel."[29]

It is significant that Canadian teachers' images of Arabs encompass the notion of "militancy against Israel," implying that the confrontations have been one-sided. Closer examination of the treatment of the Middle East peoples in the media shows that the Palestine question and the Arab-Israeli conflict are important factors in the structuring of a negative image of Arabs. This is true even of some Christian church publications which portray the Arab in "the image of a nomadic adversary and territorial intruder."[30] One children's text contains the following:

If you were to visit Bible lands today you would see that many of the people in the Arab countries are nomads . . . [moving] from place to place to find food and water . . . [living] in tents made of goat skins and camel hair. . . .

91

FIGURE 3
Location of Four Groups on a Favourable-Unfavourable Continuum

Favourable

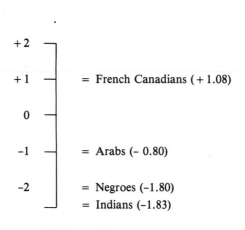

Unfavourable

Source: McDiarmid and Pratt, *Teaching Prejudice*, p. 126.

The Israelites had no transportation that could compare with the speed of the Arabian camels. They were terrified of these nomads who swooped down upon their land. They destroyed their homes and food, then dashed away on their fast camels. . . . Today the descendants of the Midianites and Arabs continue to attack the cities of Israel trying to drive them out of the land."[31]

The point that needs to be stressed here is that contemporary Canadian and Western images of Arabs are based not only on the traditional ethno centrism manifest in virtually all national groups, but also on what appear commonly to be one-sided assessments of the Arab-Israeli conflict. The caricature of Arabs stresses negatively evaluated qualities (e.g., "nomadism," "backwardness," "bad guys") in the cause of strengthening Zionist political claims.

There are Canadians who have provided other assessments of the Palestine question and the Arab-Israeli conflict. Notable among these are the late A.C. Forrest (as editor of the *United Church Observer*) and Frank H. Epp (former editor of *The Canadian Mennonite* and now President of Conrad Grebel College, University of Waterloo, Ontario), whose recent writings constitute a distinct departure from the typically negative treatment of Arabs in the Canadian mass media.[32] "When I returned to the Middle East in 1968," writes Forrest, "I was conscious of the distortion of the Arab image for which churchmen and the church press and fund raisers have been partly responsible."[33] In his *Unholy Land*, as well as other publications, Forrest has made a determined effort to present a different view of Arabs and Palestinians.

In a similar vein, Epp states:

> The Zionists, encouraged by the stance of the Christians and the policies of Christian nations, promoted dreams and visions that discounted the native population [the Palestinian Arabs], much in the same way that European immigrants to North America through the years discounted the humanity of the native Indian and Eskimo populations. The Zionists did not ask about the rights of the Arabs. The League of Nations allowed itself to be blinded by the Zionists and the big powers, which had material interests in the Middle East, all on the assumption that the Arabs were not aware, mature, alert, capable or even there.[34]

The heart of the problem, according to Epp, is that "the attempt to redress a wrong against the Jews [in Nazi Germany and elsewhere in Europe] produced a similar wrong against the Palestinian Arabs."[35] In a subsequent publication, Epp has provided a vivid portrayal of the Palestinian people.[36]

Despite efforts such as the above, the popular literature remains heavily slanted in favour of the Zionists and the state of Israel. The respondents to our survey have reflected acute sensitivity to this bias and the overwhelming majority of them contend that mass media treatment of Arabs has been unfair. The specific question asked was: "In your judgement, how fair are the mass media (newspapers, radio, TV) in their treatment of Arabic-speaking people? Four response categories were provided: "very fair," "somewhat fair," "somewhat unfair," and "very unfair." The percentage distribution of the responses is as follows:

Very fair	1.5%
Somewhat fair	17
Somewhat unfair	31.5
Very unfair	50

Moreover, Arab Canadians do not believe that they are highly regarded in Canadian society. The following question was asked of all the respondents: "In your judgement, how do Canadians generally regard people of Arabic-speaking origin?" Five response categories were provided: "very highly," "highly," "average," "below average," and "poorly." The percentage distribution of the responses is as follows:

Very highly	2.5%
Highly	14
Average	47
Below average	21.3
Poorly	15.2

Negative social attitudes towards a minority group involve not only prejudice and stereotyping, but also the potential for discriminatory treatment. The present study did not attempt to investigate claims of discriminatory treatment accorded Arab Canadians, but it is significant that when the respondents were asked: "Have you ever faced any discrimination or ill treatment because of your national or ethnic origin?" about 36% answered yes. The areas in which these respondents perceived discriminatory treatment include employment, housing, education and a multitude of public social service areas.

SUMMARY

Canada has experienced an ebb and flow in its receptivity to new immigrants. Around the turn of the century, the heavy influx of immigrants from Asia and eastern and southern Europe heightened concerns that this stream of immigration would have a negative impact on Canada's Anglo-Saxon heritage. These concerns meshed with existing stereotypes regarding the donor groups, resulting in a hierarchy of immigrant acceptability. Within this context, Arab immigrants, as people of non-Western extraction, found rising barriers against their admission. Few of the qualities attributed to Arabs were positive and most were negative. At the official level, they were regarded as undesirable immigrants who would be difficult to assimilate.

Following the end of World War II, there was a liberalization of Canada's immigration policy and large numbers of Arab immigrants have since been admitted to Canada. However, the stereotype of the Arab remains highly uncomplimentary. Analyses of Canadian media, including school textbooks, find portrayals of Arabs ranging from unsympathetic to derogatory, and frequently erroneous. Thus, a network of stereotypes shifting in content through the century, but persisting, surrounds the Arab Canadian and threatens the balance between old and new identifications.

Against this are the few accounts that treat Arabs favourably and the many rewards of the adopted country. Arab immigrants to Canada saw their move as one of opportunity and saw Canada as providing greater freedom. Also, the federal government's recently adopted policy of multiculturalism seems to have had a positive effect on the Arab-Canadian community. For these reasons, Arab Canadians continue to feel a strong affinity for Canada as a country and Canadians as a people.

NOTES

1. Between 1901 and 1913, over four million immigrants, including sizable numbers of non-British and non-Western Europeans, were admitted to Canada.
2. For a detailed discussion, see D.C. Corbett, *Canada's Immigration Policy* (Toronto, 1957); and Freda Hawkins, *Canada and Immigration* (Montreal, 1972).
3. For a concise discussion of racial attitudes in Canada, see John Porter, *The Vertical Mosaic* (Toronto, 1965), pp. 60-68. See also J.S. Woodsworth, *Strangers Within Our Gates* (Toronto, 1972). Woodsworth's book, first published in 1909, is a valuable study of the problem of the immigrant at the beginning of the present century. All references to this work are based on the 1972 edition.
4. Cf. Porter, *op. cit.*, p. 66.
5. As quoted in *ibid.*
6. As quoted in *ibid.*, p. 139.
7. *Records of the Immigration Branch* (Record Group 76), RG 76, Vol. 552, File No. 801591, Pts. 1, 2, 3: "Immigration from Syria and Lebanon, 1910-1949." (Letter from W.D. Scott to Mr. Clements, dated March 27, 1913.)
8. *Records of the Immigration Branch* (Record Group 76), RG 76, Vol. 431, File No. 642439: "Immigration for Syria and Lebanon, 1905-1910, 1913." (Letter from W.D. Scott to the Honourable Dr. Roche, dated January 16, 1913.)
9. Woodsworth, *op. cit.*, p. 205.
10. For a description of the situation of early Syrian immigrants, see Elias Karam, "Syrian Immigration to Canada," in Elias Karam, ed., *The Syrian Canadian National Review* (Ottawa, 1935), pp. 19-37.
11. Letter from W.D. Scott, Superintendent of Immigration, to the Honourable Dr. Roche, dated January 16, 1913. (See footnote 8) It should be noted that the 1910 Immigration Act gave extensive powers to the government. For example, Section 37 reads:

> Regulations made by the Governor in Council under this Act may provide as a condition of permission to land in Canada that immigrants and tourists shall possess in their own right money to a prescribed minimum amount, which amount may vary according to

95

the race, occupation or destination of such immigrant or tourist, and otherwise according to the circumstances; and may also provide that all persons coming to Canada directly or indirectly from countries which issue passports or penal certificates to persons leaving such countries shall produce such passports or penal certificates on demand of the immigration officer in charge before being allowed to land in Canada.

12. *Ibid.*
13. See footnote 7.
14. Joseph Helal, "Resumé of the History of the Syrian Canadian Association-Montreal," in Karam, *op. cit.*, p. 38.
15. *Records of the Immigration Branch* (Record Group 76), RG 76, Vol. 522, File No. 801591, Pts. 1, 2, 3: "Immigration from Syria and Lebanon, 1910-1949." (Letter from J. Obed Smith, Superintendent of Emigration for Canada (London), to Dr. Philippe Roy (General Commissioner for Canada in France), dated May 27, 1920.)
16. See, for example, a 1916 (May 30) telegram from the Canadian Lebanon Association, Vancouver, to the Prime Minister, condemning the Turkish government for contemplating "a massacre of our people in Mount Lebanon . . .," in Sir Robert Borden Papers (Manuscript Group 26 H), MG 26 H, Vol. 191, pp. 106720-106721.
17. *Records of the Department of External Affairs* (Record Group 25), RG 25, 61(a), Vol. 1845, File No. 766: "National Status of Syrians and Lebanese, 1937-38." (Telegram from the Secretary of State for External Affairs, to the Secretary of State for Newfoundland, dated January 20, 1938.)
18. Muhammad Said Massoud, *I Fought As I Believed* (Montreal, 1976), p. 11.
19. As quoted in *ibid.*
20. Norman Jaques, *House of Commons Debates*, December 17, 1945. As a member of the Committee on External Affairs, Mr. Jaques, on that day, delivered some remarks in the House of Commons on the question of Palestine. The speech shows that he was very critical of Zionist propaganda and its misrepresentation of facts. He was critical of the letter which he received from Mr. Mowat and read during his presentation in the House of Commons. (Emphasis supplied.)
21. The statement is attributed to Mr. James Peters, an Arab-Canadian leader from Toronto, in the March 23, 1961, issue of the *Toronto Daily Star*.
22. Garnet McDiarmid and David Pratt, *Teaching Prejudice* (Toronto, 1971), p. 25.
23. *Ibid.*, p. 127.
24. *Ibid.*, p. 41.
25. *Ibid.* For comparative purposes, it may be added that the terms most frequently applied to Jews include: great, faithful, just(ice), wise, genius;

the terms applied to immigrants include: hardworking, enriched Canada, contribution, skillful, problem; the terms most frequently applied to Negroes are: primitive, friendly, fierce, savage, superstitious; and the evaluative terms most often applied to Indians include: savage(s), friendly, fierce, hostile, skillful.

26. Cf. Sharon McIrvin Abu-Laban, "Stereotypes of Middle East Peoples: An Analysis of Church School Curricula," in Baha Abu-Laban and Faith T. Zeadey, eds., *Arabs in America; Myths and Realities* (Wilmette, Illinois, 1975), p. 163.

27. L.M. Kenny, "The Middle East in Canadian Social Science Textbooks," in Abu-Laban and Zeadey, *op. cit.*, p. 139.

28. As quoted in *ibid.*, p. 140.

29. *Ibid.*, pp. 138-39.

30. Sharon Abu-Laban, *op. cit.*, p. 162.

31. As quoted in *ibid.*

32. See A.C. Forrest, *The Unholy Land* (Toronto, 1972); Frank H. Epp, *Whose Land is Palestine?: The Middle East Problem in Historical Perspective* (Grand Rapids, Michigan, 1970); and Epp, *The Palestinians: Portrait of a People in Conflict* (Toronto, 1976).

33. Forrest, *op. cit.*, p. 75.

34. *Whose Land is Palestine?*, pp. 252-53.

35. *Ibid.*, p. 252.

36. Cf. Epp, *The Palestinians*.

FIVE

Economic Adaptation

Economic factors play a major role in the adjustment of new immigrants. Financial considerations act to define the success of their move, their lifestyle and life opportunities. Most immigrants are slated to enter the Canadian labour force or are dependent on the earnings of someone who will enter the labour force. The success of that entry, its level, rewards and mobility opportunities, have major ramifications for the adjustment of new Canadians.[1]

This chapter focuses on the economic adjustment of Arab-origin Canadians. It will examine their means of making a livelihood, factors influencing their occupational pursuits and the extent of their economic success. Throughout the discussion, differences within the Arab-Canadian community – for example, between the early and the post-war immigrants – will be considered and explained.

THE EARLY PIONEERS

Traditionally, newcomers to North America, from the early explorers to the immigrants, have had high hopes for financial gain. The promise of wealth, in one form or another, has acted as a lure. North America in the nineteenth and early twentieth centuries represented a promising virgin land, waiting for adventurers to capitalize on its seemingly unlimited riches. Horatio Alger stories detailing poor boys' rise to fame, power and wealth, are part of the North American tradition. Such are the stories from which immigrants' dreams are made and many Arab immigrants came to Canada with such visions.

The hope of a large number of the early Arab immigrants was to take advantage of the economic opportunities in Canada, save enough money to pay off debts incurred through their travel and return to the Old Country with sufficient money to buy a house and land. Some of them sent money to relatives left behind. It is believed that Abraham

98

ECONOMIC ADAPTATION

Bounadere was the first immigrant to send, in 1889, a bank draft (for $50) to his family in Lebanon.² As indicated earlier, the economic factor was an important motivating element in Syrian immigration to Canada because the opportunity structure in the homeland was restrictive. In separate interviews with some of the early pioneers, it was repeatedly pointed out that they and their compatriots had viewed their arrival in Canada as a temporary venture rather than a permanent move.

The diary of one early pioneer, who emigrated to Canada in 1895 at the age of 12 to join an older brother in Montreal, indicates that he was allowed to leave home at such a tender age because his mother felt there was little future for her son in his homeland. This man was married, in 1908, to a young girl who had emigrated from Lebanon. An interview with his widow indicated that when she arrived in Canada to marry, she had thought her stay would be for only a couple of years. Four years later, in 1912, she and her husband returned to Lebanon for a visit. By this time, they had achieved a considerable measure of success through business activities and their relatives urged them to return to Beirut, establish a permanent home and "live happily on their high income from business in Canada." However, the young couple never made the move back to their land of birth. They remained in Canada to make their home with their children and their children's children.

The conditions surrounding this case were not atypical. A large number of the early Syrian immigrants to Canada were very young, with no capital and with little or no formal education. To make things more difficult, many of them had no knowledge of English or French and limited knowledge of reading or writing in their native Arabic. As Karam notes, "the great majority were able to do little more than sign their own name in English and some were wholly illiterate."³ What could immigrants with such qualifications do?

Occupational Pursuits

In terms of general orientation towards work, the early Syrian immigrants were prepared to do almost anything. They were destitute and they considered their emigration as an escape from poverty. Upon arrival in Canada, the majority worked as unskilled industrial labourers or as peddlers or shopkeepers. Typically, these jobs required physical exertion, which the youthful immigrants could do, and a minimum degree of acquaintance with the Canadian culture and language. The Syrian immigrants' entry status, in general, was at the lowest rungs of the occupational hierarchy.

The Canadian-born children of Syrian immigrants, and some of the older immigrants who were interviewed in this study, noted that the peddlers and traders among them did not confine themselves to Canada's main urban centres. They carried their business wherever there were opportunities, and this meant moves to some distant industrial, commercial and mining communities. By their willingness to move about in the early phases of their settlement in Canada, these immigrants were aiding their climb up the ladder of occupational success.

Despite their rural or peasant origins, a very small proportion of the turn-of-the-century Syrian immigrants went into farming. The few who did select farming as an occupation tended to settle in the Prairies, particularly Saskatchewan. For varying reasons, Syrian immigrants to all parts of the New World eschewed the tilling of the land. Specifically focusing on early Syrian immigrants to the United States, Hitti attributes this general reluctance not to a lack of ability or knowledge about farming, but to "the isolation and lonesomeness of American farm life, the greater necessity of knowing English and starting with a fund of money, the strange food and lack of church facilities, the less abundant economic remuneration."[4]

While the factors which Hitti cites may well apply to the Syrian immigrants bound for Canada, at least two additional considerations played an important role. First, Canadian farming required co-operative family efforts, particularly in the more remote farming regions. The vast majority of Syrian immigrants lacked this important resource because they came to Canada as unattached individuals.[5] The second factor which reduced the attractiveness of farming was the direct or indirect influence exerted by Syrian immigrants already in Canada. Newcomers tended to gravitate towards those who preceded them to Canada and the net effect of this was the reinforcement of occupational pursuits other than farming.

The Dominance of Peddlery and Self-Employment: At first, very few Canadians took note of the energetic Syrian Arabs who took to the road selling their smallwares. Nor did Canadians take note of them in the industrial sector of the economy. There were relatively few Syrians in Canada in the latter part of the past century, barely visible alongside the larger immigrant groups from eastern and southern Europe. Nor was there anything distinctive about Syrian industrial workers or even peddlers. At that time, unskilled industrial workers (and also farmers) were needed by the developing Canadian economy, and door-to-door selling was not an uncommon business practice.[6] Initially, the early Syrian immigrants, in mesh with the economic needs of the new environment, did not stand out.

However, within a relatively short period of time, by about the turn of the century, a substantial number of Syrian immigrants were to be found in shopkeeping and peddlery. Given opportunity and freedom of choice, these immigrants were more inclined to engage in peddlery and other forms of self-employment than in industrial work. By 1909, it became clear to observers of Canadian immigration, such as J.S. Woodsworth, that the Syrians' chief occupational pursuits were trade and peddlery.[7] Government officials in Ottawa were also cognizant of the main occupational pursuits of Syrian immigrants, as evidenced by a statement made by the Superintendent of Immigration in 1913: "Generally speaking, Syrians are city dwellers confining their attention largely to peddling or, when their financial position justifies, opening up stores for the sale of goods of Eastern manufacture."[8] A similar observation was made by Edmund Bradwin, in his study of life and labour in the work camps (1903-1914) associated with the building of Canada's railroads:

> Men of the Levantine peoples – Turks, Syrians, and Armenians – are found only occasionally and in small numbers throughout the camps of Canada. . . . Few of the Syrians and Armenians found on construction are employed in manual work. Following the customs of their fathers, they engage as shopkeepers and small dealers.[9]

Judging from available evidence, the occupational preferences of Syrian immigrants to Canada were essentially the same as those reflected by their kinsmen in the United States and elsewhere in the New World.[10]

The precise proportion of Syrians who became vendors, peddlers, or shopkeepers is not known, but on the basis of my interviews with some of the early pioneers and their descendants, as well as the preceding accounts, it appears that the majority, or at least a very substantial plurality, followed these occupational careers. In New York, it was estimated that about one out of three Syrians went into peddling and shopkeeping.[11] The comparable proportion for Syrian Canadians was probably no less than that, and possibly much larger.

There were several reasons for the dominance of peddlery among the early Syrian immigrants to Canada. To begin with, Syria, by virtue of its strategic geographical location between East and West, has long been an important trade centre. Buying and selling is a deeply rooted activity among the inhabitants of the eastern Mediterranean region. According to Hitti, "the Syrian is a trader wherever and whenever he can be, and a laborer only where he must be. But in either case, he is industrious, acquisitive, and frugal, and therefore almost always economically independent."[12] Secondly, Canada was viewed as a land of social and economic freedom, a land of adventure, hence the preference for an occupation which would provide some freedom and independence, while giving promise of success at the same time. In addition, the socio-cultural background of early Arab immigrants, being radically different from that of the host society, strengthened ethnic bonds and enhanced moves towards joint economic ventures designed for mutual economic benefits. Finally, either because of kinship ties or clearly defined social networks established in the Old Country, newer waves of Arab immigrants tended to gravitate toward those who preceded them, seeking and/or expecting their advice and help. Thus, the twin elements of necessity and social imitation were present in the situation.

For some Syrian immigrants, peddlery was a way of life, encompass-

101

ing their total social existence. As far back as the mid-1880s, Ameen Lutfi, a Syrian wholesaler in Montreal, supplied peddlers not only with goods, but also with accommodation in a rented house, often without charge. Newcomers from Syria were given accommodation while being initiated into the trade. Men roomed with men and women with women, "except in the case of a married couple and their young children who were allotted special accommodation."[13] The arrangement proved to be profitable for all concerned. Hence, it was expanded to the point where "as many as two score or more were living under the same roof."[14] According to knowledgeable respondents, this type of accommodation was also developed in Toronto and it continued well into the second decade of the twentieth century.

The rooming house accommodation arrangement was significant in that it provided structural and community support for a specific occupation. It also nourished an associational need and created a community feeling among Syrian peddlers, both as an ethnic group and as an occupational group. Syrian women played a vital role in the success of this type of accommodation, cleaning the premises and looking after the clothing and food needs of the boarders.[15] Thus peddlery could, and at least for some, did become almost a total institution, meeting economic as well as social needs. As one Montreal respondent put it, "the early Syrian peddlers were very close and they lived close to one another. They maintained their customs in food and recreation and respect toward elders. In those early years, they would meet at the end of the day at some elder's house. They sang, danced the dabkeh, and discussed the day's events and their experiences in Canada."

The hardships involved in boarding house living, such as loss of privacy and crowded conditions, were far overshadowed by the resulting social and economic advantages. It is probably true, as some informants asserted, that the work ethic and deferred gratification pattern were strengthened within that communal rooming house work setting. Also, the ethnic fellowship resulting from these social and economic arrangements tended to mitigate the adjustment problems which Syrian immigrants faced in the new Canadian environment.

That there was demand for the services of peddlers is indicated by the growing numbers of participants, the increased variety of goods sold, and the expansion of geographical coverage. Syrian peddlers carried a wide range of goods, including Christian holy pictures and worship-related items, scapulars, shawls, beads, handkerchiefs, table cloths, yard-goods, lace, ribbon, costume jewelry, perfume, and many other items. Peddlers were essentially distribution agents, serving the interests of the producer and/or wholesaler as well as those of the housewife living not only in the city, but also in remote communities. The important role which these peddlers played in the Canadian economy cannot be overlooked.[16]

The early Arab immigrant peddlers found Quebec particularly attractive because, according to our older respondents, French Canadians were seen as being kindlier, friendlier and less likely to display feelings of superiority than English Canadians. One respondent, relating his experiences as a young Montreal peddler at the beginning of this century, spoke for many others like him when he reminisced:

I harbour nothing but gratitude and good feeling towards the French Canadians. As a young peddler I recall many instances when I could not return home at the end of the day, either because of long distance from home or heavy snowfall. At that time, roads were not cleared of the snow. I used to knock at the door of the closest house and, by gesture, ask for accommodation for the night. At that time I knew neither French nor English. In every case accommodation was gladly provided.[17]

This positive feeling towards French Canadians, together with Montreal's important position as a port city and commercial centre, may explain why the Arab community in Quebec grew steadily in size and importance. However, it should be noted, too, that the Arab Canadians' positive feelings towards French Canadians did not prevent them from expanding their business activities into English Canada.

Syrian peddlers used every means of transportation that was available. Those whose work was confined to the city, and even some of those who ventured outside the city, went on foot. As peddlery was expanded geographically, it became necessary to travel on horseback, by horse-driven wagon, or by train. The use of the automobile came later and it was associated not with peddlery, a far from admired occupation, but with "salesmanship." In any case, the Syrian peddlers worked hard, and they returned to their home base only to replenish their merchandise.

Gilbert Johnson, a former agent for the Saskatchewan Wheat Pool at Marchwell, provides a vivid description of the Syrian peddler in Western Canada:

About the turn of the century and for some years thereafter, the Syrian peddler was something of an institution in most Western settlements. Sometimes on foot, with a pack on his back and a case of trinkets and smallwares in his hand, but more often with a horse and a light wagon in summer, or with a sleigh in winter, he travelled the prairie trails in more or less regular routes, and few were the homesteads not visited periodically by one of these itinerant merchants. His arrival often provided a welcome relief from the monotony of pioneer life, and I remember one, a soft-spoken, fair-haired Lebanese, who became an esteemed friend of our family.[18]

Unlike W.D. Scott, the former Superintendent of Immigration, who had described the Syrian peddler as being a nuisance to Canadians, Gilbert Johnson paints a positive picture of this hard-working man. To quote again:

To the farm children of that period, the visit of one of these travellers (peddlers) was a gala occasion. The delighted youngsters would gather around him as he unpacked his bales of tempting yardgoods, table cloths, shawls, ribbon and neckwear. What these may have lacked in quality they made up in color and showiness of pattern. To measure yardgoods, the salesman used his nose as a base from which he extended the cloth or ribbon the full sweep of his arm. This constituted a yard. The generosity or parsimony of the vendor might be indicated by a slight deviation of the nose to the right or left of dead centre. For the children, however, the supreme moment came when he opened the case containing trays of pocket knives, mouth organs, spectacles, trinkets and perfumery. The glass sparklers in the brooches and tie pins drew admiration worthy of the finest diamonds and rubies, and the brassy rings were coveted as if they had been the gold of Ophir. When the last tray of glittering smallware had been lifted, the bottom of the treasure chest revealed a layer of less glamorous merchandise such as thread, buttons and toilet soap. Thus, for a brief hour, the drab farm kitchen was transformed into a miniature bazaar of Araby.

Sometimes the more experienced and enterprising peddlers engaged in barter. Horse hair, seneca root, hides and furs might be taken in exchange for merchandise, but this manner of business was exceptional rather than common practice. Cash was the general rule although credit was sometimes extended to trustworthy customers.

If the salesman stayed overnight or sold a substantial quantity of goods, there were usually presents all around. For father there might be a handkerchief or a stick of shaving soap, for mother an apron or a bottle of perfume; the boys were made happy with a mouth organ, a jews-harp or a pocket knife, and the girls with a length of ribbon or a necklace. Wistful eyes followed the canvas covered vehicle as it lurched over the winding trail toward the next farmstead.[19]

Peddlery could not have expanded without an accompanying system of wholesale merchandising. At first, Montreal was the main centre where peddlers could replenish their stock. The demand was heavy and some suppliers in Montreal used their own homes to store goods needed by their peddler clients. Visits by peddlers and business transactions were often part of the daily routine in these homes. Syrian business was booming in the 1890s, and "the newcomers began to gain self-confidence in proportion to their advancement in knowledge of the ways and customs (and language) of their new country."[20] Two noteworthy developments occurred at this time: first, peddlery was extended further into more distant regions and, second, an increasing number of Syrian immigrants went into storekeeping. As peddlers dispersed, Montreal was no longer a convenient supply centre for all of them. Recognizing this, Syrian businessmen branched out to other cities: Ottawa in the early 1890s and Toronto and Three Rivers in the late 1890s. Thus the foundations of Syrian immigrants' vast trade network were laid down in the closing decade of the nineteenth century.

In Montreal, Syrian wholesale and dry goods stores occupied several blocks along Notre Dame Street East. In Toronto, they concentrated on Wellington Street and later moved to York Street. Both Notre Dame and York streets, particularly the former, were the great centres of Syrian enterprise in Canada. By any measure, they contributed significantly to the well-being of the Syrian-Canadian community. It is noteworthy that in spite of new stores opening outside of Montreal, Notre Dame Street East remained a highly competitive centre because of its "superior buying facilities and proximity to source of supply."[21] It supplied other centres with merchandise, and as Syrian businesses outside of Montreal multiplied and thrived, so did the ones in Montreal.

The Path to Success and Prosperity: In the closing decade of the past century and thereafter, Syrian business activities in Canada diversified further and spread more widely. Elias Karam's 1935 account provides a record of the early pioneers' activities and it is worth quoting at some length:

Early in the nineties, a young man from Zahleh, already a seasoned traveller, having migrated to Australia where he had married, arrived at Montreal accompanied by his wife and another energetic young man. He brought a considerable amount of novelty and other fancy, old world merchandise with which, shortly after their arrival and clearance from the customs, they set up in business. The firm was known as Aboud (Charles) and Attiney (Esper). They were followed into business by Selim Elias who later emigrated to the United States. Wanis Abdelnour, as romantic and enterprising a young Syrian as ever to set foot on Canadian soil, who was one of the earliest to embark in business, took part in several organizations and reorganizations and finally established in wholesale distribution with Selim Bouziane. They opened a buying office in Manchester, England, from which base of operations this highly energetic personality was to roam for several years, over the markets of Europe to consummate some transactions, breathtaking for that period.

About the middle of the nineties, young Assaf Aziz, joined shortly by his older brother Joseph, first arrived in Montreal and went into business there, later moving to Peterboro and finally establishing themselves in Toronto, in 1898. Joseph was probably the first Syrian to go on the road, catering to Syrian and non-Syrian stores alike and the day he appeared on Notre Dame Street, showing the first commercial travellers' certificate ever issued to a Syrian, was a proud day indeed for the ambitious youth.

The original store of Ameen Lutfi had, early in the nineties, disappeared. The firm of Aboud and Boosamra replaced the firm of Aboud and Attiney, with various other amalgamations (and) reorganizations intervening.

In Toronto, the Aziz boys had been preceded by the late Selim Sheyck, a Catholic Maronite, in 1888. This Lebanese gentleman was probably the first Syrian, he was at least the first on record, to take out naturalization papers, which he did in 1892. Other Maronites followed Sheyck to Toronto, as well as Syrians of other religious creeds and places of origin. Sheyck, operating a jobbing business, catered to them. The firm of J. and A. Aziz did business with both those of their own racial element and other Canadians and prospered, until today (1935) theirs is not only the most outstanding Syrian house in Canada but also occupies a very high place in the wholesale dry goods distribution business in Canada.

In the latter part of the nineties, Roger Wakin ventured East as far as Three Rivers. The district seemed to be suitable for his business requirements and the people hospitable, and he decided to establish himself there. Shortly afterwards, he was joined by his young, ambitious nephew, A.N. Aboud. Later the Barrakets and Boumansours followed. Stores rose up, the newcomers prospered. Further developments followed.

Aboud N. Aboud, joined later by two brothers, took up wholesaling in the early part of the century, and later, set in motion the machinery of the small factory which today is known as Sterling Shirt and Overall Limited, employing several score people. The Boumansour men's furnishing business is said to be the largest store of its kind in the Province of Quebec. The Barrakets, two branches, are also successful in the retail dry goods business, as well as in real estate, owning extensive property some of which is in the heart of the business district. As a matter of fact, the Syrian-Canadian citizens of Three Rivers are, as a rule, large property owners. . . .

Out of Ottawa emerged the small community that first settled in Carleton Place and attracted a number of others to follow them. . . . In 1899 Rasheed Zahlan left this group and travelled north as far as New Liskeard, when there were but a few settlers in that section, north of which was nothing but woodland trails. In the next year and following the historic fire of 1900 in Ottawa, the Chamandy boys settled in North Bay, where the Continental Hotel, formerly known as the Cecil, stands today as a monument to their early achievement. Abraham and Aboud followed some time later and set up a retail business in Cobalt, becoming previously engaged for a short time in the wholesale dry goods business in Montreal. Rasheed Zahlan visited Ottawa in 1900, and when he returned to New Liskeard he took back with him a young man who was to become for all time one of the legendary figures of the North, Kalil "Big Pete" Farah. It was "Big Pete" who built the first hotel owned by a Syrian, who built the electric power and light plant which he later sold to the municipality, who ventured into mining and succeeded, who staked all comers who sought him, who rarely turned back friend or foe who sought his helping hand. His physical prowess was such that he volunteered to penetrate the bushlands on one occasion to arrest a criminal character, as the agent of the law when no regular constable was available.

. . . Michael Abraham, another fellow townsman, ventured into a grand opera and moving picture house, and is one of the pioneer men of Northern Ontario. A few years later, the first soft drink bottling works was started by Abe David, when barely twenty-eight years of age, although he had been already thirteen years in Canada without the benefit of parental supervision. Later he was successively established in Cochrane, where he became one of the largest real estate holders, in Iroquois Falls and in St. Catharines.

During the first ten years of this century a considerable number of Syrians moved into Northern Ontario and whenever a mining or other district opened up, or a railway extended, they were among the first to venture in. . . . Nor did the frequent bush fires that took devastating toll dampen the zeal and enterprise that was theirs. The prohibitive fire insurance rates often caused them to omit to insure and in most cases a fire left them absolutely penniless. They accepted these vicissitudes with a smile and rose up again more determined, however, than before.

In the early years of the century, probably the first attempt at agriculture by a Syrian was made when the late Elias David took up truck farming which, with his growing family of boys, he gradually developed until he was operating two farms. After the War, however, the boys gradually drifted into business and have since been successfully established as retail merchants in Cochrane and Timmins.

The Shatilla family is said to have been the first family to venture as far West as Saskatchewan where at Tessier, a few miles out of Saskatoon, they took up homesteads, built a hotel, established a dry goods business and were undoubtedly the first Syrian postmasters in Canada.[22]

Several conclusions may be drawn from Karam's account. At the same time that peddlery, in its pure and simple form (i.e., door-to-door selling), was expanding in the 1890's and 1900's, many Syrians were also establishing themselves, on a relatively large scale, in different lines of business and industry. The above quotation underlines the importance of the role of kinship and friendship in the upgrading of Syrians' entrepreneurial activities in Canada. Brothers, cousins, fathers and sons, nephews and uncles, and kinsmen worked together forming the companies that were to become leading enterprises in Canada's major urban centres. Karam's account focused not on the "common man," but rather on the "elite" of the Syrian-Canadian community, that is, those who by their resourcefulness and perseverance rose to high economic positions in Canada. This chapter in the history of the Arab-Canadian community tends often to be ignored or forgotten. However, the effects remain to the present time.

A close examination of the activities of enterprising Syrian immigrants reveals an interesting pattern of social and ecological mobility. After a few years of being on the road, a successful peddler was able to open a store and settle down. In turn, a successful shopkeeper whose business outgrew local demand in a smaller community tended to branch out and/or move to Toronto or other larger centres. Finally, successful storekeepers in larger cities tended to gravitate towards manufacturing and/or real estate. Thus room was created for new peddlers to start at the lower rungs of the business hierarchy.

Only a small amount of cash and a positive recommendation from a known person in the Syrian-Canadian community, or in the Old Country, would provide a young aspirant with a peddling job and goods to sell. "That this policy of unrestricted trust and confidence is not in strict conformity with sound economic principles cannot be denied. Nor is it denied that some, through misguidance, insufficient capitalization and the lack of other natural economic requisites, fell by the wayside, and caused considerable loss to their creditors of Notre Dame Street."[23] Despite some losses, this policy had inestimable beneficial effects on the Syrian-Canadian community.

The 1920's witnessed further occupational changes in the Arab-Canadian community. At that time, a few Syrian Canadians entered the ranks of professionals in medicine and law. Also, peddlery, the occupation to which the Syrian community owed its prosperity, was fast disappearing, due partly to the curtailment of Asiatic, hence Syrian, immigration to Canada, partly to its having been a temporary occupation for those who engaged in it, and partly to shifts in Canadian business practices which replaced peddlery by the mail order (and telephone order) business. In 1929-1930, Montreal's dry goods district lost its vigour and it was dealt a severe blow by the crash of the stock market. Only a few Syrian businesses survived the crash.

The collapse of financial enterprises at that time brought many Syrians to the brink of bankruptcy. The ones who suffered severe financial setbacks were reduced to small-scale shopkeeping or grocery store business, starting all over again. On the other hand, those who did not suffer such setbacks, or who had an abundance of resources, were able to shift and consolidate their position in manufacturing and other large-scale industrial activities. Some of the businesses and companies which were started by Syrians about half a century ago are still in existence (at times in an altered or modified form) in Montreal and Toronto. Montreal, where the first Syrian settlement was established, contains a large number of these enterprises and in an early study it was estimated that there were 20 to 25 millionaires among the old Syrian immigrants living in that city.[24]

Despite the transformation of Syrian enterprise and diversification of economic activities by the early Syrian immigrants, occupational differentiation within this ethnic group would have remained limited were it not for their Canadian-born descendants. Some second and later generation Arab Canadians followed in the footsteps of their fathers, of course, but many others moved to new occupational careers. Unlike the parental generation, the Canadian-born generations, having had the advantage of education and often higher education, faced a wide range of occupations from which to select. In the absence of statistics to show their occupational distribution, we are forced to depend on informed judgments of representatives of this ethnic group. Knowledgeable respondents and old-timers were in agreement that second and later-generation Arab Canadians have penetrated every occupational sphere. They are to be found in business and industry, real estate, insurance, the professions, the judiciary, politics, teaching, the ministry, government service, entertainment and the media, fashion and design, management, and many other fields. The heaviest concentration is in free enterprise occupations allowing for self-employment.

Relative to their numerical strength in the Canadian population, the contributions of Syrian immigrants and their descendants to the social and economic development of Canada compare favourably with those of any other ethnic group. Syrian Canadians have been, and continue to be, productive members of society. They have adapted to the economic needs of the host society and have channelled their energies accordingly. In addition, some members of this ethnic group have excelled in their fields of endeavour, thereby adding quality to their productive activity. Names of prominent Syrian-origin Canadians are to be found in virtually all of the above-noted occupational spheres.[25]

The Levantine Ethnic and the Spirit of Entrepreneurship: The early Syrian immigrants to Canada provide a notable example of an immigrant group rising by its own bootstraps. Generally speaking, the entire Syrian ethnic group experienced substantial upward economic mobility. Of course, not every Syrian immigrant fit the "Horatio Alger" ideal, but there were many who did. In an open class system, such as the one prevailing in Canada, upward social mobility is to be expected. But it might take two or three generations before a given ethnic group can transcend the disadvantages resulting from the low entry status of its forebears. In the case of Syrians, however, advancement occurred within the life span of the immigrant generation whose entry status was at the bottom of the occupational hierarchy.[26] The Syrian experience raises an important question regarding the conditions which contributed to their rapid upward economic mobility in Canada.

Judging from some of the biographies and occupational career patterns of the early Syrian immigrants, it appears that a multiplicity of factors were relevant to their success as entrepreneurs. Together, they make up what might be termed the "Levantine ethic and the spirit of entrepreneurship." These factors may be grouped under three main headings: orientation towards kinsmen, devotion to work and self-employment, and risk-taking, resourcefulness and self-denial. Each of these dimensions will be discussed in turn.[27]

Orientation Towards Kinsmen

The resources which immigrants to Canada bring with them are more than capital and physical possessions. The cultural foundations of their past can, on occasion, provide an invaluable resource in the new environment. One of the intangible, but nevertheless significant, resources which Syrian immigrants brought to Canada was a supportive network of social relations centering around their kinsmen. The word "kinsmen" is used here not only in the sense of blood relations, but also in the sense of people of their own kind. As Hitti noted in his 1924 study of Syrians in the United States: "The relation of the Syrian immigrants, not so much to his old country, as to their folks in the old country, has been kept alive and cordial."[28]

There was an element of communalism in the early Syrian-Canadian community which was of sufficient force to serve as an important resource in their economic adaptation to the new Canadian environment. Interviews with older respondents revealed the frequency with which young Syrian immigrants came to Canada to join relatives and the number of joint economic ventures by Syrian kinsmen. The banding together of fellow countrymen for mutual aid is reflected in the Arabic saying: "Strangers in a foreign land are like relatives." There were, in fact, often strong support ties, not only between blood kin but also between fictive kin.

This may explain the strong tendency of Syrian immigrants from the same village or locality in the Old Country to reside in Canada in the same area or city where their predecessors had located. In Ottawa, Montreal, Toronto, Windsor, Edmonton, Lac La Biche, Alberta, and other areas, the bulk of the Syrian immigrant population had tended to originate from neighbouring villages in the Old Country.

An interesting example of the trust and receptivity which Syrians had toward each other in the land of adoption, and also of the pattern of support given to people from the same area, concerns an immigrant group from the village of Kfermiski:

Thus, in 1893, a party of almost twenty young men and a few women after landing at a Canadian port, were wending their way to Fort Wayne, Indiana, where they had been told some Syrians known to one or more of them were living. Waiting in Bonaventure Station, Montreal, for a change of trains, one of the party spotted a man on his way in from an outside point and carrying what looked like a pack of merchandise that had been described to them before leaving Syria. He drew the attention of his companions to the fact and proceeded to accost the stranger. The latter readily admitted racial kinship and informed them that there were a considerable number of their countrymen in Montreal. Some of the party were immediately dispatched to seek further information from the local Syrian residents and on being informed by someone that conditions at Fort Wayne were at that time bad, the party therefore decided to remain in Montreal. The group being from a single village, lying between Mount Herman and Mount Lebanon, was destined to establish by that decision, the nucleus of a colony consisting not only of hundreds of immigrants from their own village, but also from the surrounding villages and hamlets of the former immediate neighbourhood in the Tyme Valley.

Some of this group later moved to Ottawa, so that, today, the majority of Syrian Canadians in Ottawa, as well as an equivalent number now settled in Montreal, claim the picturesque, mountain village of Kfermiski, Tyme Valley, Syria as the home of their forefathers. . . . In the larger community centres (of Canada, the United States, Mexico and the various countries of South America) there will be found various sectional groups in the one city, which, however, may have had their origin within a radius of fifteen to twenty miles in the homeland.[29]

The kinship orientation of Syrian immigrants does not necessarily mean absence of tension and ambivalence. As one Montreal respondent suggested, "the Syrians love each other but envy each other. They work together yet they are apart from each other. They do business with each other yet they would rather not." In any case, such hypothesized vacillating feelings aside, the supportive network of social and economic relations within the early Syrian community was an important resource influencing their successful economic adjustment in the new Canadian setting. It made it possible for them to engage in larger business undertakings than individuals, alone, could have undertaken.

Devotion to Work and Self-Employment

A second important element influencing the early Syrian immigrants' entrepreneurial ventures was devotion to work. While luck, undoubtedly, played a role, it was relentless toil which was more commonly associated with financial success. Unlike the labour activity associated with the Pro-

111

testant ethic, which sees work as a calling based on divine ordinance, the Syrian immigrants' devotion to work did not have a religious foundation.[30] Rather, it was a secular (social) response to a given environment at a particular point in time and under particular conditions.

For many of the early Syrian immigrants, devotion to work and labour was propelled by a concrete goal: to accumulate as much capital as possible, in as short a time as possible, and return to the Old Country. Thus, future plans and security were intimately linked to financial success in Canada. In this respect the Syrian immigrants' conception of the work ethic was different from some popular versions which merely emphasize the value of work for its own sake. Accumulation of capital, to Syrian immigrants, was synonymous with devotion to work. As one insightful Canadian-born respondent said, "the people back home think that the streets of Canada are paved with gold. The people here know that they must pave the streets before they get the gold."

The second element involved in the Syrian immigrants' conception of the work ethic was their preference for self-employment as traders and businessmen. Their gravitation towards peddling rather than other types of employment was due to their strong attachment to self-employment. A similar situation occurred in the United States where "criticism of Syrians as workers came from the misconception that they would not do manual labour. In truth, they did not like working for someone else and they were usually busy elsewhere in types of work that made them independent employers."[31] In the course of the present study, many Arab Canadians indicated a preference for self-employment over a job in government or industry. The prevalence of this attitude to the present time is a matter of considerable sociological interest.

Devotion to work also meant the investment of many hours a day on business and related activities. Neither the Syrian peddler, nor the shopkeeper, nor the wholesaler was content with an eight-hour work day. In many cases, the line dividing work and leisure (or business and social life) was thin indeed. It will be recalled that, in the old days, peddlers and wholesalers met in their homes at the end of the day not only to socialize but also to transact business.

In certain lines of business, the maximum daily work capacity was demanded of the entrepreneur. A relevant example is a Syrian immigrant who came to Canada in 1909 at the age of fifteen. In 1914, he opened, on borrowed money, an ice cream parlour and lunch counter in Toronto. According to this early pioneer, who was interviewed in 1974, he worked from 7 a.m. to 2 a.m., and would find at the end of the work day that his toes were bleeding and he would have to go home and soak them in hot water and salt. The payoff came at the end of four months when he was able to pay back the money he borrowed to start the business, and as well deposit $2,000 in his bank account. Some 60 years ago this was indeed a large sum of money to earn in a four-month period.

Finally, the Syrians' commitment to hard work meant the subordination of many other values to that of work. "The concept of family life as something sacred has not yet been divorced from the Syrian mind";[32] however, it is likely that work in general was given a slight edge over family. In this connection, it might be noted that the Syrian women's supportive economic role, both in and outside the home, was related not only to capital accumulation, but also to family unity within the context of economically productive activity. Also, the use of one's home, if necessary, as a place to transact business, something which was not uncommon in the early years, might have resulted, serendipitously, in reconciling familial and economic interests and values.

As indicated earlier, commitment to hard work was premised, in part, on their hope to return to their native land. It is noteworthy that even when many Syrian immigrants came to the realization, early in this century, that they were here to stay, they did not retreat from their commitment to work. The work ethic had already been internalized, and the goal of returning to Syria was replaced by the goal of a better life in Canada for them and their children.

Risk-Taking, Resourcefulness, and Self-Denial
The third and final dimension pertinent to the success of early Syrian immigrants as entrepreneurs in Canada relates to a personality syndrome which apparently was congenial to capital accumulation and success. Among the syndrome's relevant characteristics, that of risk-taking was most important. Buying and selling, land speculation, entering into partnerships, organizing and reorganizing companies, stock and bond investment, selling out and moving into a new line of business or to a new community, trusting clients, sales agents and peddlers, going without insurance in the face of a possible bush fire, and many other things had a good reward potential but an equally high risk potential.

The careers of many early Syrian immigrants were checkered, in the sense of making frequent business shifts and taking risks. An illustrative case is the Syrian who opened an ice cream parlour and lunch counter in Toronto in 1914. He then went into partnership with another Syrian man and expanded the business. Shortly thereafter, he sold out to his partner and went into the entertainment business, first buying one theatre and then buying two more – all in Toronto. In 1920-21 he sold everything and returned to Lebanon, only to return in 1929. During his period away from Canada, he was involved in several business ventures in Lebanon and Egypt. Upon his return to Canada, he joined the businesses of a relative in Kingston and his former partner in Toronto. With the latter he worked as a partner-agent collecting unpaid debts. He then bought a candy factory, a second candy factory, and after this a biscuit factory. Finally, he went into real estate where further monetary success was awaiting him.[33] The businesses which this man operated were in different areas and provinces and the last was in Montreal.

Generally speaking, there were more gains than losses resulting from risk-taking. The gains benefitted not only the Syrian businessmen, but also the Syrian-Canadian community at large. But some of the losses were heavy, as in the case of those who suffered the effects of a bush fire. Such people were forced to start all over again.

The second characteristic involved in the entrepreneurial personality syndrome is resourcefulness. At first, the majority of the early Syrian immigrants lacked the economic and other power resources that were necessary for self-employment. Yet that was not only the desired type of occupation but also the one in which many of them, in fact, later engaged. This was facilitated by certain practices, some makeshift, which, although not altogether unique to Syrian immigrants, were of definite benefit. Rooming house accommodations for new immigrants from Syria, and the use of one's home as an office and also a warehouse for merchandise, were among such arrangements. Also, the element of resourcefulness tended to surface in the process of setting up a new business, and more specifically in securing the necessary financing and outfitting it.

Again, the example of our pioneer Montreal respondent who opened an ice cream parlour and lunch counter in Toronto is relevant. With $250 in his pocket, this man looked through the *Toronto Telegram* for business opportunities. In his own words:

> I spotted a confectionary business for sale which at first seemed good. I looked at the store, saw magazines and newspapers all over the place and thought that there was a lot of stock. Mr. . . ., the owner, asked for five hundred dollars when in reality, as I was later to discover, there was only one hundred dollars worth of merchandise. I agreed to the purchase and gave him two hundred and fifty dollars as a down payment; the balance was to be paid in monthly instalments. But this money was never collected as he had already received more than it was worth. Before the owner left, he cleaned out the store and left me with virtually nothing. . . . I would sell ninety cents worth of goods a day. My breakfast consisted of toast and coffee. Next door to my shop was a restaurant where I could buy a full course meal for fifteen cents. For supper I would have cake and coffee. After three months like this, I could not pay my rent. . . .[34]

At this point this Syrian businessman decided to borrow fifty dollars. He obtained $20 from a cousin to pay the rent and wondered how he could acquire the additional money needed to turn a confectionary store into an ice cream parlour and snack bar. "I remembered," he said, "that (a man) who lived in Toronto had a brother who had borrowed $75 from my father in the old country. I went to him to collect this debt and he gave it to me."[35] He then added:

> I now had seventy-five dollars to make a new start. My first step was to visit the Adam's Linoleum Company and arrange for a new

floor. It cost me ten dollars down and ten dollars a month until the bill was paid. I now needed a small soda fountain and began to check the second hand stores. I found one and bargained with the man for twenty-five dollars – once again ten dollars down and five dollars a month. I then bought eighteen tables with chairs for ten dollars down and the rest on time. The place was now fitted with the necessary equipment and I had what seemed to be a beautiful ice cream parlor. . . .[36]

In his subsequent business ventures, the experiences of this Syrian immigrant reflected good management and resourcefulness. Without these elements, in his case and in the case of many other Syrian immigrants like him, commitment to hard work would not answer all his problems.

The third element which proved to be of cardinal importance in capital accumulation and success was self-denial. In Canada, the United States, and elsewhere in the New World, Syrian immigrants were frugal, planning for the future, ascetic, and almost puritanical in their orientation. It was their determination and future orientation that forced even the Syrian factory worker to avoid worldly pleasures and wastefulness and save for his future goals. Again, there was no religious foundation for this orientation akin to the one associated with Calvinism.[37] Rather it was a social response to a set of conditions associated with their personal background and the new Canadian environment.

To sum up, it should be noted that this analysis of the "Levantine Ethic" is an ideal-typical characterization against which the realities of the early Syrian community in Canada, and specific Syrian immigrants, can be measured. It is based on the inductive method of analysis which involves generalization through experiences. Clearly, not every Syrian immigrant exhibited the "Levantine Ethic," and in many cases it was a question of degree rather than a question of presence or absence of this ethic. There were, however, many commonalities in the experiences of these immigrants suggesting the existence of a pattern. The position taken here is that certain values and ethical principles appear to have guided the behaviour of the early Syrian pioneers. These included a unique orientation towards family and kinsmen, commitment to hard work and preference for self-employment, and a collection of personality traits such as initiative and risk-taking, resourcefulness, and self-denial. Together with Canada's facilitative environment, these values and ethical principles, termed the "Levantine Ethic," were important factors in the relatively rapid upward social mobility of the early Syrian immigrants.

THE POST-WAR IMMIGRANTS

During the period following World War II, the ranks of the early Syrian pioneers and their descendants were swelled by the influx of a large number of immigrants from the Arab world. In terms of educational and occupational characteristics, and also country of origin, the recent Arab immigrants were a heterogeneous group. They were significantly different from the early pioneers, although there were similarities in the economic adaptation of the two groups. This section will focus on current aspects of the economic adaptation of the Arab Canadian community. The occupational intentions of post-war Arab immigrants will be considered, followed by a discussion of economic adjustment problems, incomes and change in social position.

Occupational Intentions

The best available information on the economic activities of post-war Arab immigrants is that made available through immigration interviews at the time of entry into Canada. These data are published annually by the Department of Manpower and Immigration. Although not all immigrants, Arab or otherwise, pursue the occupations which they reported at the time of entry to Canada, information on intended occupations is a relatively valid indicator of behaviour. For example, a recent longitudinal survey of over 2,000 immigrants shows that 69% of the respondents "had jobs in the occupations they intended to follow when they arrived."[38] Also, "almost half of the respondents had held only one position since their arrival, and almost three-quarters had held no more than two jobs."[39]

Table 12 shows the intended occupations of immigrants from the Arab world by country of last permanent residence for the period 1956-74.[40] In this table, the category "professional" includes such occupations as manager or administrator, engineer, lawyer, physician or surgeon, as well as occupations in mathematics and related fields, in the physical, life and social sciences. As a general rule, the occupations covered by this category require university or post-secondary training. "Lower white collar" includes bookkeeper or cashier, stenographer, sales clerk and kindred occupations. "Service" occupations include protective service, food and beverage preparation, lodging and other accommodation services, personal service, and apparel and furnishings service. Farmers or farm workers are included under the category of "farm." Finally, the category of "blue collar" includes all those who work with their hands – whether skilled, semi-skilled or unskilled. While the distinction between "professional or semi-professional" and "lower white collar" is useful for certain purposes, the two categories may be combined under the title "white collar workers" and compared with "blue collar workers."

It will be observed that of a total of 44,120 Canada-bound immigrants from the Arab world during the period 1956-74, exactly 20,600 persons, or about 47%, had planned to enter the labour force. The percentage of Arab immigrants destined for the labour force is almost identical to that reported for other immigrant groups.[41] In comparison, about four out of 10 Canadians were in the labour force in 1971. The percentage of entrants to the labour force varies considerably among Arab national

TABLE 12

Intended Occupations of Arab Immigrants to Canada by Country of Last Residence, 1956-1974

PERCENTAGE DISTRIBUTION

Country of Last Residence	Professional	Lower White collar	Service	Farm	Blue collar	Not Stated	Total Percent	Total Workers	Total Immigrants	Percent Non-workers
Algeria	57.97	17.39	10.14	3.62	9.42	1.45	100	138	221	37.56
Arabia	19.49	16.91	13.60	8.09	40.07	1.84	100	272	536	49.25
Bahrain	31.43	48.57	2.86	—	14.29	2.86	100	35	92	61.96
Egypt	39.21	37.15	3.44	0.17	17.71	2.32	100	8,033	17,104	53.03
Iraq	39.56	23.59	3.44	—	30.47	2.95	100	407	892	54.37
Jordan	20.31	20.69	5.11	0.38	46.36	7.15	100	783	1,562	49.87
Kuwait	47.77	22.68	3.78	—	24.74	1.03	100	291	579	49.74
Lebanon	21.65	17.22	12.37	4.88	38.82	5.06	100	6,863	14,396	52.33
Libya	56.64	27.43	2.65	—	12.39	0.88	100	113	274	58.76
Mauritania	60.00	40.00	—	—	—	—	100	5	12	58.33
Morocco	20.76	45.70	8.95	0.30	22.12	2.16	100	1,989	5,139	61.30
Qatar	9.09	54.55	—	—	36.36	—	100	11	22	50.00
Saudi Arabia	56.76	23.42	—	1.80	17.12	0.90	100	111	247	55.06
Sudan	55.10	33.67	2.04	—	9.18	—	100	98	228	57.02
Syria	22.56	17.24	5.83	1.20	47.77	5.40	100	1,166	2,391	51.23
Tunisia	40.07	14.80	18.41	1.08	23.10	2.53	100	277	406	31.77
Yemen	50.00	37.50	—	—	12.50	—	100	8	19	57.89
Total	30.17	28.30	7.50	1.96	28.54	3.53	100	20,600	44,120	53.31

groups. It is highest among immigrants from Tunisia and Algeria, and lowest among immigrants from Bahrain, Morocco, Libya, Mauritania and Yemen. For the two countries which sent the largest majority of Arab immigrants to Canada, namely Egypt and Lebanon, the percentage is about the same as the average for the total Arab immigrant population.

Table 12 shows wide differences in the occupational intentions of post-war immigrants from the Arab world. For example, of the five Arab countries which supplied over 90% of these immigrants (Egypt, Lebanon, Morocco, Syria, Jordan), Egypt provided the most highly professionalized immigrant labour force entrants. Nearly four out of 10 immigrants from Egypt intended to follow a professional or semiprofessional career, and an almost equal proportion had plans for white collar occupations. In comparison, only two out of 10 immigrants from Lebanon, Morocco, Syria and Jordan were professionally inclined, and an almost equal proportion (higher for immigrants from Morocco) intended to pursue a white collar career. The remainder, in each case, had plans for blue collar occupations.

Among those intending to follow blue collar occupations, there is a spread in terms of participation in various parts of the job sector. For example, they include labourers and unskilled workers in the construction and other industries, municipal and provincial public works, department stores, universities and hospitals, transport and communications, and in varied service occupations – both as wage earners and small-scale owners and operators; as well as factory workers, machine operators, carpenters, mechanics, among other types of skilled and semi-skilled work.[42] While there is no occupation to which a disproportionate number of Arab Canadians have gravitated, in many cities they now represent an identifiable portion of the work force in such occupations as taxi driving, small-scale storekeeping and grocery business, restaurant-keeping, hair styling and barbering, and hotel work. In Lac La Biche, Alberta, mink ranching has for many years been dominated by Lebanese immigrants. Besides this very limited occupational concentration, Arab immigrants, not infrequently, work in twos and threes in many parts of the job sector due to the influence of kin and social networks in finding a job.[43]

The evidence suggests that post-war Arab immigrants, at all levels of the occupational hierarchy, seemed to have had a preference for self-employment and trade. Like their earlier counterparts, some of them have gravitated to self-employment, often starting on a small scale and later expanding the enterprise as opportunities arise. Despite the fact that even the enterprises which have been expanded are still small by Canadian standards, they are large enough to secure economic security and prosperity for their owners. Judging from the results of interviews with Arab ethnic leaders, as well as informed opinions regarding occupational choice patterns in Arab communities across Canada, the "Levantine

Ethic" seems to be no less prevalent today than at the turn of the century.

Overall, the intended occupations of post-war Arab immigrants to Canada were high ranking. Table 12 shows that over 30% of these immigrants intended to pursue professional careers in Canada, and an additional 28% to enter white collar occupations. About 29% of these immigrants planned to pursue blue collar occupations, and less than eight per cent had plans to follow careers in the service industry. A very small proportion of the post-war Arab immigrants to Canada, less than two per cent, reported that they had plans for farming occupations. The balance, about 3.5%, did not state their intended occupations.

At this point it is interesting to note the Canadian norm. The 1971 Canadian Census shows the following distribution of the labour force for Canada: about two out of 10 workers were in professional or semi-professional occupations, a further two out of 10 were in lower white collar occupations, less than five out of 10 workers were in blue collar occupations, and the remainder were engaged in primary occupations (agriculture, fishing, hunting, logging, mining and quarrying).

The relatively high occupational intentions of post-war Arab immigrants to Canada resembled those of other immigrant groups during this period. Relevant to this, the first report of the longitudinal survey of the Department of Manpower and Immigration states: "By occupation, the largest proportion of all the new workers entered managerial, professional or technical fields, followed by craftsmen and clerical and sales occupations. . . . To a large extent, immigrants were able to realize the occupational intentions they held prior to arrival in Canada."[44] Thus, in terms of occupational and educational qualifications, and more generally occupational placement, post-war immigrants to Canada, including those from the Arab world, were significantly different from their turn-of-the-century counterparts. With reference to Arab immigrants, the main similarities in occupational choice between the earlier and more recent waves concern the small proportions who went into farming, persistence – albeit to a much lesser degree – of a low occupational entry status, and continued preference for trade and self-employment.

Problems of Economic Adjustment

While the majority of post-war Arab immigrants to Canada appear to have adapted well to the Canadian economy, a certain number of them have faced difficulties. Unfortunately, there is no information on the average time taken for Arab immigrants to start work in Canada, or on the extent of unemployment or underemployment in this immigrant group. However, we have information which, though unsystematic, might assist in identifying some important aspects of problems faced.

One of the most pressing problems for some Arab immigrants was finding a job. For example, examination of the records of the Arab Community Centre in Toronto, established in 1972 to assist Arab immigrants in their adaption to the new environment, showed that there were many cases of immigrants requiring job placement assistance. This type of assistance was sought by nationals from different Arab countries, and by both men and women, of varying ages. Language difficulties and lack of skills were often cited as the main problems underlying poor economic adjustment. To these two factors in economic maladaptation, we might also add the high unemployment rate in Canada in recent years.

Because of their limited facility with the language, many of those who called on the Centre asked for help in dealing with government agencies, including Manpower and Unemployment Insurance Commission officials. Usually, it was the appropriate branch of the Department of Manpower and Immigration that provided concrete assistance in finding a job, and in skill and language training.

Another problematic aspect of the economic adjustment of some Arab Canadians is underemployment. According to the records of the Arab Community Centre in Toronto, as well as the interviews from this study, some Arab immigrants with post-graduate education are engaged in menial labour. There are professionals whose economic activities are considerably mismatched with their training and even less fortunate professionals who find themselves unemployed.

At least two factors, in addition to the factors cited above, are relevant to the unemployment and underemployment of high level immigrant manpower. The first factor, influencing an undetermined number of them, is lack of Canadian experience. The feelings of some Arab Canadians are represented by one of those interviewed who asked rhetorically: "If I am refused a job because of lack of Canadian experience, how will I ever get that experience without ever getting a job?"

The second factor in the economic maladaptation of high level manpower is lack of recognition of qualifications obtained outside of Canada. Medical doctors from Egypt, for example, have not been allowed to practise medicine without passing qualifying examinations or obtaining additional training in Canada. The same is true of engineers, lawyers and others in technical fields. As a consequence of this, some professionals from the Arab world have drifted to lower white collar occupations, while others work as night guards or in factories. Given the prevalence of professionals among them, immigrants from Egypt, in particular, were adversely affected in their economic adaptation and many of them indicated their extreme disappointment concerning this situation.

The impediments in the economic adjustment of Arab immigrants are similar to those reported for other immigrant groups.[45] Certain job barriers (such as language difficulties and lack of skills) are within the control of individual immigrants, while others (such as the high unemployment rate, lack of Canadian experience and lack of recognition of qualifications) are beyond their control. Regardless of the locus of con-

TABLE 13

Relationship Between Occupational Status and Income

Annual Income	Occupational Status* Low	High
Less than $5,000	19%	6%
$5-9,999	50	26
$10-19,999	28	48
$20,000 or more	3	21
Total %	100%	100%
(N)	(113)	(144)

*Occupations receiving a score of less than 50 on Blishen's Socio-Economic Index were defined as "low" status; those receiving a score of 50 or more were defined as "high" status occupations.

trol, the net effect of these job barriers is to weaken some Arab immigrants' adaptation to the Canadian economy. On the whole, however, the post-war Arab immigrants' economic adaptation to the new Canadian setting has probably been no less effective than that of the early Arab pioneers. But the adaptive experiences of the two waves of immigrants are qualitatively different.

Income in Canada
A survey conducted by the author yielded information on incomes of Arab Canadians by means of the following question: "In which of the following broad income categories did your total family yearly income from all sources fall last year (1973)?" Four response categories were provided. Of 325 persons who responded to the question, 14% checked the first category (less than $5,000), 33% checked the second category ($5,000-$9,999), 40% checked the third category ($10,000-19,999), and 13% checked the category of "$20,000 or more."

Annual income was most strongly associated with occupation, as would be expected. The respondents' occupational status was dichotomized as "high" or "low" on the basis of scores obtained on Blishen's Socio-Economic Index.[46] Table 13 shows the relationship between occupational status and income. It will be observed that respondents with high status occupations were seven times as likely as those with low status occupations (21% of the former compared to three per cent of the latter group) to report an annual income of $20,000 or more. Contrariwise, 19% of those with low status occupations and only six per cent of those with high status occupations earned less than $5,000 per year.

The relationship between length of residence in Canada and income is shown in Table 14. Income tends to improve considerably with length of residence. For example, of those who had been in Canada five years or less, four per cent reported an annual income of $20,000 or more; of those who had been here 6-10 years, 12% earned a similarly high income;

121

TABLE 14

Relationship Between Length of Residence in Canada and Income

Annual Income	Length of Residence		
	5 years or less	6-10 years	Over 10 years
Less than $5,000	23%	13%	6%
$5-9,999	40	31	21
$10-19,999	33	45	46
$20,000 or more	4	12	27
Total %	100%	100%	100%
(N)	(115)	(96)	(52)

and of those who had been in Canada more than ten years, as many as 27% had an annual income of $20,000 or more. The percentages are reversed in the case of low income respondents (those earning less than $5,000 per year).

There was no difference in income distribution between those who were born in Canada and those who were naturalized Canadian citizens. However, compared to the remainder of the respondents, the Canadian citizens (by birth or naturalization) were four times as likely to have an annual income of $20,000 or more. Contrariwise, the respondents whose status was still that of "Landed Immigrant" were three times as likely as the Canadian citizens to report an annual income of less than $5,000. These differences are more a function of occupation and length of residence than of citizenship *per se.*

Further analysis of income shows noteworthy differences among respondents from different parts of the Arab world. Table 15 shows the relationship between Arab region of origin and income. For present purposes, the respondents were grouped under three regions of origin: Near East (consisting of all countries east of the Mediterranean); Egypt; and North Africa other than Egypt. It will be observed that 44% of the respondents originating from North Africa (other than Egypt) earned less than $5,000 per year, compared to 15% of those originating from Egypt and only 10% of those originating from the Near East. The situation is reversed when region of origin is considered in relation to the high income category: 13% of Near Eastern Canadians, 17% of Egyptian Canadians and none of African Canadians earned $20,000 or more annually. The combined effects of such factors as place and length of residence in Canada, education and occupation account for these differences. Also, income tended to be slightly higher among men than women, among older than younger respondents and among Ontario than Quebec residents.

TABLE 15

Relationship Between Arab Region of Origin and Income

Annual Income	Region of Origin		
	Near East	Egypt	North Africa Other than Egypt
Less than $5,000	10%	16%	44%
$5-9,999	37	18	48
$10-19,999	40	49	9
$20,000 or more	13	17	00
Total %	100%	100%	100%
(N)	(219)	(83)	(23)

Financial Position Before Immigration

The Arab immigrants' financial position in the home country was measured by the following question: "Before you came to Canada, did you consider your financial situation in the 'old country' to be: 'below average,' 'average,' 'above average,' or 'wealthy'?" Of those who responded to the question (N-272), only seven per cent checked the category "below average," 41% checked the category "average," 40% checked the category "above average," and 13% checked the category "wealthy." It should be emphasized that the above responses were based on the respondents' *perceptions* of financial standing prior to immigration. It is noteworthy that over nine out of 10 Arab immigrants to Canada perceived their financial position in the country of origin to be average or better. These results, together with earlier accounts, again confirm that the post-war Arab immigrants' economic motivations were qualitatively and quantitatively different from those affecting the early Syrian pioneers.

There were no differences in perception of financial standing prior to immigration by sex, age, or length of residence in Canada. However, about 69% of immigrants from Egypt perceived their former financial position to be "above average" or "wealthy," compared to 45% of immigrants from the Near East and 30% of immigrants from North African states (other than Egypt) making similar claims.

An interesting question is whether the incomes derived in Canada are in any way associated with perceived financial standing prior to immigration. Relevant data are provided in Table 16.

Table 16 shows a positive relationship between income and perceived financial standing prior to immigration to Canada. It will be observed, for example, that 29% of those who perceived their prior financial position to be "wealthy" reported an annual income of $20,000 or more. In

TABLE 16

**Relationship Between Perception of Financial Standing
Prior to Immigration and Income**

	Perception of Financial Standing		
Annual Income	Average or Below	Above Average	Wealthy
Less than $5,000	18%	13%	14%
$5-9,999	42	27	21
$10-19,999	33	48	36
$20,000 or more	7	12	29
Total %	100%	100%	100%
(N)	(126)	(105)	(28)

contrast, 12% of those who regarded their prior situation to be "above average" and only seven per cent of those whose prior situation was perceived to be "average or below average" checked the same high income category ($20,000 or more). Contrariwise, 60% of those who perceived their financial position in the home country to be "average or below average," and only 35% of those who perceived themselves to be "wealthy" had an annual income of less than $10,000 (combining the percentages for the lowest two income categories). On the basis of this evidence, it appears that there is a tendency for those who were among the economically advantaged in the home country to have a position of relative economic advantage in Canada also.

SUMMARY

The economic adaptation of the early Arab immigrants was often linked with a keen desire for economic and occupational success. Many of the early Syrian immigrants entered the labour force through peddlery, an independent but relatively low status occupation. Through devotion to hard work, frugality and reciprocal support, the three elements of what I have termed the "Levantine Ethic," peddlers often experienced a steady rise in their economic fortunes and a broadening of their entrepreneurial functions.

Some post-war Arab immigrants have followed a pattern similar to that of the early pioneers, exhibiting the same sacrifices in terms of time, thrift and interpersonal reciprocity. However, the post-war immigrants entered Canada with higher average educational and occupational qualifications, and the majority of them planned to follow professional and other white collar careers. Thus the economic/occupational characteristics of the typical Arab immigrant have been changing.

Economic adaptation is a central life concern, relevant not only to the material but also the social, psychological and spiritual well-being of the individual immigrant and his/her ethnic community. Throughout the years, Arab immigrants and their descendants have entered all levels of the occupational hierarchy, some of them achieving renown in their respective fields. The generally successful economic adjustment of Arab Canadians has had ramifications in other spheres. For example, it has facilitated the development of a favourable attitude towards Canada and provided the resources necessary for the development of ethnic institutions, both religious and secular. Also, in the Old Country, stories of financially successful Arab immigrants have provided an incentive for yet more Arabs to seek admission to this country, and Arab-Canadian communities, on their part, have been receptive to new immigrants. The relative economic security of this ethnic group reflects the important role of a facilitative environment for achievement.

NOTES

1. For a recent study of immigrant adaptation, see Department of Manpower and Immigration (Canada), *Immigration and Population Study: Three Years in Canada: First Report of the Longitudinal Survey on the Economic and Social Adaptation of Immigrants* (Green Paper on Immigration, Vol. 4) (Ottawa, 1974).
2. Jose El-Idd, *Jowlat fi Al-'Alam Al-Jadid* (Travels in the New World) (Buenos Aires, 1959), p. 613 (Arabic).
3. Elias Karam, "Syrian Immigration to Canada," in Elias Karam, ed., *The Syrian Canadian National Review* (Ottawa, 1935), p. 31.
4. Philip K. Hitti, *The Syrians in America* (New York, 1924), pp. 72-73.
5. For a discussion of the challenge of the wilderness in Canada, see Donald Creighton, *A History of Canada* (Boston, rev. ed., 1958).
6. For a brief discussion of Canada's immigration policy and manpower needs at that time, see Department of Manpower and Immigration, *The Immigration Program* (Green Paper on Immigration, Vol. 2) (Ottawa, 1974), pp. 1-17.
7. J.S. Woodsworth, *Strangers Within Our Gates* (Toronto, 1972), p. 138.
8. Records of the Immigration Branch (Record Group 76), RG 76, Vol. 431, File No. 642439: "Immigration from Syria and Lebanon, 1905-1910, 1913." (Letter from W.D. Scott to the Honourable Dr. Roche, dated January 16, 1913).
9. Edmund Bradwin, *The Bunkhouse Man* (Toronto, 1972), p. 108.
10. Cf. Philip M. Kayal and Joseph M. Kayal, *The Syrian-Lebanese in America* (Boston, 1975), Ch. V, pp. 89-111.
11. Lucius Hopkins Miller, *Our Syrian Population: A Study of the Syrian Population of Greater New York* (Columbia University Library, N.Y., and N.Y. Public Library, Widener Collection, Harvard University, 1904), as quoted in Kayal and Kayal, *op. cit.*, pp. 101-102.
12. Hitti, *op. cit.*, p. 69. According to a Montreal respondent, who report-

edly became a millionaire after a humble beginning as a peddler, Syrian immigrants traded with each other just as they did with non-Syrians. He recalled an incident in which a certain item was traded among several Syrian peddlers, finally again reaching the original peddler and being offered to him for sale at twice the price for which he had sold the item in the first instance!

13. Karam, *op. cit.*, p. 21.

14. *Ibid.*, p. 22.

15. *Ibid.* Several of the early pioneers interviewed in this study acknowledged the Syrian women's supportive economic role in the new environment.

16. The same is true of the role of Syrians in other parts of the New World. With reference to the United States, for example, a recent publication states: "A Syrian peddler filled an important vacuum in the American economy, and his disposition to travel served him well." See Kayal and Kayal, *op. cit.*, p. 99.

17. To this date, Arab Canadians have strong positive feelings towards French Canadians. Because of their minority status, French Canadians are believed to be more sympathetic towards Arabs and Palestinians (a minority group at home and abroad) than are English Canadians.

18. Gilbert Johnson, "The Syrians in Western Canada," *Saskatchewan History*, 12 (1959), p. 31.

19. *Ibid.*, pp. 31-32.

20. Karam, *op. cit.*, p. 25.

21. *Ibid.*

22. *Ibid.*, p. 26-29.

23. *Ibid.*, p. 31.

24. The 1973-74 telephone directory, *Dialogue Oriental* by Elie Bacha, provides a listing of Arab-Canadian business establishments in Montreal. See also Baha Abu-Laban, "The Arab-Canadian Community," in Elaine C. Hagopian and Ann Paden, eds., *Arab-Americans: Studies in Assimilation* (Wilmette, Ill., 1969), p. 32.

25. I have decided against a listing of such outstanding Arab Canadians, partly because the listing will necessarily be incomplete and partly because of the absence of acceptable criteria on the basis of which a given name may be included or excluded. Suffice it to note that many of these Arab Canadians are nationally, sometimes internationally, prominent.

26. For a discussion of the entrance status of different immigrant groups and of limitations on social mobility of ethnic groups, see John Porter, *The Vertical Mosaic* (Toronto, 1965), pp. 60-103.

27. Omitted from the discussion is a consideration of the opportunity structure prevailing in Canada at the turn of the century. It is here assumed that the Canadian opportunity structure accompanying economic development at that time was not only an empirical fact, but also equally open, or equally impermeable, to all the "new" immigrant groups (i.e.,

the ones who came from countries other than those of Western Europe and the United States).

28. Hitti, *op. cit.*, p. 87.
29. Karam, *op. cit.*, pp. 23-24.
30. For a discussion of the Protestant ethic, see Max Weber, *The Protestant Ethic and the Spirit of Capitalism* (New York, 1958).
31. Kayal and Kayal, *op. cit.*, p. 98.
32. Hitti, *op. cit.*, p. 80.
33. About two years after my interview with him, this respondent published a book which contained his biography. See Sheikh Muhammad Said Massoud, *I Fought as I Believed* (Montreal, 1976), pp. 3-9.
34. *Ibid.*, pp. 6-7.
35. *Ibid.*, p. 7.
36. *Ibid.*
37. For a discussion of the Calvinistic movement, see Weber, *op. cit.*, pp. 95-154.
38. Department of Manpower and Immigration, *Three Years in Canada, op. cit.*, p. 32.
39. *Ibid.*, p. 35.
40. No information is available for Arab immigrants to Canada for the period 1946-1956. The number of these immigrants was very small.
41. The results of the longitudinal survey on the economic and social adaptation of imigrants show that "half of the 16,531 immigrants who came to Canada in 1969 were destined to the labour force." Cf. *Three Years in Canada, op. cit.*, p. 5.
42. For case studies containing occupational distributions for selected Arab communities, see Abdelmoneim M. Khattab, "The Assimilation of Arab Muslims in Alberta," M.A. Thesis, Department of Sociology, The University of Alberta, 1969; Denys R. Reed, "The Arab Community in Toronto," unpublished manuscript, 1973; Louise E. Sweet, "Reconstituting a Lebanese Village Society in a Canadian City," in Barbara C. Aswad, ed., *Arabic Speaking Communities in American Cities* (Staten Island, N.Y., 1974), pp. 39-52; and Nadia Hanna Wassef, "The Egyptians in Montreal: A New Colour in the Canadian Ethnic Mosaic," M.A. Thesis, Department of Geography, McGill University, 1977.
43. Sweet, *ibid.*, p. 45.
44. *Three Years in Canada, op. cit.*, p. 6.
45. *Ibid.*
46. See Bernard R. Blishen, "A Socio-Economic Index for Occupations," *Canadian Review of Sociology and Anthropology*, 4 (1967), pp. 41-53. Occupations with a score of 50 or higher were classified as "high," whereas those with a score of less than 50 were classified as "low."

SIX

Institutional Development: Religion, Associations and Newspapers

The most pressing problem facing new immigrants to Canada is that of making a living while adapting to the new environment. Following an initial period of adjustment, which varies in length for different individuals and groups, immigrants tend to turn their attention to the founding of ethnic institutions and organizations to replace the ones which have been left behind. Examples of these institutions include churches, mosques, schools, social, cultural and economic organizations, and newspapers. The institutional development of an ethnic group in Canada is always a matter of degree, ranging from a high level such as that characterizing Jews or Ukrainians, to a low level such as characterizes immigrants from the United States. The pervasiveness, openness, and persistence of these institutions are important elements of ethnicity and thus a factor influencing acculturation and assimilation into Canadian society.

The institutional development of a given ethnic group is determined by many conditions, chief among which are group size and inclinations, geographical distribution, and capacity or willingness to support specialized ethnic institutions. The Arab Canadians provide an example of a relatively small, heterogeneous, geographically-spread ethnic group which could not support certain kinds of ethnic institutions in Canada, such as parochial or private schools as distinct from language or Sunday schools. Nor could the early or post-war Arab immigrants depend on their welfare on ethnically-based ecomomic institutions confining their services to their own kind. As individuals and as a group, they simply had to integrate with the host society in major institutional spheres such as the economic, educational and political.

What they could and did develop, however, were varied religious institutions and voluntary associations the survival of which was not decisively determined by absence of Arab immigrant concentrations in urban neighbourhoods. They also published newspapers, either as organs of religious or secular organizations, or as the personal enterprises of ethnically-committed individuals. The admixture of religious and secular elements in some of the Arab Canadian organizations and newspapers makes it advisable to provide a unified analysis of these institutional developments.

INSTITUTIONALIZING THE FAITH

It will be worthwhile to emphasize, at the outset, two points regarding institutional developments undertaken by the early and more recent Arab immigrants to Canada. First, the Arab-Canadian community was not isolated from its ethnic counterpart in the United States. There, the Arab immigrants were numerically larger, at least ten times as strong, and thus potentially more capable of taking a leading role in developing ethnic institutions, which they did. Despite the eventual institutional self-sufficiency of the two North American-Arab communities, the links between them have remained to the present time. The earliest and most formalized of these links were in the sphere of religion, but they were not confined to the spiritual realm. Another aspect of these links was (is) the frequent crossing by Arab Americans of the Canada-United States borders on a temporary as well as permanent basis. At the turn of the century, for example, a good number of the Syrian settlers in the prairie region of Canada came from the United States.

Second, the earliest phase of institutional development of the Syrian-Canadian community was in the sphere of religion, followed by the development of secular organizations and then newspapers. The starting date of these developments was not the same for different Arab Eastern religious groups, but the sequence of development tended to be the same for all of them.

Although the process of institutionalizing the faith had priority over other aspects of institutional development, it did not occur immediately upon the arrival in Canada of the early Syrian immigrants. For one thing, these immigrants came to Canada not as communal religious groups, but rather as individuals who happened to belong to one religious faith or another. Although religion played a role in their migration, its role was minor and the immigrants themselves were not religious zealots. To be sure, they were alienated from the Turkish Muslim rulers, but on the whole they came to Canada mainly in search of economic opportunities, often expressing the belief that their return to the ancestral homeland would follow after they had achieved their goal of obtaining some measure of economic security. Given Canada's radically different socio-cultural and climatic conditions, they faced serious adjustment problems which did very little, initially, to change that belief.

During the beginning period of Syrian settlement in Canada (1880's and 1890's), the spiritual needs of the pioneers were met by Eastern (Russian) Orthodox rite, Latin rite, and even Protestant churches and clergymen. Syrian priests began to arrive in New York and Montreal, as well as other American cities, as early as the 1890's, but not in sufficient numbers and denominational variety to stabilize the situation. At that time, the geographical mobility of Syrian peddlers and business men was a complicating factor. As a result, there was, perforce, an ecumenical spirit among the early Syrian immigrants. Some of the older pioneers interviewed in this study affirmed that there was a considerable amount of crossing of lines among the Orthodox, Melkites, and Maronites. No less important, however, was the absorption of an undetermined number of Syrian immigrants into Canada's established Protestant and Catholic churches. The memory of certain Syrian families who crossed denominational lines was still fresh in the minds of Syrian Canadian clergymen interviewed in 1974.

Around the turn of the century, the overwhelming majority of Syrian immigrants to Canada (and the United States), or over nine out of ten, were affiliated with the Antiochian Orthodox, Melkite, and Maronite churches. The Muslim and Coptic components of this early wave of immigration were negligible. Of the three main religious groups accounting for the majority of the early Syrian immigrants to North America, the Orthodox had to face the greatest challenge. The Melkites and Maronites, being part of the Catholic church, were not alone in North America. Although they were, and still are, Eastern Rite Catholics, the Latin church was their home away from home. In contrast, the Orthodox immigrants were separated from the Mother Church in the Arab East and, in view of the nationalistic orientation of Eastern Orthodoxy, they had no real or putative "mother" church in the new environment. A recent publication recalled that the ecclesiastical head of the Syrian Mission of the Russian Church, who was consecrated in 1904 as Vicar Bishop of the Russian Archdiocese, aimed at "preserving the life of Grace in Orthodoxy among the faithful, for already they (Orthodox immigrants from Syria) were receiving the attention of other religious groups who sought them as proselytes."[1]

For Syrian immigrants to Canada, the three main factors instigating the development of religious institutions were recognition of the proselytization efforts of the established religious groups, commitment to their own respective religious groups, and developing optimism about their future in the adopted land. The influence of these factors reached its peak in the opening years of the present century. At that time, the founding of Syrian churches, after the seed of Arab Eastern Christianity had been planted in Canadian soil, was a main preoccupation of this immigrant group. The founding of mosques and Coptic churches did not come until much later. The following pages will tell the story of how the larger Arab Eastern religious groups evolved in this country.

THE ANTIOCHIAN ORTHODOX CHURCH

There are four Antiochian Orthodox churches in existence in Canada today, two in Montreal (St. George Orthodox Church and St. Nicholas Orthodox Church), one in Ottawa (St. Elijah Orthodox Church), and one in Toronto (St. George Orthodox Church). These churches are part of the Antiochian Orthodox Christian Archdiocese of New York and All North America. Combined, they have a total membership of about 2,000 families (or 8,000-10,000 individuals). The Antiochian Orthodox membership is made up largely of Lebanese and Syrians and, to a lesser degree, Palestinians, Jordanians, Egyptians, and others, dispersed throughout Canada, but with concentration in the above cities.

The process of institutional development of this religious group started in the United States, more specifically in New York City, where the Syrian Orthodox immigrants were more numerous and earlier in time of settlement than in Canada. The situation of the Syrian Orthodox immigrants in North America was precarious at first. For example, in 1892 their first priest, Father Constantine Tarsy of Damascus, arrived in New York. He stayed for a short period of time and then returned to Damascus feeling that his co-religionists could not financially support their own church in America. In the same year, another Damascine priest, Father Christopher Jabara, landed in New York and set out to work among his people. But the local Arab Orthodox community rejected him for espousing what they regarded as heretical beliefs.[2] He returned to Egypt.

In order to satisfy their spiritual needs on a regular basis, the early Orthodox immigrants from the Arab East looked to the already established Russian Orthodox Church in North America for leadership. In 1892, this church founded a Syrian Mission with jurisdiction over Canada and the United States. The Syrian immigrants' recourse to the Russian Orthodox Church was inspired by the traditional, protective, role which Russia, as a European power, had played in behalf of this religious community *vis-à-vis* the Ottoman rulers. In addition, this Church was well organized, being the first to be established in North America.

The centre of gravity for the Syrian Orthodox community in Canada was Montreal. Its first Orthodox priest, Father Ephraim Deebs, was appointed by the Russian Bishop of Alaska and All North America in 1898. He was succeeded by Archmandrite Meletius Karroum of Latakia in 1901, and by Father George Mahfouz in 1903. The latter was appointed in Montreal because he originated from Rachaya, the village from which came the majority of Montreal's Syrian Orthodox community. Canada's first Syrian Orthodox Church, St. Nicholas, was founded in Montreal in 1905 as a result of the efforts of two societies: one for men (The Commission) and one for women (Ladies' Benevolent Society). The first parish priest was Father Oftimos Ofeish, later to become Archbishop.

The founding of St. Nicholas Orthodox Church occasioned a schism within the ranks of Montreal's Syrian Orthodox community. The conflict revolved around choice of a priest, as well as family and village loyalties. The dissenting segment of this immigrant community established two new societies and resolved to build their own church.[3] In 1910,

131

the second Orthodox church, also named St. Nicholas, was established. At this point, community conflict recurred over the naming of the new church and the matter was taken to court. Wisely, the presiding judge allowed the two churches to retain the name of their patron saint, one to be called St. Nicholas Syrian Orthodox Church of Montreal and the second St. Nicholas Syrian Orthodox Church of Canada. However, upon relocating in 1939, the former church renamed itself after the Patron Saint of Syria, St. George.

In broader context, the early history of the Syrian Orthodox community in North America was marred by dissent and disharmony. Particularly stormy were the years 1915-1934 which saw sharp disputes over maintenance of loyalty to the Russian Orthodox Church as opposed to entering the jurisdiction of the Antiochian Patriarchate. In 1927, the Syrian Mission of the Russian Orthodox Church became independent and, by then, the majority of Syrian Orthodox parishes in the United States had transferred or were about to transfer allegiance to the Patriarch of Antioch.[4] In Canada, the parishioners of St. Nicholas Orthodox Church of Montreal (later St. George) were among the last to do so, transferring to the jurisdiction of the Antiochian Patriarchate in 1934. According to a church publication, from this point "peace and harmony prevailed among the Orthodox community" in Montreal.[5]

The Antiochian Orthodox community of Canada has been, and still is, active both spiritually and socially. For example, as early as 1908, an Arabic-language newspaper, *Al-Shehab*, was started in Montreal by Michael Zarbatany, who was later ordained to the priesthood of the Syrian Orthodox Church. In 1935, St. Elijah Orthodox Church of Ottawa sponsored the publication of *The Syrian Canadian National Review* – the first collection of articles on the history of the Syrian-Canadian community. In Montreal, St. Nicholas and St. George churches played host, twice, to Syrian Antiochian Orthodox archdiocese conventions: the 11th and 29th annual conventions in 1956 and 1974, respectively. At the local institutional level, each parish performs a number of different spiritual and integrative (socio-cultural) functions through its standing committees and affiliated organizations as SOYO (Society of Orthodox Youth Organizations). Finally, the civic activities of this community in Canada have included, among other things, the charitable Ladies Aid Society, and the founding of the Cedars Home for the Aged in Montreal and the Cedars Cancer Fund (in support of cancer research at Montreal's Royal Victoria Hospital).

THE MELKITE CHURCH

The Melkites, or Byzantine Rite Catholics of the Middle East, were numerous among the early Syrian immigrants to Canada. Like their Antiochian Orthodox complement, they were attracted to Montreal and from there some of them moved to other major cities such as Toronto and Ottawa. According to their current leader in Canada, Monseigneur George Coriaty, there were about 60-70 Melkite Catholic immigrant families in 1890. By 1911, the size of this religious group grew to about 3,000 persons.[6]

Since the Melkites are in communion with Rome, forming part of the Catholic church, they looked to this church for some leadership and assistance in spiritual matters. At the same time, they maintained an uninterrupted line of communication with the Melkite Patriarch. As early as 1892, the Patriarch asked Father Boutros Shamy to accompany some 250 Syrian Melkite immigrants to Canada and assist them in preserving their faith, as well as their cultural and linguistic traditions. Father Shamy became the first priest of Montreal's evolving Melkite community. On November 23, 1892, representatives of this community petitioned Monseigneur Fabre for the use of a church building and a residence for their new priest. Shortly thereafter, arrangements were made for them to practise their Eastern Melkite rite at Notre-Dame de Bonsecours. Services were celebrated there and later at other church centres until they purchased their own church.

Because of its relatively large size, Montreal's Melkite community was able to purchase its own church building before the other Melkite communities in Ottawa and Toronto could do so. With the arrival of their second priest, Father Simone Nasre, in 1911, the pioneers and the new pastor gave serious thought to the idea of securing a physical structure for the community to own. After much hard work and financial sacrifices, in 1923 the Melkite community of Montreal purchased the present site, which used to belong to the Church of England. A short time later, the building was destroyed by fire and rebuilt in 1924. This was how Saint Sauveur Melkite Church of Montreal came into being.

At present, Saint Sauveur is one of the largest churches serving the Arabic-speaking people of Canada. According to its pastor, the membership list grew from 160 families in 1922 to 200 families in 1945, 420 families in 1960, and to a high of 3,000 families in 1974. It is apparent that the phenomenal growth of this church occurred in the 1960's and 1970's during which period large numbers of Egyptian immigrants settled in Montreal. By 1974, the national origins of its membership were as follows: about 60% Egyptian, 30% Lebanese-Syrian, and 10% other groups. Because of the early date of its founding as well as its vigorous leadership, the church has attended to the spiritual needs of the Melkite-Catholic communities in Ottawa, Toronto and elsewhere in Canada. In 1972 its present pastor, Monseigneur George Coriaty, was appointed Patriarchal Vicar for all of Canada. Several priests assist him in his pastoral work.

More recently, the Ottawa and Toronto Melkite communities have acquired their own resident priests. In Ottawa, in 1961 Saints Peter and Paul Church was founded and a resident priest appointed, after a long period of dependency on a visiting priest from Saint Sauveur Melkite

133

Church. In Toronto, where the church has had a longer history than that of Ottawa, Our Lady of Assumption was able to engage a resident priest in 1968. During the two years preceding this appointment, Monseigneur Coriaty visited the Toronto community regularly, both to do pastoral work and to provide assistance in the rejuvenation and integration of the community.

Adherents of the Melkite Catholic faith are not confined to Montreal, Ottawa and Toronto, although these three cities account for a large majority of this religious group. The remainder are scattered in other parts of Quebec and Ontario, as well as in the major urban centres across the country.

Associated with the institutional development of the Melkite community in Canada was the development of numerous men's and women's organizations and youth groups:

> Avec le développement de la Colonie la vie paroissiale se fait plus intense, des associations et des oeuvres se créent dans un but d'entraide tant materielle que morale. Les Dames auxiliaires s'occupent de l'entretien de l'Eglise et des ornements sacerdotaux. Le Centre d'Accueil reçoit les nouveaux arrivants et essaie de les diriger. La Société de bienfaisance prend soin des vieillards. La Chorale forme des members qui contribuent à la solennité des offices en leur gardant la force d'expression de la langue et de la musique. Les mouvements de jeunesse, le catéchisme, la Légion de Marie, inculquent aux enfants et aux jeunes gens la langue, les traditions et le folklore du pays. Cela est nécessaire pour 'faire le pont' entre l'éducation des parents et celle des enfants et maintenir la cohésion dans la famille.[7]

St. Sauveur community's most ambitious project yet was the founding of the Bois-de-Boulogne Community Centre in Montreal. Several years of work and planning went into this project which was brought to a successful completion in 1974. The Centre is designed to provide day care facilities for children of working parents, a place for youth and adults' social and cultural activities, and assistance for newcomers to Canada. Other outstanding activities of St. Sauveur community are the Immigrant Aid Society and the Quebec-Middle East Friendship Association.

Communication within the Melkike community in Canada, and between it and other groups, has been enhanced by a well-designed and managed national quarterly magazine, *Trait d'Union*. This publication commenced in 1964 and celebrated its tenth anniversary in 1973. *Trait d'Union* features Melkite community news from different parts of Canada and a variety of articles dealing with such topics as religion, the Middle East, visiting dignitaries and religious leaders, social and cultural activities and issues being confronted in the new environment.

THE MARONITE CHURCH

The early Maronite immigrants to Canada were not as numerous as those of the Orthodox faith. However, like the other Syrian immigrants, they settled first in Montreal, and from there moved in large numbers to Ottawa, Toronto, the Windsor-Leamington region and the Maritime Provinces – particularly Halifax and Sydney and, to a lesser degree, St. John and Charlottetown. Relatively few Maronites ventured into Western Canada. There is no record of a Maronite church being established in Montreal during those early years, partly because of the immigrants' movement to other parts of Canada and partly because of the likelihood of their assimilation into Roman Catholicism. St. Maron Church in Montreal is a development of the late 1960's.

In Toronto, a St. George Maronite Society was established in the early 1920's and a Maronite church (located at Shuter and Victoria streets) was functioning under the leadership of Father Sabalany.[8] In fact, Father Sabalany opened and directed the first Arabic-language school in Toronto.[9] Following the demolition of the structure in which the church was housed, no attempts were made to relocate, and by the 1930's the St. George Maronite Society went out of existence. From that point on, the Arab associations which were established in Toronto were "secular," e.g., the Canadian Young Lebanese Club and later the Ladies Auxiliary of the Canadian Young Lebanese Club, but the memberships were largely comprised of Maronites.[10] The assimilation of many into the Roman Catholic Church was almost inevitable.

Elsewhere in Canada, including Halifax, Sydney, St. John and Charlottetown, the pioneer Maronites established social, cultural and benevolent societies rather than churches, except in Windsor. The Windsor community benefitted from the generosity of one of its successful members. A 1935 Syrian-Canadian publication, referring to the "beautiful Maronite Church at Windsor," provides the following description of its benefactor, a man named Louis Peters: "Shy and retiring to a fault, at a meeting of·fellow Maronites at Windsor, at which was being discussed ways and means of providing funds to build a church, he quietly nudged a friend, and whispered in his ear requesting him to announce that he would pay the total cost. . . ."[11] The resulting church building, St. Peter's Maronite Church, continues today to serve the approximately 3,000 Maronites of Lebanese origin in the Windsor-Leamington region.

The development of autonomous Maronite religious institutions was attenuated due to absorption by the Roman Catholic Church. Compared to its Melkite complement, the Maronite community in Canada, as well as the United States, was more ready to accept Roman Catholicism (although both communities are administratively linked with Rome).[12] According to a knowledgeable Arab Canadian, "most of the Maronites assimilated easily to Roman Catholicism and joined whatever church that happened to be close by."[13]

The most notable recent development was the establishment in 1969 of St. Maron church in Montreal, prompted by the influx of large numbers of Maronite immigrants from the Arab East. The two main components of the post-war wave of Maronite immigration to Canada came from Egypt and Lebanon. The Egyptian component, comprised largely of descendants of nineteenth century Lebanese immigrants to Egypt, arrived in Canada in the 1960's and 1970's. The Lebanese component, arriving mainly from 1972-1977, is composed largely of people fleeing the civil war in Lebanon. A sizable portion of this latter group were admitted to Canada as visitors, but special arrangements have been made to change their status to that of Landed Immigrants. It is estimated that about 6,000 Maronite immigrants have arrived in Canada in the past two decades.[14] The majority of these immigrants have gravitated toward Montreal, due to their knowledge of French language and culture.

By 1974, St. Maron church had approximately 600 families on its membership lists, of whom about six out of 10 were from Egypt.[15] Under the leadership of the two Maronite priests, now resident in Montreal, the community's activities are both religious and social. According to Wassef:

> . . . the religious ones include Sunday mass, which is celebrated in Arabic and Syriac. Religious comments at the end of the mass are conducted in French. Again, French is the language often used by members of this community. A group of 20 ladies called 'confrerie des soeurs' is responsible for the other religious activities, such as organizing prayers and religious education for children. Meanwhile, they help during Sunday mass, along with a youth group which participates in the church chorale.
>
> The social activities of the community are relatively limited. They consist mainly of organizing parties, and are in the hands of 'les dames auxiliaires' and the youth group. The latter formed a theatrical group called 'al Safa' that presents very successful plays.[16]

The numerical base of the Maronite community and its recent expansion in Canada have contributed to the development of some distinctly Maronite religious organizations to meet the needs of this Eastern Christian group.

THE COPTIC ORTHODOX CHURCH

The largest component of post-war Arab immigration to Canada was from Egypt, and the overwhelming majority of Egyptian immigrants arrived in the 1960's and 1970's. Among the things which these immigrants brought with them was the Coptic faith, one of the most recent additions to Canada's religious mosaic. The Coptic church in Canada is still in pro-

Ruth Barkett, Kalthoom Peters, and Rose Tobias, c. 1920, Toronto.
(James Peters)

Peter Tobius at Long Branch, c. 1922-23. He specialized in meat in his butcher shop and general store. (James Peters)

Lebanese immigrants onboard ship before landing in Canada, January, 1952. (Hassan Jabara)

January 1, 1947, citizenship ceremony in Ottawa, whereby Palestine-born Naif Hanna Azar takes the oath to become a Canadian citizen. (Public Archives Canada)

The Macham brothers, Jacob, Abraham, and Isaac (sitting) in 1907 at Ottawa. (Multicultural History Society of Ontario)

Visiting Bishop Germanos Shahadi in 1915 at St. Barnabas Anglican Church. (Multicultural History Society of Ontario)

Melkite community from Zahler, Lebanon, photographed in front of their church in Toronto at 223 Jarvis St., c. 1927. (Multicultural History Society of Ontario)

Coptic Pope Schnoda III on a visit to Montreal, May-June, 1977. (Arab News of Toronto)

Resurrection celebration at a Catholic-Arab Church, San Sauvé, Montreal. (Arab News of Toronto)

Faiz Peters and Sadie Peters, Toronto, c. 1932. (James Peters)

Naiffe Stephen, a Toronto community leader, c. 1936. (James Peters)

Fred, Rose, and Helen Salloum at Neville, Saskatchewan. (H. Salloum)

Fred Burke in 1943 at Jasper, Alberta. (H. Salloum)

A street-corner scene on the prairies. (H. Salloum)

Hassan Jabara, Windsor, 1953.
(H. Jabara)

Annual dinner of the Ottawa Muslim
Association. (Multicultural History Society
of Ontario)

London, Ontario, Moslem mosque. (Victor Aziz)

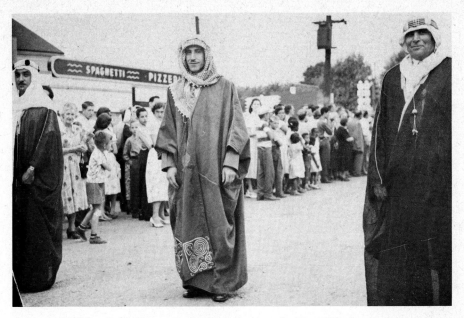

H. Jabara, M. Nasar, A. Deeb, Lebanese, during a Windsor parade.
(H. Jabara)

Lebanese-Canadian float, May 13, 1937, Kirkland Lake, Ontario.
(Multicultural History Society of Ontario)

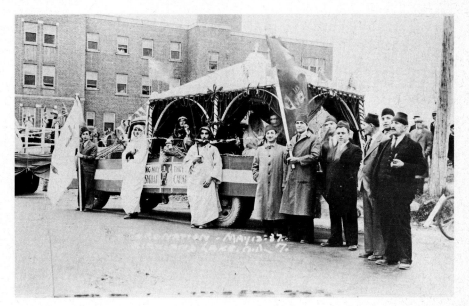

Mr. James Peters, 1945. Photo taken in Germany just after the war.
(James Peters)

H. Salloum and James Peters at the Baghdad Pavilion,
Caravan, Toronto, 1975. (H. Salloum)

An Egyptian dancer in Montreal. (Arab News of Toronto)

cess of development, as is the Coptic Orthodox Church Diocese of North America. Because of the short history of this church in North America, the present discussion will consider issues involved in transplanting Coptic Christianity into the new environment.

The spiritual needs of Coptic communities in North America were met, at first, by a patriarchal representative dispatched from Egypt once a year. This proved to be an inadequate arrangement due to the growing size and geographical spread of these communities. Thus, the Coptic Orthodox Patriarchate decided to appoint permanent priests in North America. The first priest, Father Morcos, was ordained in 1964, and the second, Father Nakhla, in 1967. It is significant to note that these two priests were based in Toronto and Montreal, respectively. By September, 1974, seven more priests had been ordained in different parts of the United States.

The church was registered in Canada in 1965. Its first chapter was founded in Toronto in that year, and the second chapter was founded in Montreal in 1967. Both churches started with small memberships, but by 1974 the lists had expanded to include 362 families in Toronto and 400 families in Montreal. The first parish priest served Hamilton, London and Kitchener, in addition to Metropolitan Toronto, and he also visited Western Canada once a year. The second priest served Montreal; Sherbrooke, Ottawa, Boston, Pittsburgh and St. Louis. Given their responsibilities, the two priests had full schedules and one of them indicated that "in the early days it was like missionary service rather than parish work."

Two sets of problems have confronted the new church in Canada. The first set of problems pertains to short term issues which are taken for granted by the established churches: place and time of worship. For example, the Toronto Coptic priest at first could not find a place to worship on Sunday and as a result he was forced to hold services on Saturday. Later, he used a kindergarten for Sunday services, but his congregation did not find small children's chairs to be exactly comfortable. The situation improved a little in the next stage when a small chapel in a church was acquired for Sunday service. Because of the chapel's small capacity, the church was finally moved to a rented structure where services are held regularly on Sunday afternoon. Like the Toronto church, the Montreal one was housed in a rented structure until recently.

The second set of problems faced by the church involved basic changes in some aspects of its operation. The Coptic clergymen, for example, felt it would be wise to modify the church's traditional musical style in order to "appeal to the Western ear." A highly qualified ethnomusicologist was engaged to work on this problem. Second, the church is creating an English Service Book and considering the creation of a French Service Book. The shift from Arabic to English is total for Sunday School children, the new generation of Egyptian Canadians that has little or no knowledge of the ancestral language. For adults, English is used par-

137

tially, except in Ottawa where it is used regularly. Finally, the traditional sex segregation in seating during church services has been abolished.

Not all Coptic immigrants were on the membership lists of the two churches. When asked about this matter, the priest felt, first, that some people prefer to go to churches closer to their home; second, that there has been some loss of membership due to intermarriage; third, that some people simply do not know of the existence of the church, being too involved in adapting to the new environment; and, finally that the church's two-hour service might be too long for some people.

Church activities include the founding of the St. Mark Club, Home Study Groups, and a number of committees with specialized functions. In addition to the Religious Education Committee, there is a Newcomers' Committee and a Social Activities Committee. The latter committee takes charge of such integrative activities as picnics, plays, and charter flights to Egypt. Although the church was not involved in such activities in Egypt, it is in its interest to facilitate them in the new environment. Thus, the Coptic Orthodox Church is performing important functions for the benefit of its members and, where necessary, adapting to the demands of the new environment.

THE ISLAMIC MOSQUE

Throughout the entire history of Arab immigration to Canada, Muslim immigrants were a fraction of the total volume of newcomers. It will be remembered that in 1931 there were only 645 Muslim residents, probably mostly Arab, spread throughout different regions of Canada. Small size and relatively even geographical spread underlay the slow development of mosques and related Muslim institutions. Another factor of possible influence in impeding the institutional development of the Muslim community in Canada inheres in Islam. Specifically, Islam lacks the priesthood which is both prevalent and elaborate in Christianity. This fact makes it possible for a given Muslim to be self-sufficient and discharge his basic religious obligations (e.g., praying five times a day, fasting during the month of Ramadan, etc.) without having to have an intermediary between him and God. The leading of prayer in a group, say on Friday noon, which is of equal significance to the Sunday Service in Christianity, could be accomplished by the group's calling on any one of its members to act as imam (religous leader). Moreover, there are minimal restrictions in Islam on where an individual or a group can pray.

Despite the above, the Islamic faith cannot thrive without institutional supports such as an imam, a mosque and associated benevolent societies. In a non-Islamic environment such as Canada, these community resources are particularly important. Also, the arrival of children and community growth often strengthen the need for the founding of institutions which would perpetuate the faith. As Dr. Ilyas Ba Yunus noted, "living as an Islamic family within the non-Islamic society is strainful. It demands conscious efforts and sacrifices. Those who are concerned should start by creating a community of the like-minded among themselves."[17] Thus, to build a mosque and to select an imam for the group is to begin to develop the Muslim community and institutionalize the faith. The mosque would provide a meeting place for the group and an imam would be able to lead prayer, facilitate group solidarity, provide religious and language instruction, solemnize marriages, arrange for burials according to the Islamic tradition, and mediate in family and community disputes.[18] Traditionally, imams have been accorded high status and looked upon as community leaders.

Canada's first mosque, Al-Rashid Mosque, was erected in Edmonton, Alberta, in 1938. At that time Edmonton had approximately 20 Lebanese Muslim families who worked together on this project. For the Alberta Muslim pioneers, the Great Depression had its positive aspects. At that time, business was slow and Edmonton's Arab Muslims, who were in business for themselves, met regularly to discuss common problems and ponder the future. The idea of building a mosque crystallized in those meetings. A new association was formed under the name of the Arabian Muslim Association and a building permit was obtained in May, 1938.[19] Also, a fund raising campaign was launched and through the generosity of Canadian friends and other Arab-origin Canadians, both Muslim and Christian, in Alberta and Saskatchewan, the mosque was completed in November, 1938.

Further institutional development of the Arab Muslim community in Canada was not forthcoming until after World War II. In the 1950's and thereafter, the need for mosques and religious associations became pressing as a result of the arrival in Canada of large numbers of Muslim immigrants.

Parenthetically, it should be noted that among those arriving in the post-war period were Druse immigrants, largely from Lebanon. However, due to the relatively small size of this religious community in Canada, the Druse have not developed their own distinctive religious institutions. Being affine with the Muslim tradition, they have depended on Muslim religious leaders to solemnize marriages and provide other services as needed.

Quebec and Ontario, and to a lesser degree Alberta, claimed the large majority of the new Muslim arrivals. In Alberta, an atypical situation has developed whereby Arab Muslims (and Druse) now outnumber Arab Christians. In contrast, in Canada at large, Arab Christians today outnumber Muslims by a ratio of three to one.

Characteristically, the post-war Muslim immigrants to Canada were of mixed national origins, including Arabs, Pakistanis and, to a lesser degree, Indians, Yugoslavs, Albanians and Bulgarians, among others. They were all bound together by commitment to the Islamic faith – a religion which embodies the conception of a unified Islamic nation (*Umma*) regardless of ethnic origin. In practice, many Muslim groups did emphasize religion over nationality. For example, in a recent study of Pakistani Canadians, Awan observed: "Although Pakistani immigrants wish to preserve their identity as a people with their own language, culture and special traditions, still they show a greater desire to be known as a religious community than an ethnic, political entity."[20] The multi-ethnic characteristic of Canada's Muslim community has provided its members with many challenges, but this has not deterred them from continuing to work together as a religious minority in Canada.

Presently, Islamic mosques and/or organizations are to be found in Newfoundland (St. John's), Nova Scotia (Dartmouth), Quebec (Montreal and Ville St. Laurent), Ontario (Ottawa, Toronto, Hamilton, London, Windsor, Kingston, Hespeler, and Thunder Bay), Manitoba (Winnipeg), Saskatchewan (Saskatoon and Regina), Alberta (Edmonton, Calgary and Lac La Biche), and British Columbia (Vancouver).[21] These mosques and organizations are usually managed by officers elected by their respective memberships.

The most recent development worthy of note was the founding in 1972 of the Council of Muslim Communities of Canada. The CMCC grew out of a firm belief in self-help, and a feeling that it alone could undertake a coherent, national approach to the issues facing the Canadian Muslim community. Affiliated with it is a large number of Muslim associations across Canada. The following list of committees organized within the CMCC should provide an idea about the scope of current activities: Education, Youth, Women's, Religious Affairs, Public Relations, and Publications. The CMCC is a member of the Federation of Islamic Associations in the United States and Canada (with headquarters in Detroit) and works in co-operation with the Muslim Students' Association of the United States and Canada (with headquarters in Gary, Indiana).

Several newsletters (mostly in English but some in Arabic), published by Muslim associations in practically all of the major centres, keep the memberships informed of Muslim celebrations and holidays, ongoing activities, programmes and future plans. A major quarterly magazine, *Islam Canada*, published by the Council of Muslim Communities of Canada, has been in existence since 1972. It features a variety of articles dealing with religious, educational and political matters, news of Muslim communities in Canada and around the world and essays interpreting Islam and providing advice on how Muslims can adapt to the Canadian environment.

Brief mention should be made here of the dilemma of leadership, of imamship, faced by Muslim communities in Canada. There are two aspects of this dilemma, one financial and the second cultural. With reference to the financial aspect, Muslim communities often lack a qualified imam due to lack of sufficient funds. In fact, financial limitations have often impeded institutional development and the introduction of new programmes. Under a special state policy, Egypt has, on occasion, supplied imams to selected communities in Canada, but this has not eliminated the problem. The second aspect of the leadership dilemma concerns the type of imam most suitable to serve in Canadian cities. According to Muslim respondents, the most desirable type of imam is the one who combines a high level of religious training with intimate knowledge of the North American way of life. It is generally believed that this type of imam could most effectively reconcile the Islamic faith with the new environment. In reality, this type of imam is not frequently encountered for several reasons, including the fact that Islamic theological seminaries for the training of imams are not available either in Canada or the United States.

Muslims in general, and Canadian Muslims in particular, believe that their faith is good for all time and places, and any contradictions between it and the North American environment are more apparent than real. As one spokesman asserts, "failures in Islam today are due to the failure to put original Islam into practice."[22] While Islam is inflexible in matters relating to proscriptions (e.g., drinking of alcoholic beverages and eating pork) and moral standards, it is believed to be flexible and pragmatic in the way it allows a Muslim to meet his religious obligations in the face of unusual circumstances. A few examples will illustrate this point. In Canada, if a Muslim is prevented by his work from praying five times a day, at specified intervals, he may combine these prayers at the end of the day. Also, if a Muslim is prevented by his work from observing the major weekly group prayer on Friday noon, he is allowed to make up for that either on Friday evening or Sunday noon. The latter group prayers, of which that at Sunday noon is the more common, are aspects of Islamic adaptation to the new environment. The reactions of Muslims interviewed in the course of this study confirm the following statement: "One can conclude that the Five Pillars of Islam can be observed easily in North America if the believer sincerely wants to do so and that the religion which has its origin in seventh century Arabia seems flexible enough to be adapted to twentieth century city life here."[23]

THE ADAPTIVE ROLE OF RELIGIOUS INSTITUTIONS

Religious pluralism is one of the main characteristics of Canadian society. The Canadian religious mosaic includes scores of religions which seek to bring spiritual meaning to the lives of their members. The Eastern Christian churches and the Islamic mosque are part of this mosaic. For these Arab Eastern religions, as for many non-mainstream ones, Canada has provided a great challenge. The response to this challenge has varied in details and intensity, but all of these Arab Eastern groups were one in the desire on the one hand to facilitate members' integration with the Canadian community, and on the other to maintain a link with the ancestral heritage.

The first aspect of the above goal, that of facilitating adaptation to the new environment, was undertaken in a number of different ways. To start with, it should be noted first that both the Eastern Christian churches and the Islamic mosque were adaptive, in the sense that they looked after the members' spiritual and psychological needs. However, this strictly religious role was soon to be expanded to include a socially adaptive element. At the turn of the century, there were few government services available to immigrants, and thus these religious organizations had to function as immigrant aid societies, the chief and often sole counsellor being the priest. Even today, despite the substantial expansion of government services to immigrants, these religious organizations have continued to assist new immigrants in the transition to the Canadian way of life.

The magnitude of the task facing the Middle East religious organizations multiplied manifold as a result of the heavy influx of Arab immigrants to Canada during the post-war years, particularly the 1960's. In Montreal, for example, the Saint Sauveur Melkite Church formally established an immigrant aid programme manned by the parish priest, together with assistants and volunteers. Likewise, the priests of the recently established Coptic Orthodox churches in Montreal and Toronto were called upon to help large numbers of immigrants from their native Egypt. Assistance to new immigrants was also provided by other parish priests and by imams in different regions of Canada. The needs of post-war Arab immigrants varied considerably, given their heterogeneity and the multiplicity of reasons underlying their immigration. Among the issues on which they sought help were employment, housing, family counselling, translation of documents, facilitation of professional qualifications, certification, mediation with Canadian government agencies, and mediation with appropriate Arab consulates in Canada to obtain or certify documents, renew passports, etc.

Another way by which Arab-Canadian religious organizations facilitated the adaptation of members was reflected in institutional shifts regarding the language of liturgy. At the turn of the century, the dominant language was Arabic. However, in the course of time the church brought English or French, as the case may have been, into partial use. This was necessitated, in part, by the situation of Canadian-born children of Arab immigrants. The degree to which English or French was used varied from church to church, but it tended to increase as the immigrant generation in the congregation felt more secure with the new language. By the 1950's or early 1960's, the shift to the new language was more or less complete, the more common of the two official languages being English. Saint Sauveur Melkite Church (Montreal) provides an example of a major church where the shift was largely in the direction of French.

When the post-war Arab immigrants began pouring into Canada, there was a noticeable retreat by the older churches from the newly acquired liturgical language. For example, St. George Orthodox Church (Toronto) reintroduced Arabic in 1969, and presently the congregation worships half in Arabic and half in English. The congregation of Ottawa's St. Elijah Orthodox Church worships almost exclusively in Arabic. In contrast, Montreal's St. Sauveur Melkite Church has continued to use mainly French in its liturgy. It is clear that the return to the native language was neither universal nor complete, it being determined by certain demographic characteristics and expectations of the membership.

With reference to more recently founded religious institutions, such as the Coptic Orthodox churches and Islamic mosques, the predominant language to this date has been Arabic. English is used occasionally, but with a steadily increasing frequency. Again, the arrival of the "new" second generation is an important factor in current shifts to English. Not surprisingly, the Sunday School programmes in the Coptic church are almost exclusively in English. Similarly, where second generation Muslim children have been involved, religious training and instruction by imams has often been in English (or at least mixed).

It is clear from the above that in the earlier period of this century, as in the post-war years, the trend was for newly founded religious institutions to introduce English or French in their liturgy. Whereas the older institutions went all the way, substituting English or French for Arabic and then reintroducing Arabic in differing degrees to appeal to the newly arrived post-war immigrants, the religious institutions founded in recent years are still at the early stage of assimilating English or French to appeal to new second generation Arab Canadians. Whether the newly founded institutions will experience the same developmental processes as the older ones will be influenced by a number of different factors, including Canada's immigration experience in the near future. The point to be made, however, is that these religious institutions have been flexible regarding their language of worship and this has, undoubtedly, enhanced their adaptive role *vis-à-vis* Arab Canadians.

The third and final way by which the religious institutions under study attempted to facilitate adaptation to the new environment was through church integration with, but not full assimilation into, the host community. This pattern characterizes the Arab experience in North America. In the United States, Orthodox clergymen, for example, were eager to establish seminaries for the training of their own priests in America in order to assure "the continuity of Orthodoxy here and its progressive integration into American life."[24] Archbishop Antony Bashir (1936-1966) was firmly convinced of "the necessity of adjusting his church to the needs of American life in which his people were active participants." To this end, he employed different means such as the founding of church-related organizations, involving the congregations in the reorganization of the archdiocese, linking his church with other national

Orthodox churches (by co-founding the Federation of Orthodox Bishops) and with American Christian churches (through membership in the Federal Council of the Churches of Christ), and even accepting into the archdiocese three western rite parishes.

Like their Orthodox counterparts, the leaders of Arab Eastern Catholic and Coptic churches and of Islamic mosques, in varying degrees, were also committed to integration. This was apparent from interviews with various leaders and from examinations of their organizational activities and publications. The notice of an "immigrant church or mosque" did not carry as much appeal as seeing their own institutions integrated into the context of the larger Canadian religious mosaic.

Turning now to the other side of their adaptive role, the Christian churches of Arab origin in Canada have served (and continue to serve) as a vehicle for preserving the cultural heritage and maintaining a religious link with the ancestral homeland. The church leaders have viewed the beliefs and values of Eastern Christianity as not only valid, but also fundamentally compatible with the basic value systems of North American society. On the other hand, they have acknowledged the existence of socio-cultural differences between the North American and Middle Eastern societies as a source of challenge and a prime motive for adaptation to the new setting. Consider, for example, the following statement made by the Antiochian Orthodox Church of North America: "Given the contemporary world and its radically secular approach to life, Orthodox theology is called to its greatest challenge. We do not need a 'new' theology which is 'uprooted' from the depths of our tradition and catholicity: what we more nearly need is a way of applying these truths and that lifestyle. . . ."[25]

For Muslims, the link with the heritage has been maintained through the Islamic mosque. Research evidence indicates that the presence of an imam in the group tends to strengthen commitment to Islam and associated precepts.[26] As indicated earlier, Muslims share in common the belief that the Islamic way of life is not irreconcilable with many elements of the Canadian value system and existing social patterns. Consider, for example, the following prescription given by the Islamic Foundation of Toronto: "Our personal conduct and social-business relations must reflect the life style of Prophet Muhammad (Peace be Upon Him). We should be truthful, responsive, just, generous, friendly, respectful, concerned with the social issues of our time and active in a responsible way. Our words or actions must not defame or hurt others."[27] Significantly, Islamic publications in Canada appear to serve the double purpose of cultural preservation and of easing Muslims' transition to the Canadian way of life. With reference to the latter goal, they regularly feature interpretations of Islamic codes of behaviour in such areas as family life, role of women, education and hygiene, for the purpose of emphasizing that Islam is not an altogether alien religion to Canadian society.

THE FOUNDING OF SECULAR ASSOCIATIONS

The Early Period

Over a century ago Tocqueville noted that Americans were characterized by their readiness to form a committee or an association when faced with a pressing issue or problem.[28] For early Syrian immigrants to Canada, the most pressing need was the development of religious institutions. Non-sectarian associations were viewed with less urgency, for several reasons. First, at that time the Syrian community was very small and many of its members were in constant contact with each other, thereby satisfying their associational and communication needs. Second, these needs were also met informally as a by-product of their economic activities and the boarding-house type of accommodation. Third, the early pioneers had little time for administering voluntary associations, partly because of their long work days and partly because of their continuous movement.

The founding of secular associations became more urgent when the newly established sectarian institutions fragmented the Syrian community in a way not unlike the situation experienced in the Old Country. More to the point, the internal conditions of this ethnic group after World War I were different from those prevailing in the 1900's: the community grew considerably, the Canadian-born generation not only arrived but was also maturing, and certain pressures of the Canadian environment were being felt more by the community as a whole. In short, the group was ripe for further institutional development.

In 1919, Montreal witnessed the founding of a Syrian men's association, the Syrian National Society of Canada, the goals of which were to promote the social, political, and educational welfare of the Syrian community. In addition to providing opportunities for social and cultural functions, this Society helped establish a united front for dealing with two pressing issues facing the community at that time. The first issue was the federal government's restrictive policy regarding Asian, hence Syrian, immigration to Canada. The second issue concerned a special school tax levy imposed on parents of Orthodox children in Quebec as a result of their having been grouped under "a certain minority classification set by the School Board."[29] The Society claimed credit for convincing the Canadian authorities that the Syrians belonged to the white race, and for succeeding in appeals for the removal of the school tax levy in Quebec.[30]

Within a period of 12 years from the founding of the above society, three other organizations were founded in Montreal, two by the younger generation Syrians and one by women. In 1923, a group of young Syrian men between the ages of 18 and 23, operating out of the International Branch of the YMCA, formed the Syrian Canadian Society. Except for the fact that it served the younger generation, the objectives of this organization paralleled those of the older one. The second development among

145

Syrian youth was the founding in 1931 of the Echo Club. This club was founded by a mixed group of younger men and women and its objectives were mainly social and literary. The third organization to appear in Montreal, the Syrian Ladies Aid Society, was founded in 1930 to provide relief for needy Syrian families.

The instigator for the development of a non-sectarian Syrian women's organization was a visiting Lebanese educator, Mary Kassab, of Al-Ahliya School in Beirut. According to a former president of the Syrian Ladies Aid Society, Mary Kassab noticed that all the welcoming committees, organized on the occasion of her visit to Montreal, represented the churches. In a gathering of Syrian women the visiting educator asked, "Isn't there a non-sectarian women's organization in town?" By her question and comments, Mary Kassab was said to have sown the seeds for the Syrian Ladies Aid Society. Another interesting aspect of this development was the opposition it received from priests. One of the former presidents of the Society noted: "The priests used to say that we had no poor Syrians in Canada." However, through facts and figures, the Syrian women finally were able to convince their clergymen of the need for such a society, one of the accomplishments of which was the founding, in post-war years, of the Cedars Home for the Aged.[31]

In 1933, the above-named organizations amalgamated to form a new association, the Syrian Canadian Association, subsequently renamed the Lebanese Syrian Canadian Association (LSCA) in order to reflect the national identity of the large majority of its members.[32] At present, the LSCA is housed in a large, handsome building unequaled by any other similar Arab community structure in Canada. Some idea of its character is reflected in the following description:

> The cornerstone of the present site on Jean Talon was laid in 1946 with the building not being occupied until 1947. Dining room facilities were opened and became a very welcomed addition.
>
> Throughout the years, the LSCA has endeavoured to initiate programs to promote continued fellowship amongst the men, women and children of the community. Bowling Alleys were installed in 1949, they sponsored Arts and Crafts classes, Little League Baseball, Cubs, Boy Scouts and Girl Scouts.
>
> The Scholarship Fund was established in 1957 and the Association's aid to underprivileged children. Renovation of the present site took place in 1972 at which time the Bowling Alleys were removed and a health Club, complete with a Steam Room, Sauna, Whirlpool and Exercise Room were installed on the lower level. . . ."[33]

In Toronto, as in Montreal, the founding of sectarian organizations (such as the Syrian Orthodox Society and the Maronite Benevolent Society) preceded the development of secular institutions. However, by about the mid-1930's, at least six non-sectarian organizations were in existence

146

in Toronto. These included the Syrian Canadian Association, the Syrian Young Men's Club, the Syrian Girls' Club, the Canadian Young Lebanese Club, the Syrian-Lebanese Ratepayers' Association, and the Lebanese Liberal Association. It was through these organizations that the Syrian community of Toronto launched its social and cultural programmes. The value of these organizations to the Syrian ethnic group was expressed by the *Syrian-Lebanese Mercury*, in 1937, as follows: "These organizations must remain integral parts of our lives, serving the good at all times and consolidating the elements of Syrian and Lebanese culture in order to weave them into the entire fabric of Canadian life."[34]

Despite calls for consolidation and co-operation, the Syrian organizations in Toronto continued to operate independently of each other. They undertook social and recreational functions and on certain occasions, such as annual picnics or Christmas parties, a larger segment of the Syrian community participated.

Similar organizations were founded by the early Syrian pioneers in Vancouver, Winnipeg, Ottawa, Windsor, and in such cities in the Maritime region as Saint John, Halifax and the Sydney/Glace Bay region. In none of these localities, however, was institutional development as strong as in Montreal or Toronto. To this date, these two cities account for the larger proportion of Arab-Canadian organizations.

Before turning to a discussion of the institutional development of the Arab-Canadian community during the post-war period, reference should be made to the formation in 1943 of the Canadian Arab Friendship League. Founded in Montreal through the efforts of a Druse immigrant named Sheikh Muhammad Said Massoud, then a prosperous business man, the League had branches in major urban centres and a national secretariat with a guiding and co-ordinating function. Among the League's "charitable and patriotic" objectives were improvement of Canadian-Arab relations and protection of the integrity of the Arab-Canadian community "against unjust attack, racial discrimination and misrepresentation." In the main, the founders of the League concentrated attention on advancing the Arab viewpoint and defending the Arab image against Zionist representations. To this end, the League published a monthly magazine, *The Canadian Arab*, starting in 1945, and created the Canadian-Arab News Service. Moreover, Sheikh Massoud undertook to issue a weekly Arab-Canadian newsletter which was sent free to every newspaper in Canada.[35]

To sum up, the formation of secular organizations in the early Syrian community of Canada tended to follow the development of religious institutions. Montreal and Toronto, in particular, witnessed the founding of numerous organizations by the local Syrian immigrants and their descendants; however, some modest development occurred in other metropolitan centres from coast to coast, where there were sizeable Syrian settlements. The objectives of these non-sectarian organizations were diverse, but they tended to revolve around charitable, social,

147

cultural and, to a lesser degree, political goals. Overall, the organizations established by the early pioneers functioned to integrate their members with the larger community and to perpetuate some sense of ethnic community and pride in ethnic heritage.

The Post-war Period

The institutional development of the Arab-Canadian community was carried further in the post-war period, particularly in the late 1950's and beyond. Undoubtedly, the arrival of post-war Arab immigrants was a main factor in the formation of new organizations in virtually all metropolitan centres. Scores of organizations were founded by the newly arrived Arab immigrants, and some of these organizations were formed in co-operation with the early pioneers or their descendants.

Rather than enumerating the large number of Arab-Canadian organizations which came into being in the past quarter century, their varieties and functions will be discussed, with examples. Judging from available evidence, a number of principles were involved in the formation of post-war Arab organizations in Canada. For example, some of them were formed under the label "Arab," while others were formed under a more particularistic label such as the name of the Old Country or even ancestral village. Also, some of these organizations were limited to a particular age group, occupational group, or sex, while others were formed with no such restriction on membership. In terms of scope, some of them were oriented toward a charitable, social, cultural or political goal, while others combined several different functions. Finally, while most of them were formed strictly as local associations, at least two of them had a broader geographical coverage.

In recent years, one of the most important developments has been the emergence of a type of association projecting a decidedly "Arab" name and image. Formed under a variety of labels (e.g., "Canadian Arab Friendship League," "Arab Canadian Society," "Canadian Arab Club," etc.), this type of association is to be found in Montreal, Toronto, London, Hamilton, Windsor, Sudbury, Edmonton, and Vancouver. In certain cities, such as Montreal and Toronto, there may be two or more Arab associations in existence. Typically, friendship associations are open to Canadians of Arab origin (and sometimes to their non-Arab friends) regardless of country of birth or religious affiliation. The membership mix, by country of origin and religion, may vary from one place to another, depending on the dominant characteristics of the founding group and the local Arab-Canadian community. This is why in cities like Montreal and Toronto, where the Arab-Canadian community is quite heterogeneous, there is more than one such association.

Arab-Canadian friendship associations tend to combine, in varying degrees, social, cultural, political and, on occasion, charitable goals. Generally speaking, these associations attempt to foster better under-

148

standing between the Canadian and the Arab peoples and to defend the Arab-Canadian community against attacks from the outside. Typically, this is accomplished through a variety of programmes and functions such as annual banquets, visiting speakers, picnics, cultural displays and/or folk dancing, Arabic classes for children, and immigrant assistance.

Somewhat related to the above is the type of association formed by Arab students in virtually all major Canadian universities. Arab students associations and those serving the local Arab-Canadian community often co-sponsor cultural events and visiting speakers. The goals of student and Arab-Canadian friendship associations are essentially similar, except that the former tend to be more politicized than the latter.

The more particularistic organizations have invoked country of origin or even a narrower factor as an organizing principle. As indicated above, the early pioneers established "Lebanese" and/or "Syrian" organizations, and a number of similar organizations were established by postwar immigrants from these two countries. In Canada, the largest number of Arab-Canadian organizations bearing the old country's name are the Syrian and Lebanese. Next in frequency are the Palestinian organizations (or committees) of which at least three are in existence in Montreal (Palestine Arab Association, Association Québec-Palestine, and Solidarity Committee with the People of Palestine), and one each in Toronto (Arab Palestine Association), Ottawa (Canada-Palestine Committee) and Quebec City (Comité Palestine de L'université Laval). The main goal of these Palestinian organizations has been to provide information about and defend the national rights of the Palestinian people.

Also related to the narrower organizing principle are two recently formed, Montreal-based, Egyptian organizations, Circle St. Mark and Circle Heliopolis, open to graduates of St. Mark College in Alexandria and to Egyptian-origin Maronites, respectively. Finally, it is not uncommon to encounter, particularly among Lebanese immigrants across Canada, organizations carrying the names of such ancestral villages as Rachaya, Ain Hersha, Hasroun and Yanta. Apart from their social and integrative functions, these organizations aim at fostering continued loyalty to and material support for the ancestral village.

There are also Arab organizations comprised of certain age, sex, or occupational categories. Among such organizations are women's auxiliaries and youth associations, already discussed in connection with religious institutions. Less common are occupational or professional associations. The sole known example of this type is the Arab Canadian Professionals Association which was established recently in Ottawa. In addition to pursuing cultural objectives, this organization seeks to strengthen the links among Arab professionals in Canada. Folkloric groups represent another type of Arab organization. A prime example of this type is the Arab Folklore Group in Toronto. This organization pursues the goal of sharing aspects of the Arab culture with Canadian peo-

149

ple. Similar groups exist in other parts of Canada, such as the Arabian Knights in Edmonton, except that they tend to function under the umbrella of a previously established association.

Immigrant aid societies constitute yet another category of Arab-Canadian organizations. One of the largest is the Arab Community Centre of Toronto, formed in 1972 with grants from private and public sources. In addition to its information service for Arab immigrants, the Centre pursues broad social, cultural, recreational and educational goals. Since its inception, it has been publishing a newsletter in Arabic and English.

In 1963, a unique cultural organization was formed, the World Lebanese Cultural Union (WLCU), with branches in the different parts of the New World including Canada. This integrative organization came into being in response to initiatives taken by the government of Lebanon and had the following goals: "To carry the message of love and peace among mankind; strengthen friendship and mutual understanding; and enlarge cultural, economic and touristic exchanges."[36] A non-sectarian and non-political organization, the WLCU is committed to building bridges between Lebanon and her descendants abroad.

Finally, the year 1967 witnessed the formation of the Canadian Arab Federation which now consists of a national executive and board of directors and 13 associations in Montreal, Quebec City, Toronto, Hamilton, London, Windsor, Sudbury, Edmonton and Calgary. The Federation arose, in part, as a result of the challenge of the Six Day (Arab-Israeli) War. It aims to co-ordinate and unify the activities of Arab organizations in Canada, foster friendly relations and mutual understanding between the Canadian and Arab peoples, advance the Arab viewpoint and defend the rights of Arab Canadians, and provide financial assistance to Arab refugees. From its inception, the Federation embarked on a vigorous programme involving a large annual convention, visiting speakers, public announcements, mail contacts and preparation of briefs for political and government leaders in Canada. The Federation has been one of the most vocal Arab organizations in Canada on the question of national rights for the Palestinian people.

In conclusion, it should be noted that, collectively, Arab-Canadian organizations have been active on many different fronts: social, cultural, religious, educational, political, recreational, and charitable. While they have provided avenues for co-operation among Arab Canadians, they have also been arenas of dissent and, on occasion, intense conflict. Differences among groups of Arab Canadians have often emerged in connection with the issue of establishing organizational priorities and leadership recruitment. Some of the differences are of a long-standing nature as they inhere in the varied political orientations which immigrants brought with them from the Old Country and transmitted to their descendants.

Despite the above, Arab-Canadian organizations are given considerable community support. The survey of Arab Canadians conducted by the author in Toronto and Montreal yielded information on organizational participation, ethnic and otherwise, by means of the following question: "Are you a member of any social, religious, political, professional organizations or unions?" Space was provided for listing the names of Arab-Canadian and other (non-ethnic) organizations of which the respondent was a member, and for specifying length of membership, committee involvement and office holding.

A substantial minority, or about 43% of the respondents, indicated that they were members of one or more organizations, ethnic or otherwise. The most active joiners came from the ranks of higher income, educational and occupational categories. About five out of 10 Egyptian respondents, four out of 10 Near Eastern-origin respondents, and two out of 10 North African (other than Egyptian) respondents were joiners. Also, active participation in associations was positively related to length of residence in Canada. Thus, those who had been in Canada for over 10 years were almost twice as likely as those who had been here for 10 or less years to belong to associations. The differences by province of residence, age and sex were very small (in favour of the Ontario rather than Quebec residents, the age group "31 and over" rather than the younger one and males rather than females).

About one-third of the total sample listed at least one Arab-Canadian organization to which they belonged. The results show essentially the same pattern of relationships between participation in Arab-Canadian associations and the selected background variables, as those discussed above. The only exception is that the participation rate in ethnic associations was highest among respondents of Near Eastern origin (four out of 10) rather than Egyptian respondents (three out of 10). The North African (other than Egyptian) respondents remained the lowest joiners, with two out of 10 of them holding membership in ethnic associations.

NEWSPAPERS AND PERIODICALS

The third and final major institutional development occurring in the Arab-Canadian community concerns the Arab-language press. The first Arabic-language newspaper to appear in Canada, *Al-Shehab*, originated in Montreal in 1908. It was published by a young Syrian immigrant, Michael Zarbatany, who came to Canada at the age of 18 in 1902. In 1910, this bi-weekly newspaper ceased publication due to insufficient community support. A subsequent attempt involving the publication of a new periodical, *Al-'Alamein* (The Two Worlds), did not fare any better for essentially the same reason – limited circulation.

Almost a quarter century later, *The Syrian-Lebanese Mercury*, an English-language monthly periodical under the editorship of a young

151

Canadian-born Arab, James Peters, was started in Toronto. The main purpose of this magazine was to instill pride in the ancestral heritage, disseminate news of the local Arab community, and feature articles on the Arab world. Again, the *Mercury* was a short-lived periodical ceasing publication in 1938. This publication is particularly interesting because it started after the Syrian community had established firm roots in Canada. At that time, the immigrant generation was fairly well established and secure, except for the universal uncertainties of the Great Depression, and second generation Arab Canadians were growing to maturity. Thus, it was possible for the *Mercury* to portray aspects of ethnic community life as well as express attitudes and concerns of a relatively stable Syrian community. Among the attitudes expressed in the magazine was a strong commitment to the Canadian political system and way of life, coupled with pride in ethnic heritage and an explicit multicultural orientation.

In 1945, a new monthly magazine, *The Canadian Arab*, was published by the Canadian Arab Friendship League of Montreal, under the editorship of Sheikh Muhammad Said Massoud. Its chief goal was to advance the Arab viewpoint in Canada and "neutralize," to use the editor's word, Zionist claims to the land in Palestine. *The Canadian Arab* was published mostly in English, with a short Arabic-language editorial section. In his recent autobiography, Massoud noted: "Some 5,000 copies were printed monthly, and sent to government officials, religious leaders, club organizers, university professors, teachers, doctors, lawyers and businessmen, so that Canadians in general would be aware of the fact that Palestine is an Arab and not a Jewish country."[37] *The Canadian Arab* ceased publication in 1948.

The next major move to start a new publication was made in 1962 when the Canadian Arab Friendship Society of Toronto published a semi-annual periodical in English, *The Middle East Digest and Newsletter*. For the length of its existence, 1962-68, the *Digest* was edited by James Peters (the ex-editor of the *Mercury*) who was later joined by Habib Salloum, another prominent figure in Toronto's Arab community. Among other things, this magazine featured articles on Zionism, Palestine and the Arab world, as well as critical commentaries on the reporting of Arab news by the Canadian media, analyses of United States – Middle East policy, and literary contributions. For a while, the *Digest* was the only major periodical serving the interests of the Arab-Canadian community. Although it was a politically-oriented publication, its scope was broad.

In 1964, the Eastern Catholic community, led by St. Sauveur Church of Montreal, embarked on the publication of *Trait d'Union* – a bi-monthly magazine which is predominantly French with some materials in English. The main features of this magazine have been discussed in the preceding section on the Melkite Church. At the present time, *Trait d'Union* is the oldest surviving periodical undertaken by any segment of the Arab-Canadian community.

The period 1965-70 witnessed the emergence of four new periodicals, of which three were published by individual Arab-Canadians and the fourth by the Federation of Arab Canadian Societies (later the Canadian Arab Federation). In 1966, Joseph Lahoud founded the *Middle East Journal* in Montreal and, three years later (1969) Raymond Kneider founded the *Arab World Review* in the same city. Both of these monthly newspapers were, and still are, published in Arabic, French and English. In 1970, Ahmad Mourad started his bi-weekly newspaper, *The Source*, in Western Canada. Published in Arabic and English, *The Source* made its debut in Vancouver and, shortly thereafter, was moved to Edmonton and then to Ottawa where it has continued to be published. The fourth publication, *Arab Dawn* originated in Toronto in 1969. It was published quarterly in Arabic, English and French. *Arab Dawn* briefly ceased publication due to financial and other difficulties, but it re-appeared in a new format in October, 1977.

The above-noted periodicals share several characteristics and diverge from each other in editorial policy and political orientation. The *Middle East Journal* (MEJ) features articles about different parts of the Arab world, but gives particular coverage to Lebanon. In addition, it provides news about the ethnic community in Montreal, particularly the Lebanese-Syrian portion. Social and cultural functions undertaken by local ethnic organizations and churches are often featured pictorially. Finally, the MEJ exhibits pride in ethnic identity and supports Canada's policy of multiculturalism. The *Arab World Review* (AWR), in comparison, respresents a broader political scope and features more articles about different Arab regions including the (Arab) Gulf states and oil-rich Saudi Arabia. As the title suggests, its underlying orientation is one of pan-Arabism and this informs its analysis of issues, such as the Arab-Israeli conflict, coming within its purview. Like the MEJ, the AWR is also a social and cultural newspaper. It covers news about the local Arab community and supports the federal government's policy of multiculturalism.

In contrast to the above, *The Source* was founded specifically for the purpose of disseminating information about the dispossessed Palestinian people. Wide-ranging issues are featured in the newspaper, but priority is given to the Palestinian cause. Among the topics discussed are the history of the Arab-Israeli conflict, Zionism, the Palestine Liberation Movement, and the conditions of the Palestinian people in the occupied territories and in refugee camps. It also publicizes the activities of Arab-American individuals and organizations dedicated to the Palestinian cause. The news coverage of Canada and of the local Arab community is quite restricted.

A publication of the Canadian Arab Federation, *Arab Dawn* represents an altogether different type of periodical. While it shares some of the concerns expressed in other Arab-Canadian newspapers, it is more of a national medium dedicated to principles of human rights and the protection of the integrity of the Arab-Canadian community. Examination of its contents reveals concerns about such matters as prejudiced treatment or portrayals of Arab Canadians, violations of their human rights and biased reporting of Arab news in the Canadian media. However, critical analyses of Canada's Middle East policy figure prominently in this periodical, and a substantial portion of space is devoted to varied aspects of the Palestine problem. For several years now, *Arab Dawn* editors, together with other Arab-Canadian representatives, have met regularly with members of parliament, political party leaders and Ministers of External Affairs to present the Arab side of the Middle East conflict and underline the national rights of the Palestinian people. The magazine carries no commercial advertisements and its community news department emphasizes civic participation, not social and ceremonial activities.

Since 1970, the range of materials potentially available to Arab Canadians has expanded considerably due to the appearance of a number of periodicals and newsletters. Of these media, two are devoted to political analysis of the Palestine question and defense of the Palestinian people: the Toronto-based *Free Forum*, published monthly in Arabic and English by the Arab Palestine Association; and the Montreal-based *Fedayin*, published bi-monthly in French and English by the Association Québec-Palestine. These periodicals were started in 1972 and 1973, respectively. The *Jerusalem Times* was started in Vancouver in 1973, but it ceased publication within about four years.

Two other periodicals are still publishing. These include *Islam Canada* (1972), already discussed in an earlier section, and the *Arab Community Newsletter* (1973), published by the Arab Community Centre of Toronto. This latter periodical serves the common interests of Toronto's large Arab community and encourages the socio-economic and cultural adaptation of Arab immigrants to Canada. Published quarterly in Arabic and English, it features community news, cultural and ethnic events, and Arabic art and literature.

In 1974, a major Arab-Canadian journal, *ARC* (*Arabic Reinforcement Culture*), made its appearance in Montreal and has been publishing monthly, in Arabic, French and English, ever since. It features news about Montreal's Arab community, particularly its Egyptian portion, and its contents are primarily social, cultural and literary in nature. A major goal of ARC's has been the maintenance of a link with the ancestral culture and homeland, on the one hand, and the successful integration of Arab immigrants into the Canadian society.

In addition to the above, a large number of newsletters are printed by Arab Canadians in virtually all the major urban centres. These include monthly, bi-monthly, quarterly, or semi-annual communications from religious organizations, non-sectarian associations and even individuals. They cover a wide range of topics and concerns, similar to those covered by the more established Arab-Canadian media.

To sum up, only four newspapers and periodicals were started by Arab Canadians in the first half of this century and none of them survived beyond a few years of existence. Further moves to develop ethnic newspapers did not occur until the 1960's and 1970's. Of the 12 major publications initiated in the past 15 years, ten are still publishing (bi-weekly, monthly, bi-monthly or quarterly). As a general rule, the Montreal-based newspapers are published in Arabic, French and English, whereas those originating outside of Quebec are published in Arabic and English. The majority of the publications are sponsored by established organizations, whether religious or non-religious, and only a few of them are owned and published by individual Arab Canadians.

There is little information on the actual effects of these media either on the Arab-Canadian community or the larger society. However, they have such stated objectives as enhancing mutual understanding of Arabs and Canadians and strengthening the bonds of friendship between the two peoples, promoting the Arab culture and developing pride in ethnic identity, facilitating the social, economic and cultural adaptation of Arab immigrants to Canada and, more generally, serving the interests of the ethnic community.

SUMMARY

The Arab-Canadian community has undergone a moderate degree of institutional development involving mainly religious organizations, secular associations and newspapers. In the Arab East, the church and mosque are, by tradition, focal points for community activity. Accordingly, once there was an adequate numerical base capable of their support, priority was given to the development of religious institutions. The founding of secular organizations and newspapers had to await the institutionalization of faith. Both the religious and secular ethnic institutions have provided a link with the ancestral land, reinforcing the maintenance of cultural and linguistic identity. At the same time, they have played an important adaptive role, encouraging acculturative change and integration with the host society. In these institutional spheres, the Arab-Canadian community is differentiated from the larger society. Overall, however, the community's existence as a separate entity is partial rather than complete.

NOTES

1. See the special book prepared on the occasion of the 29th Annual Convention of the Antiochian Orthodox Christian Archdiocese of New York and All North America, held in Montreal, August, 19-25, 1974. (No pagination) Henceforth, this reference will be identified as "29th Annual Convention. . . ."

155

2. In a book which Father Jabara published in English in New York, he stated that "the Jewish, Christian and Muslim religions were one religion and that the Torah, the Gospel and the Koran were one book." This caused the Syrian Orthodox community to repudiate him. See the special book prepared on the occasion of the 25th Anniversary of St. George Orthodox Church of Montreal, May 30, 1965 (no pagination). Henceforth, this reference will be identified as "25th Anniversary. . . ."

3. The men's society was named the Syrian Orthodox Benevolent Society, and the women's was named the Syrian Ladies' Benevolent Society.

4. The conflict within the Orthodox community during that period resulted in the formation, in 1936, of the Antiochian Diocese in Toledo, Ohio, with support from the Russian Orthodox Church. However, the majority of Arab Orthodox parishes in the United States, and all four in Canada, came under the jurisdiction of the Antiochian Orthodox Christian Archdiocese of New York and All North America. For more details regarding the conflict, see Elaine C. Hagopian, "The Institutional Development of the Arab-American Community of Boston: A Sketch," in Elaine C. Hagopian and Ann Paden, eds., *The Arab-Americans: Studies in Assimilation* (Wilmette, Ill., 1969), pp. 67-83.

5. See "25th Anniversary. . . ."

6. Lily Sabella, "En Remontant Le Cours de L'Histoire," *Trait d'Union*, Vol. 4, No. 4, 1967, p. 5.

7. *Ibid.*, pp. 5-6.

8. See *The Syrian-Lebanese Mercury*, Vol. II, No. 18, February 25, 1938, p. 2. The St. George Maronite Society was brought to my attention in Mr. James Peters' September 8, 1977, letter to me.

9. *Ibid.*

10. This information was provided in Mr. James Peters' September 8, 1977, letter to me.

11. See Elias Karam, ed., *The Syrian Canadian National Review* (Ottawa, 1935), p. 57, and p. 56 under the biographical sketch of Father Farah.

12. For information regarding the situation of the Maronite community in the United States, see Philip M. Kayal and Joseph M. Kayal, *The Syrian-Lebanese in America* (Boston, 1975), pp. 39-40.

13. Quoted from James Peters' September 8, 1977, letter to me.

14. This estimate is distilled from different sources, including telephone interviews (dated October 7 and 8, 1977) with Mr. Henry Hechema, President of the National Council of the World Lebanese Union (Montreal) and Father Francoise Eid, pastor of St. Maron Church (Montreal). Today, it is estimated that there are about 20,000 Arab-origin Maronites in Canada, distributed as follows: about 40% in the Maritime provinces, 30% in Montreal, 15% in the Windsor-Leamington region, and the balance (15%) in Ottawa, Toronto, and elsewhere.

15. In her recent study of Egyptians in Montreal, Wassef notes that in 1973 there were 580 families on the membership lists of St. Maron Church. See Nadia Hanna Wassef, "The Egyptians in Montreal: A New Colour

in the Canadian Ethnic Mosaic," M.A. Thesis, Department of Geography, McGill University, 1977, p. 182.
16. *Ibid.*, p. 183.
17. As quoted in *Islam Canada*, Vol. 1 (June, 1972), p. 17.
18. In addition to being a place of worship, the mosque in North America has been used for different functions, including community and board meetings, public lectures, dinners and celebrations of religious holidays, weddings and funerals.
19. Cf. Abdelmoneim M. Khattab, "The Assimilation of Arab Muslims in Alberta," unpublished M.A. Thesis, Department of Sociology, University of Alberta, 1969, pp. 22-23.
20. Sadiq Noor Alam Awan, *The People of Pakistani Origin in Canada* (Ottawa, 1976), p. 35.
21. *Islam Canada* regularly carries the names of Islamic organizations affiliated with the Council of Muslim communities of Canada.
22. Ismael al-Faruqi, *Al-Fajr*, 2 (1969), p. 6, as quoted in Emily Kalled Lovell, "A Survey of the Arab-Muslims in the United States and Canada," *The Muslim World*, 63 (1973), p. 149.
23. The quotation appears in *ibid.*, p. 150.
24. Cf. "29th Annual Convention . . . ."
25. *Ibid.*
26. Khattab, *op. cit.*, p. 44.
27. As quoted in *Islam Canada*, Vol. 1 (June, 1972), p. 14.
28. Alexis de Tocqueville, *Democracy in America* (New York, 1956), p. 198ff.
29. Joseph Helal, "Resumé of the History of the Syrian Canadian Association – Montreal," in Elias Karam, *op. cit.*, p. 38.
30. *Ibid.*, p. 39.
31. The story told in this paragraph was related to me by the society's ex-president, Mrs. Emilia Boosamra, of Montreal, in an interview August 13, 1974.
32. Helal, *op. cit.*, p. 38.
33. See "29th Annual Convention . . . ."
34. Vol. 1, No. 6, February 15, 1937, p. 3.
35. For further details, see Sheikh Muhammad Said Massoud, *I Fought As I Believed* (Montreal, 1976).
36. Joseph R. Haiek (ed.), *The American-Arabic Speaking Community: 1974 Almanac* (Los Angeles, 1974), p. 45.
37. Massoud, *op. cit.*, p. 18.

SEVEN

Arab-Canadian Family Life

By Sharon McIrvin Abu-Laban

The family is a basic institution in all societies. It is the one institution which is likely to be an integral part of the Arab immigrants' baggage. Family ties serve as a constant reminder of the homeland, of origins; they are a link between the old and the new. For the recent immigrant, kin ties in the new country can sustain one in adjustment, be a solace in culture shock, or restrict the extent of adaptive change possible. Family relationships, more than any others, touch the individual intimately and continuously. The individual who immigrates to Canada from a very different culture, such as that of the Arab world, may find that although old ways are often at odds with the new culture and strangers may react to him/her as a stereotype, family members never treat each other this way. The history of the individual is most often mapped within the framework of a family; there the individual exists as a known entity, with a unique, not stereotyped, past.

It is within the family, also, that second and third generation Arab Canadians learn of ancestral origins. Stories and customs which differentiate kin from non-kin lay the groundwork for ethnic awareness. Even if physical differences begin to merge with the larger society, even if distinctive language is lost, there are the idiomatic expressions, the unique foods, the holiday celebrations or the family reminiscences which are reminders of ethnic heritage. Second and third generation Arab Canadians can find representations of their ancestral origins in the manners, values and customs of parents or grandparents. These may reverberate from one generation to the next in the behaviour and forms of kin intimacy, child rearing, interacting with a loved one, reciprocating in time of need or attending to generational differences.

Arab-Canadian families mirror a blending of the old and the new. This is not a singular fusion but instead reflects differences in origin, generation, birthplace, sex and education. In order to understand the syntheses, it is necessary to examine the counterpoint between the past and the present, the Arab family patterns which provide the base and the Canadian family patterns which nurture the contemporary reality. The impact of family forms from the Arab world, mate selection, marriage relationships, kin ties, authority patterns, male-female interactions and child socialization have produced some patterns and trends which are distinctive in the family life of Canadians of Arab origin.

EMERGING PATTERNS OF MATE SELECTION

Marital Choice
Mate selection is vitally important to the family building processes of all societies. For Canadians of Arab origin, both Christians and Muslims, the traditional ethnic pattern of mate selection stands in sharp contrast to the usual Canadian practices. For example, in Arab families, the power and influence of the larger family unit is dramatized through the continued existence of the institution of arranged marriage. Usually the choice of spouse is not left to the whims of individual decision or romantic love, but instead is a decision made (sometimes arbitrarily) by parents and other senior family members, particularly males. Traditionally, prospective partners would not have been consulted regarding their own preferences. For a young woman to have indicated a preference, or even worse an attraction, to a particular man, would have been a violation of the modesty code which demanded strict segregation of the unmarried female from either knowledge of or observation by eligible males. Such seclusion, previously symbolized by the veil, particularly among Muslims, meant that dating and courtship, as known in Canada, were virtually non-existent.

Further reflecting the importance of familism in mate selection in the Arab world has been a pattern of preferential marriage between a man and his father's brother's daughter (the daughter of his paternal uncle). This marriage form is seen by analysts as serving to further strengthen ties within the larger family unit.[1] At one time, access to a patrilineal parallel female cousin was regarded as a young man's rightful marital option. Second to this type of marriage, there has been a preference given to marriage between other first cousins. Such practices still exist in the Arab world but are on the decline, most dramatically in urban areas. Among earlier Arab immigrants to Canada, marriage to relatives was common.

These traditional, ideal patterns of mate selection are undergoing some degree of change in the contemporary Middle East, in particular in urban areas and among the better educated. Increasingly, young people have the opportunity to see and know each other casually, and, increasingly, children are not only consulted by their parents, but may have veto power, if not even make the actual selection of their own spouse. While changes are occurring, the predominant pattern, in dramatic contrast to Canada, is still one of relatively strict control over male-female interaction, with family elders playing a major role in mate selection.

The marriages of most turn-of-the-century Arab Canadians were arranged, in some manner approximating the traditional pattern just described. This is also true of many of the more recent immigrants, who were married before their arrival in Canada. In the general Canadian view, such arranged marriages may seem like an obstacle to personal happiness and an incredible imposition on the freedom of the individual. The Western emphasis on love as the appropriate rationale for marriage assumes that one "falls into" love before marriage and, hopefully, remains in love throughout marriage. It should be noted that love is not necessarily absent in marriages which have been arranged by parents. Romantic love is not only recognized but celebrated in the poetry, songs and stories of the Arab world; however, it may make its appearance at a different phase in the mate relationship than in the West. We do not have reliable comparative evidence to support the common Western assumption that marriages of "free choice" are more successful than marriages which are arranged by family elders.

It should be noted further that, while the power of Arab parents in the selection of a mate for their children may seem extraordinary, even in Canada mate selection is not completely "free." If this were the case, we would find people of diverse backgrounds randomly mated; such is not the case. Socialization patterns and social pressure, much of it parent inspired, actually guide Canadian children, from an early age, towards the "appropriate category" of mate. Hence, without obvious intervention from parents, we find that people are more likely to marry someone of the same ethnicity, religion, age, social class and even neighbourhood.[2] Canadians rarely search the farthest corners of the earth for a "one and only" spouse. Their search is impeded by opportunity, social pressure, time and funds. In the West, as in the East, Cupid's wings are clipped by life's practicalities.

Despite this, for the young Canadian of Arab background the kind of parental intervention in mate selection typically found in the Middle East would be sharply at odds with the ideals of the larger culture and repeated messages of the mass media. The North American climate emphasizes freedom of choice and freedom of search in mate selection, while the Arab tradition emphasizes parental control, guidance and restrictions on the premarital quest.

While, for the most part, Arab-Canadian parents, even those of the first generation, have adapted themselves to the change in definitions regarding mate selection, they share with most other Canadian parents the sometimes frustrated hope that their child will find the "right" mate; the role of parent to a marriage-ready child has some pan-cultural strains. Previously unanalyzed data, from a survey conducted by Abdelmoneim M. Khattab provide some interesting information regarding Muslim Arab Canadians in the Province of Alberta.[3] The data are derived from a questionnaire distributed to 251 Muslim Arab-Canadian adults over the age of 18 residing in Edmonton and the small community of Lac La Biche, Alberta.[4] Respondents (mostly first generation immigrants) were asked about their attitudes towards "parents selecting mates (husbands or wives) for their children." A total of 54% of the respondents were in disagreement with arranged marriage. However, 36% of the respondents supported the practice. The wording of the question allows for the possibility that people who are in agreement with the practice still might not invoke it in their own family situation (words do not always correspond with deeds). Agreement with the practice of arranged marriage, however, sets the stage for potential problems between parent and adult child, should the child indicate interest in a partner not approved by the parents. It is not that the Arab-Canadian parent is likely to demand the right to arrange an adult child's marriage, but that the parent may attempt to exert more direct influence than would the average Canadian parent.

Arab-Canadian parents find themselves in a culture where children have extensive contact with eligible young people of the opposite sex and support is given to individual freedom in mate selection. The current group of parents of marriageable children finds itself, increasingly, using the influence technique common to most other Canadian parents: indirect pressure.

Attitudes Towards Intermarriage

Social pressure and socialization often lead the "free" individual towards an endogamous (within group) marriage. Respondents in the Toronto-Montreal survey were asked which category of person would make a better spouse for a person of Arabic-speaking origin in Canada. Forty-two per cent of the respondents said ethnicity was of no importance; 32% said it was better to be married to someone from the Old Country; 15% said it was better to be married to an Arab person brought up in Canada; seven per cent indicated an Arab-origin spouse of unspecified nativity; and only four percent said it would be better to be married to a non-Arab. Hence, a total of 54% of the respondents selected some form of ethnic endogamy as the ideal in marital selection.

The respondents who said ethnicity was of no consequence invoked love and interpersonal understanding as the major considerations in the choice of marital partner. Those respondents who indicated a preference for an Arab-origin person brought up in Canada tended to emphasize the potential help in adaptation which could be provided by such a spouse. Such spouses were seen as empathizing with adjustment problems and possibly providing "the best of two worlds." A young, second generation woman expressed the feeling of many in this group in saying that "they would have a common culture (Arab) and share common Canadian values."

161

Of those respondents who indicated that it was better to marry someone who was born in the Old Country, most (58%) justified their answer
by saying that there would be fewer differences between husband and
wife. Sixteen per cent felt that a spouse from the Old Country would be
more understanding and empathetic. For example, a respondent who
came to Canada at the age of eight and reported that he remembered
"nothing" about Lebanon, nevertheless answered that it would be better
to marry someone from the "Old Country . . . because we share the
same mentality." A more recent immigrant, an Egyptian Christian man,
indicated that it would be better to marry someone from the Old Country
because she "would still retain a woman's respect for a man. Canadian
women are too domineering. Women . . . should be . . . equal but not
domineering." It is interesting that the female role figures prominently
for many Arab-Canadian respondents when assessing the most desirable
ethnicity for a mate. Nadia Wassef, in her recent study of Egyptians in
Montreal, found a conservative sector of young men who:

> fear the liberated Canadian girl, and hence only want to marry an
> Egyptian. In order to be sure she is truly Egyptian, not influenced
> by western thoughts and ideas, they would go looking for her in
> Egypt and rarely think of the Egyptian girl resident in Canada. This
> phenomenon actually became prominent in recent years. This in-
> termediate position of the Egyptian girl lessened her chances for
> marriage in Canada, especially to an Egyptian, as compared to her
> changes in Egypt.[5]

It is interesting that while some male respondents in the Toronto-
Montreal survey were very explicit in asserting that Arab-origin women
made better wives than Canadian women, not a single respondent said
Canadian women made better wives than Arab-origin women, nor did
any respondent evaluate the specific husband qualities of Arab-origin
men in contrast to non-Arab-origin men.

Although groups tend to push towards some form of endogamy, there
are natural limitations on the degree of success possible. The probability
of in-group marriage is limited by specific social structure factors. For
example, the size of the group is important; smaller ethnic groups are
usually more likely to intermarry than larger ethnic groups. The sex ratio
also plays an important role. In the early phases of the development of
the Arab-Canadian community there were disproportionate numbers of
men and they either had to look back to the homeland for a bride (which
many did) or else intermarry with non-Arab-origin women in Canada.
Currently, although some people may aspire to ethnic endogamy, appropriate candidates may be few in number and dispersed. In some cases,
religious organizations have attempted to fill this gap by acting as match-
makers.

For example, the Muslim Students' Association of the United States
and Canada has developed a marriage application form aimed at

facilitating endogamous marriages. The confidential form asks basic background information questions of every applicant, requires a picture and instructs the applicant to: "Please write a brief summary of yourself – include your interests, religious outlook, activities, profession/studies, future plans and anything pertinent." The applicant is also instructed, on a separate sheet of paper, to write "a brief summary of what you are looking for in a husband/wife, e.g., her/his background, religious outlook, education, nationality, what you expect from him/her in marriage and anything which you may feel is important." These applications are then sent to a marriage committee. One Toronto religious leader indicated that initially they had difficulty getting any women to submit applications and, even now, only some 10% of the applicants are female.

Similar concern has been manifested by Christian groups. For example, although many Coptic Christians came to Canada in established family units, among the unmarried adults men outnumbered women. Hence, some young Coptic men have had difficulty finding brides in Canada. For this reason, among others, the church initiated charter flights back to Egypt to facilitate contact with Egyptian women and, it was hoped, eventual marriage.

For Arab Canadians of all religious backgrounds, annual conferences and other special social-cultural or religious gatherings provide opportunities for young adults to meet potential marriage partners. Parents sometimes sacrifice time and money, and travel long distances, to ensure that older children in the family can attend. Such functions facilitate contact between young people eligible for marriage and contribute to the incidence of in-group marriage.

In the course of interviews in connection with the Toronto-Montreal study, a prominent Christian leader suggested that intermarriage with a Canadian tends to isolate the individual from the ethnic community. He further stressed that it was important to recognize that "Canadian women's values are different from Arab women's values." (Note that this continues to be a theme running through the data on the Arab-Canadian family.) This particular respondent indicated that while he viewed in-group marriage as important for first generation Egyptians, he did not see ethnic endogamy as being as important for later generations of Arab Canadians. According to an Arab-Canadian priest in Montreal, some 1,200 marriages involving Egyptian Canadians took place in his church between 1960 and 1970, and of these an estimated 57% were intermarriages.[6] Most of these were with French Canadians, while only some eight per cent were with English Canadians.

Generally Christian religious leaders tend to be more tolerant of intermarriage between their members and Canadians of different Christian backgrounds, particularly for the second and third generations. Muslim leaders, on the other hand, are more likely to regard intermarriage with non-Muslims as a threat to the faith. The pressures toward in-group marriage remain strongest for those of the Islamic faith. Yet even here, dramatic parental intervention is probably rare. Barclay's study of 20 Muslim Arab-Canadian males indicates that, while the men expected their children to seek parental approval of their choice of spouse, only two out of the 20 respondents suggested that they would actually disown a child who married outside the faith.[7]

The extent of intermarriage varies by generation and over time. As Canadians of Arab origin become increasingly similar to the larger society, the term intermarriage may be a misnomer, or, at least, carry a different meaning. However, pressures toward endogamy will continue to vary by religion and sex; such pressures will be stronger for Muslims, particularly females, than for Christians.

THE ROLES OF MEN AND WOMEN

The differential expectations and constrictions on the behaviour of men and women are important considerations in examining family life. Traditional patterns in the Arab world placed extreme restrictions on the behaviour of females. This has had impact on the division of labour (both inside and outside the home), on the lines of familial authority and on the control of personal conduct. In contrast, in contemporary Canada attitudes and expectations regarding male/female roles are in an extreme state of flux. The shifting social climate has borne witness, in recent years, to such phenomena as a large increase in the percentage of married women who are gainfully employed; the legalization of abortion; and a sharp upswing in the numbers of unmarried couples who are living together. Yet in Canada, while verbalizations regarding equality are frequently heard, there continue to be large differences in power, prestige and finances between the sexes. In the middle of such conflicting messages regarding sex roles, Arab Canadians, understandably, often reflect an ambivalence regarding "appropriate" male/female behaviour.

The Division of Labour and Power

Traditionally, Arab husbands have been loathe to have their wives working outside the home, receiving an independent income and away from the surveillance of male kin. Women were viewed as weak and gullible; hence, gainfully employed women were seen as being vulnerable to sexual exploitation, particularly if under the supervision of a strange male. In actuality the closely supervised, home-bound wife has been an ideal; in practice its implementation has been class-linked. For reasons of sheer survival, the cloistering of the female was and is difficult to effect by the poor and disadvantaged. For the contemporary educated elite, this ideal is being increasingly challenged on ideological grounds.

The early Arab-Canadian pioneer women who came to Canada during the latter part of the last century often helped their husbands with their work, either directly by engaging in business transactions, or indirectly with behind-the-scenes assistance. Since many couples dreamt of accumulating enough savings to return to a financially comfortable life in the land of their birth, dedication and sacrifice on the part of both marital partners was seen as hastening that dream's realization. As a further contribution, the early immigrant women often kept boarders. In an era when household chores were exceedingly arduous, many pioneer women not only cared for their family's needs, but also made further financial contributions by cleaning, laundering, mending and cooking for lodgers in their homes.

While these early immigrant women contributed many hours of work in addition to their customary family responsibilities, this was not done in a context which challenged the traditional division of labour and authority within the family unit. The husband-father remained as the acknowledged head of the family and the authority figure, subject only to the nuances of power and influence common to the internal functioning of any individual family. Similarly, during this period the larger Canadian social context supported the authority of the husband-father. In contrast, contemporary Arab immigrants find themselves in a setting which stresses equality between husband and wife, and, under conditions where both husband and wife are gainfully employed, pays at least lip service to an equalization of task sharing in the home (an ideal which, in actuality, is far from being realized in Canadian families).[8]

Gainful employment for married women is a sometimes contentious issue for Arab Canadians, as it is for the general Canadian public. The Alberta survey found that 50% of the respondents were favourable to a woman having a job outside the home; 45% were against such outside employment and only five per cent were undecided. While this illustrates a shift from the traditional ideal of a home-bound wife, in terms of actual employment only a small percentage of the women were in the labour force (26% in Edmonton and nine per cent in the small community of Lac La Biche, below the Canadian average). The actual employment figures may be seen, however, more as a reflection of local opportunities, stage in the family life cycle and individual inclinations than rejection of the propriety of married women's employment per se.

Illustrative of the changing attitudes towards employed wives is a recent article in *Islam Canada*, a newsletter for the lay public. An Islamic scholar argues that Islam does not restrict a woman solely to the homemaking role.[9] Sajida Alvi notes historic examples of outstanding Muslim women in various spheres of public life and argues that "there is no fundamental conflict between the creative activity of women in the home and their increasing participation in social and economic life and public affairs."[10] However, the author stresses the necessity for an employed wife to exercise good planning, to be sure her involvement in work is not at the expense of her family and to have a "co-operative" husband. It is probably significant that no operational definition of a co-operative husband is provided. Researchers find that even in the most "liberated" of households and societies, task sharing in the home is slow to appear.

Certainly attitudes towards sex roles are undergoing change. In a brief presented at the Heritage Ontario Conference in 1972, the Arab-Canadian delegates affirmed a belief in sexual equality in the work place: "In those many areas of life where the sexes can be equated, they should and must be. Much remains to be done in this direction, for women still do not receive equal pay for equal work, and are not promoted on an equal footing with their male colleagues."[11] The attitudes of contemporary Arab Canadians towards wives' employment differ from those of their early twentieth century counterparts. For the earlier immigrants and their descendants, there is now the common exposure to the larger Canadian social climate with its altering definitions of appropriate male-female roles. The more recent Arab immigrants, many highly educated, were themselves often in the vanguard of social change in the Middle East. In their home countries many of the well educated have been vocal in urging equal female participation in the labour force and in the political sphere. However, formalized government assertions regarding husband-wife equality are rare. It is not that Arab wives are lacking in power and influence, but that this power and influence is not likely to have formal legitimization. Similarly, in the Alberta survey of Arab Canadians, 78% of the respondents (male and female) agreed with the statement that the father or husband should be the final authority in the family; only 18% disagreed.

It is important to distinguish between increasing acceptance of wives' employment outside the home and husband/wife equality in the home. The increasing tolerance on the part of Arab Canadians of achievement behaviour and labour force participation of women meshes well with the "Levantine Ethic" of hard work, scrimping and sacrifice, which has characterized many generations of Arab Canadians. Yet the fact that such contributions are now in a contemporary context which challenges traditional lines of authority can put additional strains on the adjustment of the immigrant couple. For example, a prominent community leader of Egyptian origin observed that among recent immigrant couples problems seemed to surface when the wives were employed full time outside of the home. In his perception, new marital tensions were introduced by the greater freedom and independence possible for the working wife.

The records of the Toronto Arab Community Centre suggest the strains such couples may face.[12] In one example, a new immigrant woman, with two small children and a full-time job on an assembly line, found herself returning home at the end of the day to a husband and brother-in-law who expected her to do single-handedly the traditional cooking, cleaning and child care commonly expected of a good wife and mother. In Canada, in sharp contrast to her native Lebanon, she did not have relatives from her lineage either to help her physically with the demanding tasks, support her emotionally or intervene on her behalf. Close kin in proximity give a wife protection and influence, even in the most patriarchal areas of the Middle East. However, in Canada this woman was alone, faced with a severe marital problem and able to communicate adequately only in Arabic. Fortunately, she was able to turn to the Community Centre staff to mediate between her and the larger community (vis-à-vis welfare officials, day care centres, landlords, etc.) and also to mediate between husband and wife (traditionally an extended family task) regarding issues relating to separation, child support and eventual marital reconciliation.

This case illustrates tensions which may be compounded for an immigrant couple in a setting where customary husband-wife roles are undergoing re-examination and there is an attenuation of traditional supports which would have buttressed evolving role definitions. In the Arab world, the larger family units (both the husband's and the wife's) which participated in the initial procedure of mate selection would take it upon themselves to arbitrate and hopefully settle disputes between marital partners. In contrast, Arab-Canadian immigrant couples in Canada may find themselves having to rely heavily, or even solely, on their own interpersonal skills in order to settle disputes.

Shifts in the roles of women of necessity have implications for husbands. Wassef's study of Christian and Muslim Egyptian immigrants indicates an altering of the division of labour in the home. Wassef found that the husbands clean windows, shovel snow and mow lawns, jobs which are familiar activities for many Canadian men but unfamiliar to Egyptian husbands.[13] In further contrast to their activities in Egypt, the wives reported that in Canada their husbands were much more likely to contribute to the general housework (sometimes to the shock of their visiting relatives), particularly when the wife was also employed outside the home. Unfortunately, we do not have information on the amount of time given, only that time is given. Information from several cross-national studies would suggest that an equal sharing of household tasks is unlikely, even if the wife is gainfully employed.[14]

Research evidence suggests, however, that in North America a woman's participation in the labour force appears to be associated with greater influence within the family, and this is also likely to be the case for Arab Canadians.[15] It is possible that in Arab-Canadian marriages public declarations of husband-wife equality will *follow* rather than precede wive's labour force participation. This may occur primarily as a consequence of shifting intra-family dynamics resulting from increasing numbers of gainfully employed wives and secondarily as an eventual

167

product of assimilation into the verbalizations of the larger Canadian society.

Personal Conduct

The personal conduct of females continues to be a theme of concern on the part of Arab-Canadian respondents. Such concern, particularly on the part of first generation immigrants, reflects the salience of this issue in the Middle Eastern heritage. Traditionally, in the Arab world the behaviour of a female is closely controlled and her chastity carefully guarded, both as a symbol of family honour and as a necessity for her selection in marriage and the maintenance of the marriage. As a result, until recently a vast majority of Arab women experienced severe restrictions on their activities and this continues to be true for a sizeable proportion of Arab women today. Both the dress and behaviour of women are carefully monitored and they are prohibited from even chaperoned dating, until after they are engaged to be married, if even then.

The early Arab immigrants to Canada reflected much of this traditional attitude in their rearing of daughters. It was an attitude which, at the turn of the century, was not extremely discordant with dominant Canadian norms. In an interview, an older Christian woman reported that the early Syrian immigrants believed in the firm upbringing of girls. While Syrian boys had freedom, girls were much more restricted. Their reputation and purity were regarded as "sacred" and there was a constant fear of any waywardness on the part of a girl, which would make her unacceptable as a bride for a Syrian boy. As an indication of the extent of this control, the respondent reported, with pride, that her daughters had been "properly raised" and until they were 18 years old they "did not know anything other than the way to school and the way home from school."

Such attitudes are undergoing change in the contemporary Arab East, particularly among the urban educated. Similarly, among Arab Canadians there are variations by generation in restrictiveness toward daughters. The same first generation pioneer declared with disappointment that the third generation had changed greatly. "Now Arab-origin Canadian girls do not speak Arabic and their mothers, perhaps because of bad feelings regarding the way they were raised, do not apply to their children the same rules we applied to them."

Respondents in the Toronto-Montreal survey were concerned about what they saw as the permissiveness of youth in Canada. This concern was particularly directed towards the behaviour of Canadian females. Some informants indicated a wish that they could send their daughters to the Middle East, during their adolescence, because teenage years in Canada are seen as particularly trying for parents. For some Arab-Canadian parents, particularly recent immigrants, there can be an intergenerational collision of values. Disagreements often centre on restrictions placed on the behaviour of daughters and on modesty in dress. For some parents, even the Canadian commonplace of a sleeveless dress or a bathing suit may be an issue leading to family tension.

In the Alberta survey, 59% of the respondents were against a Muslim woman wearing a sleeveless dress and 77% were against a Muslim woman wearing a bathing suit. Such reactions to wearing apparel represent the most conservative of Arab-Canadian response. Even in the contemporary Middle East, one finds Arab women dressed in a wide variety of styles, ranging from the most time-honoured and concealing to *avant garde* and revealing European fashions.

Parental Arab-Canadian attitudes towards boy-girl interaction can also be in sharp contrast to the dominant Canadian pattern. Barclay found, in his interviews of 20 Arab-Canadian Muslim men, that all except one regarded it as unacceptable to date without a chaperone.[16] Wassef, in her study of Christian and Muslim Egyptian Canadians in Montreal, found strong parental disapproval towards girls dating (although under pressure parents allowed it for boys).[17] The Alberta survey found that 53% of the respondents were against Western dancing for a Muslim man, 57% were against Western dancing for a Muslim girl, and 62% were against Western dancing for a married Muslim woman. And, given the usual Canadian practice, it is indicative of the inescapable discomfort some parents must feel that 46% of the respondents were against boys and girls studying together in the same high school.

Sleeveless dresses, bathing suits, dancing and co-education are not the most pressing concerns for most Canadian parents of teenagers. However, for parents of Arab background, problems can arise in attempting to reconcile the prevailing teenage behaviour patterns in Canada with parental fear of waywardness on the part of daughters and their definitions of female propriety. Wassef reports that Montreal Egyptian Canadians exhibit major differences in attitudes towards sons and daughters.[18] While fear of losing "complete control" makes parents prone to increasing tolerance of the son's behaviour (e.g., with regard to staying out late at night, as well as dating practices), parents' attitudes towards daughters are much more restrictive. Wassef reports that daughters are allowed neither to stay out late nor to have a boy friend. Female respondents under 25 years of age who had been in Canada for seven to 10 years reported that a gap existed between parental and societal expectations, "often . . . [placing] . . . them in a real dilemma. They also implied that their family's regulations always stood as a wall between them and the Canadian society."[19] This description of contemporary parental differences in the treatment of sons and daughters almost parallels the description of the rearing of daughters given earlier by a first generation pioneer respondent. In both time periods concern about the appropriate behaviour of daughters was high, their conduct was extensively monitored and sons were allowed far greater freedom, yet the two time periods described are separated by over half a century.

As mentioned earlier, restrictions on the behaviour and dress of female family members are tied to concern not only with family honour, but also about the marital prospects of a daughter. Traditionally, if a young woman's reputation was in doubt, she would have been rejected as a marriage partner. The Alberta survey suggests the possible reality of this fear for Muslim parents who wish to encourage an endogamous marriage for their daughter. Twenty one per cent of the respondents were against "a Muslim young man marrying a non-virgin girl"; an additional 42% were strongly against such a marriage, giving a total of 63% of the respondents disapproving.

While it is true that the majority of the Alberta respondents disapproved of brides with premarital sexual experience, 22% of the respondents regarded the marriage of a Muslim male to a sexually experienced female as acceptable and a further 10% were undecided. Thus, 32% of these Muslim Arab Canadians were undecided or disagreed on the necessity of female virginity at the time of marriage. This represents a sharp departure from traditional ethnic values which stressed the necessity of female virginity.[20]

Nevertheless, in the Toronto-Montreal survey, Canadian "permissiveness" with regard to female sexual expression emerged as a frequent complaint of both Christians and Muslims. We can expect change in Arab-Canadian families, even those of the first generation, and greater tolerance relative to their traditional counterparts in the Middle East, both as a result of their Canadian exposure and, possibly, as a reflection of selective features operating in the immigrant experience. However, first and second generation Arab-Canadian families, in particular, are likely to remain on the conservative side of the tolerance continuum when it comes to female sexual expression and definitions of decorum and propriety with regard to female behaviour.

KINSHIP TIES

The Role of Family in Immigration

The sense of familism in the Arab world encompasses the individual in a web of reciprocities and obligations which extend well beyond the conjugal unit to encompass not only parents and siblings but also grandparents, nephews and nieces, and aunts, uncles and cousins of various degrees. The web of reciprocities can be confining, restraining and demanding, require personal sacrifice and interfere with individual privacy, but at the same time provide the warmth of dependable human contact, interpersonal supports, comfort in crises, solace in loneliness and the assurance of commitment. As Prothro and Diab note, in the Middle East "one turns to a member of the family for assistance in almost any area, whether it be a question of health, financial need, quest for a wife, employment, admission to school, starting a business, forming a corporation, or even emigration."[21] In contrast to the West, not only is there a wider range of people who can invoke family obligations but, as well, there are more legitimate avenues of assistance and emotional support available to the individual.

The immigrant experience for Arab Canadians often involves not only a change in geographical place but the leaving behind of many family members of emotional import. The Toronto-Montreal survey attempted to gauge the importance of kin support in attracting the individual to Canada and facilitating immigrant adjustment. Respondents who had been born outside of Canada were asked about their mode of entry into this country. Of those who responded to this question (269 people), 45% came as "independent immigrants"; nine per cent came as visitors; six per cent came as students and 40% came to Canada as immigrants sponsored by relatives already in the country.

The wish to help people who are defined as relatives sometimes runs afoul of Canadian immigration laws. Louise Sweet cites an example from an Arab-Canadian Druse community which illustrates some of the sacrifices people may go through to help otherwise unsponsorable relatives emigrate.[22] A financially successful Arab-Canadian businessman who had no children of his own wished to help his Lebanon-based nephew by bringing him to Canada to join him in his work. At that time, under Canadian law, the uncle could not sponsor his nephew as an immigrant. The father of the young man in question (and brother to the Arab-Canadian businessman) was himself a wealthy businessman, and at that time a father could support his son as an immigrant; however, the father was based in South America. With two to three years of sacrifice and planning the young Lebanese man was finally brought into Canada as an immigrant. The father of the young man left his lucrative business in South America, came to Canada under the sponsorship of his Arab-Canadian brother, established residence and then himself sponsored his son to come from Lebanon as an immigrant. Once the young man was established in business with the Arab-Canadian uncle, his father returned to his own business in South America. While this is an extreme case, it illustrates not only the problems of attempting to confront Western definitions of kin responsibility, but also a more rigorous fulfillment of family obligations than usually is found in Canada.

Family ties influence not only the decision to emigrate but also the choice of a location in Canada. The Toronto-Montreal survey asked people why they selected a specific destination upon entry into the country. By far the single most important motivating factor was kinship. Forty-five per cent (122) of the respondents indicated that their selection of destination was based on the fact that relatives were living in the area already. Similarly, 41% (107) of the respondents indicated that relatives had provided help at the time of their arrival in Canada. In contrast, friends were of help to respondents in nine per cent of the cases and people from the same home town in only one per cent of the cases. Although people from the same general village areas are sometimes

171

found in broad geographic clusters in Canada, it appears that kinship ties are a far more salient form of help than ties of common community of origin. (It should be noted, however, that in small villages in the Middle East, many people trace common kinship, hence the neighbour and kin categories overlap.) A somewhat surprising finding is that 34% of the respondents indicated that they received no help at all at the time of their arrival in Canada. It appears that one either receives help from relatives or goes without.

What type of assistance might new immigrants need? Provision of accommodation was the most frequently mentioned item (28%) with financial help running a close second (24%). The questionnaire response indicates only the first item in what might have been several forms of help. Hence, financial help or housing help does not preclude advice and psychological help. In fact, these would probably be included.

Contact with Relatives in the Old Country

Help given at time of entry into Canada is often reciprocated by help given to other immigrating kin. Respondents in the Toronto-Montreal survey were asked, "Have you ever assisted or sponsored any relatives or friends from the Old Country to immigrate to Canada?" Thirty-two per cent of the respondents had given such help. Eight per cent of the respondents had given help three or more times.

Aid is also given to relatives abroad. The question was asked of all respondents, foreign and native-born, "Do you send money to relatives in the old country?" (see Table 27). Of the foreign-born, 50% had sent money to relatives in the Old Country. Of the Canadian-born respondents, a total of 22% had sent money to relatives in the Old Country at one time or another. We do not have information on the relationship between the sender and the receiver, nor, importantly, on the needs of relatives in the Old Country to access whether there are expressed needs which are being ignored by Arab-Canadian relatives. Certainly there are kin in the Old Country who have no need for the largess of their Canadian relatives. However, the fact that one-half of the foreign-born and over one-fifth of the Canadian-born had sent money to kin abroad illustrates not only the reciprocity one might anticipate with the first generation immigrant but, in addition, feelings of responsibility beyond the first generation.

Maintenance of kin contact through correspondence is also impressive. Comparing Canadian-born with foreign-born Arab Canadians on the question of correspondence with relatives or friends in the Old Country, we find that of the Canadian-born, a total of 44 per cent had some type of correspondence. Of the foreign-born, 90 per cent maintain correspondence. These findings suggest a sizeable maintenance of contact with relatives abroad, not only for the foreign-born (which might be expected) but also for the Canadian-born respondents.

172

Kin Support and Interaction

As indicated earlier, in the Arab world the web of kinship responsibilities and reciprocities is strong and extensive. In the early years of Arab immigration, support from kin was particularly important in establishing oneself financially. Sometimes "distant" relatives sought each other out for co-operative business ventures. Non-kin relationships which were strengthened by joint business ventures sometimes became even closer through eventual marriage with the sister or daughter of one's partner.

Intergenerational supports are traditionally recognized in the Arab world and the flow of support between the generations is two-way. Thus, parents helped children but in their adult years sons were expected to provide for the comfort and support of their aging parents. However, the financial support of parents contradicts some basic norms in North American society which stress independence for the young as well as for the old. In Canadian society, for the dependent older parent to need and receive help may be looked upon as a loss of dignity rather than an affirmation of dignity. Arab Canadians have had to adjust to these differing definitions. The early pioneer immigrants, who in their homeland would have expected their adult sons to support them in old age sometimes found it necessary to alter their expectations. In the words of one middle-aged second generation respondent, "Arab parents soon learned that in Canada they had to be [more] independent of their children. One just didn't hand his house over [to his sons] when he became feeble . . . sons often moved away."

Among more recent immigrants, those few who immigrated in advanced age with their children sometimes find life lonely and isolating in Canada. The severity of the winters, the geographical distance from others with similar interests and their children's active involvement in their own Canadian adaptation contribute to the sense of isolation. A Christian priest indicated in an interview that in his congregation the older people who had recently immigrated to Canada with their adult children are often bored if their children are employed. There is no one to talk to and little to do and the older people find themselves waiting for Sunday in order at least to be able to go to church. In a similar way, life can be particularly difficult for the immigrant woman who is a full-time homemaker. She may feel isolated from the extensive visiting common in the Middle East, as well as finding herself far away from relatives and friends.[23] Television aids the home-bound new Canadian in learning or improving the language, but it may be a pallid substitute for the warmth of human companionship.

Respondents in the Toronto-Montreal survey indicate some concern about the quality of interpersonal relationships in Canada. For example, although several respondents mentioned the advantage of Canadian pensions and social assistance in old age, at the same time they perceived less emotional security and less respect for elders in Canada than in the Arab world. In the words of one respondent: "Back home there is respect and family ties of young towards old . . . Man is here (in Canada) alone, on his own. Back home, I fell sick and a friend brought me food every day for ten days without asking for anything."

The smooth functioning of Canadian government relative to governments in the Middle East and the protective and supportive system of social services are greatly admired. Yet there is an ambivalence as well, for these services may not only supplement but replace traditional family and friendship supports. Thus, some respondents perceive a weakness in Canadian family ties and interpersonal supports in contrast to their home countries:

> [Canadian] social ties are very weak, not strong enough to hold brotherhood or friendship.
>
> – man of Jordanian origin

> Canadians are individualistic. No one wants to bother himself with the problem of others.
>
> – man of Egyptian origin

When respondents in the Toronto-Montreal survey were asked to indicate the three things which they liked most about their country of origin, strong family bonds and interpersonal relationships in the Old Country were mentioned first by 32% of the respondents. In response to a similar question concerning those things the respondent liked most about Canada, only one person out of 274 mentioned interpersonal relationships.

PARENT-CHILD RELATIONS

Children are highly valued in the Arab world. The parent role is viewed as an important and expected transition in the marriage relationship. There is a preference for male children, as they are seen as carrying on the family line and, potentially, providing security to their parents in case of need. It should be noted that the preference for sons does not preclude viewing daughters as part of an ideal family.[24] Children, in general, are treated with fondness and affection, by both men and women.

Child Bearing and Rearing

Consistent with the high value placed on child bearing and a preference for large families, birth control has been a contentious issue. Techniques have long been known through folk knowledge; however, at the official level, particularly through religious publications (both Christian and Muslim), birth control has been controversial. In recent years prominent leaders (from both religions) have argued that birth control is not contrary to religious teachings; nevertheless, the Alberta survey found that 47% of the respondents were against Muslims practising birth control.

Estimating the average number of children among Arab-Canadian married couples is problematic. In Canada as a whole, the 1971 census found the average number of children per family to be 1.7.[25] Across the country there is variation in the average number of children per family, with higher averages in rural than in urban areas and lower averages in Western Canada. The current Arab-Canadian family size can be determined and related to specific characteristics. However, it is quite possible that completed family size may be different. In the Toronto-Montreal sample of Arab Canadians the average number of children varied on characteristic dimensions. The average number of children for foreign-born people was 1.8; for the Canadian-born the average was 1.5. Quebec residents had a lower average number of children (1.38) than Ontario residents (2.0); those with an income of $20,000 or more annually had a lower average number of children (1.61) than people with less than $5,000 annually (2.5); those possessing a university degree had a lower average number of children (1.29) than those without a degree (2.14); and all Christian groups combined had a lower average number of children (1.84) than the Muslims and Druse combined (2.07). (The category of "other" was omitted from the analysis.) The variations along the lines of education and socio-economic status are similar to what would be expected in the Canadian population as a whole. However, it should be repeated that these figures represent current averages and not completed family size.

Prothro's landmark research on child rearing in Lebanon indicates that Arab parents treat the newborn child with warmth and indulgence and are permissive of dependency in children. However, "aggression against parents is most severely frowned upon. The good child is thought of as one who is obedient and polite. . . . There is little permissiveness for making noise, fighting, or even playing in the home. . . ."[26] The traditional definition of a polite Arab child contrasts distinctly with Canadian norms. This is reflected in Goode's description of socialization in the Middle East:

> . . . the child is taught to show great deference to both parents, and especially to the father. The Arab boy was taught not to sit down when his father was standing, and to get up when his father approached. If he had begun smoking, he could not do so in his father's presence (nor, in many regions, in the presence of his elder brother). He could not dispute with his father in an argument.[27]

The respondents in the Toronto-Montreal survey were often critical of what they regarded as Canadian permissiveness with regard to the rearing of children, particularly females and adolescents. In the words of one woman of Palestinian origin: "[In Canada] parents care about their kids until they are sixteen, after that the kids are left on their own."

Research findings which contrast adolescence in the United States with

175

adolescence in Lebanon illustrate the thrust of many Arab-Canadian respondents' concerns. For example, comparative research on teenage behaviour found that Lebanese students had a higher level of concern about potential parental disapproval, a lower degree of concern about peer approval and greater concern about school, homework and educational values than American students.[28] Further, Lebanese teenagers were more likely to engage in non-commercial social activities where they were under the supervision of adults (e.g., at home, at school or in clubs), rather than to seek the privacy and mobility of a car or to use commercial activity centres with minimal adult supervision. In addition, when asked to list the friends they "run around" with, over one-third of the Lebanese students listed relatives, mostly cousins, among their best friends; hence their peer group was partly a kinship group as well. All of this suggests an Arab adolescence which is more closely oriented to parents, teachers, and kin, and more controlled than in Canada at large.

Alternate Agents of Child Socialization

In contrast to the Arab world, in Canada there are more alternate sources of socialization which are potential competitors with the family for the loyalty of the young. In Canada the teenage peer group is not usually a kinship group; hence the young person is exposed to a variety of non-family influences. In Canada peer pressure appears to be of greater magnitude. Similarly, values promoted through the Canadian school system may be different from parental values, particularly those of first generation parents. Likewise, messages through the mass media directly or through innuendo often downgrade Arab ways, and this acts as another challenge to parental traditions and family norms.

The school may emerge as a counter-socializing force for some Arab-Canadian children. Despite the secular character of Canadian schools, children of minority religious backgrounds may feel estranged from their classmates. Christmas and Easter celebrations and programmes are deeply ingrained in the school culture. Such festivities are difficult to avoid, classroom assignments may centre around them (e.g., Christmas plays, programmes, cards and songs), and they are often placed in a context which does not acknowledge the holidays of other religious groups, notably Eastern Christianity or Islam.[29]

Teachers, as important agents of socialization, may be ignorant of the Arab world and its customs. Parents of Arab origin of all religious persuasions reported examples of ignorance and/or insensitivity on the part of teachers *vis-à-vis* their Arab-Canadian pupils. Thus, during the October 1973 Arab-Israeli war, some children perceived that their teachers acted differently towards them. At the eight of the 1973-74 energy crisis, a parent reported that a Grade Two teacher said to her class, which included a seven-year old Arab immigrant child, "Maybe we should go to war against the Arabs." A generalized lack of knowledge about life in the Middle East can place Arab-Canadian children in awkward situations relative to their teachers. Interviews revealed examples of teachers assuming that an Arab-Canadian child "must" be a vegetarian (apparently, confusing aspects of the Hindu faith with religious practices in the Arab world), that an Arab-Canadian child would not be a Christian (failing to realize there are Christian Arabs), that "obviously back home" an Arab-Canadian child's father would have worn "shoes that turn up at the toe" (confusing historical dress variations with the clothing worn in the contemporary Arab Middle East), that an Arab-Canadian child would not want to associate with a child who is Jewish (confusing anti-Semitism with the Arab-Israeli conflict), and that a Muslim child would not believe in God (ignoring the fact that the God of Islam, Judaism and Christianity is the same, although the Arabic word for God is Allah).

Even for the most acclimatized of parents, whose values and behaviour are similar to the Canadian mainstream, there is the reality that their children are exposed to the same biases and negative interpretations regarding Arab ethnicity as are other Canadian children (see Chapter 4). Parents are faced with attempting to interpret and sometimes defend divergent family practices characteristic of the Middle East. With respect to Muslim families, Barclay has argued that "the close identification of being Arab with being Muslim tends to have negative repercussions with the second generation Canadian-born who tend to react against Arabism and in so doing to reject everything associated with it, including Islam."[30]

Inter-generational problems may arise with respect to definitions of appropriate behaviour, male-female relationships, family obligations and respect and obedience towards elders. Khattab notes that "in the field of marriage and mate-choice particularly, conflicts arise and children sometimes ridicule the cultural patterns which their parents brought from the Old Country. An expression often heard from members of the second generation when opposed by their parents, especially in matters of marriage and mate-selection, is 'I am in a free country.' "[31]

First generation Arab-Canadian immigrants must make many adjustments in adapting to the Canadian way of life, including the area of parenting. Wassef, in her study of Egyptian Canadians in Montreal, notes that parents have given their children considerably more freedom than they would have had if they had never left Egypt, yet not as much freedom as is perceived to be given by Canadian parents generally.[32] All of her respondents said that they would approve of (although not suggest) their son's working as a paper boy or their daughter's working as a baby sitter (if they knew the family involved), and that they would allow their children to have jobs in the summer. In Egypt, children of this socio-economic background would not have been allowed such activity.

These shifts in attitudes towards children working are significant. Although parents reflect some apprehension about the possibility of losing influence over their children if they are financially independent, such awareness of potential problems appears to sensitize them to danger signals rather than thrusting them into obstinacy and a position rigidly contrary to the Canadian cultural pattern. Generally, the socialization practices of first generation parents are neither typically Canadian nor typically Arab but are of a blend which produces a blend – Arab Canadian.

SUMMARY

The forms of Arab-Canadian family life vary by generation, place of birth, length of stay in Canada, position in the development cycle, religion, education and marriage homogeneity. The first generation parent faces particular challenges as he/she, relying on family experience from a very different setting, attempts to socialize children into successful roles in Canadian society, sometimes in the face of counter forces which arouse ambivalence in the child. For Canadians of Arab heritage, regardless of generation, there are some family patterns which emerge that are linked, sometimes distantly, to family life in the Arab world itself.

On the average, Arab-Canadian families reflect a more conservative attitude towards female conduct; are more outwardly conservative regarding husband-wife equality; are increasingly using indirect pressure rather than direct pressure to influence their child's choice of mate; may press toward endogamy, but more for first generations than later ones, more for Muslims than Christians and more for females than males; value children highly and attempt to exercise relatively more control over their behaviour; and are more bound into a web of kinship reciprocities. Kinship help has often aided Arab immigrants in their adjustment in Canada; all left relatives behind in order to emigrate but some joined relatives in Canada. The continued maintenance of contact with kin in the Old Country is significant, even beyond the first generation. There is frequently a feeling, perhaps idealized, that interpersonal and family supports are stronger in their ancestral lands than in Canada.

For Canadians of Arab origin, as for other Canadians, family life provides warmth, support and commitment as well as discomforts, demands and restrictions. Arab Canadians differ in their experiential distance from their ancestral origins, yet characteristic if sometimes subtle Middle Eastern family practices are often transmitted from one generation to the next. Children and adults can, with varying degrees of success, forget, ignore, conceal or rebel against these origins. However, whenever they explore family history they are led back to their Arab roots. Family memories and the bonds of kinship link them with the present, but also irrevocably with the past.

NOTES

1. See Fuad Khri, "Parallel Cousin Marriage Reconsidered: A Middle Eastern Practice that Nullifies the Effects of Marriage on the Intensity of Family Relationships," *Man*, 5 (1970), pp. 597-618; and Robert Cresswell, "Lineage Endogamy among Maronite Mountaineers," in J. G. Peristiany, ed., *Mediterranean Family Structures* (London, 1976), pp. 101-114.
2. Several studies have documented the relationship between propinquity and mate selection. There is a strong likelihood that marital partners, at the time of their first date, lived within approximately one mile of each other. See Alfred C. Clarke, "An Examination of Residential Propinquity as a Factor in Mate Selection," *American Sociological Review*, 17 (1952), pp. 17-22.
3. These data will henceforth be referred to as the Alberta survey. Khattab's larger study is reported in "The Assimilation of Arab Muslims in Alberta," M.A. Thesis, Department of Sociology, University of Alberta, 1969.
4. Khattab, then the Imam (religious leader) of the Mosque in Edmonton, used records from the Edmonton Mosque to survey all known adult Arab-Canadian Muslims in Edmonton and Lac La Biche (with a response rate of 83%). In order not to bias responses, the Imam's name was not connected with the interviews, which were conducted by a team of trained Arab graduate students from the University of Alberta.
5. Nadia Hanna Wassef, "The Egyptians in Montreal: A New Colour in the Canadian Mosaic," M.A. Thesis, Department of Geography, McGill University, 1977, pp. 219-220.
6. *Ibid.*, p. 218.
7. Harold B. Barclay, "The Perpetuation of Muslim Tradition in the Canadian North," *Muslim World*, 59 (1969), p. 71.
8. Cf. Martin Meissner, *et al.*, "No Exit for Wives: Sexual Division of Labour and the Cumulation of Household Demands," *Canadian Review of Sociology and Anthropology*, 12 (1975), pp. 424-39.
9. Sajida Alvi, "Options Beyond the Home," *Islam Canada*, 2 (October, 1973), pp. 9 and 4.
10. *Ibid.*, p. 9.
11. Arab-Canadian Delegates, "Brief No. 16," presented at Heritage Ontario, June 2-4, 1972, p. 3.
12. This is derived from a systematic investigation of the records of the Toronto Arab Community Centre, covering the period from its inception to the summer of 1974.
13. Wassef, *op. cit.*, p. 213.
14. See Meissner, *et al.*, *op. cit.*; Elaine Haavio-Mannila, "Convergences between East and West: Tradition and Modernity in Sex Roles in Sweden, Finland, and the Soviet Union," in Martha T. Shuch Mednick, Sandra Schwartz Tangri, and Lois Wladis Hoffman, eds., *Women and*

Achievement: Social and Motivational Analyses (New York, 1975), pp. 71-84; and Alexander Szalai, ed., *The Use of Time* (The Hague, 1972).

15. See Robert O. Blood, Jr. and Donald M. Wolfe, *Husbands and Wives* (Glencoe, 1960).
16. Barclay, *op. cit.*, p. 72.
17. Wassef, *op. cit.*, p. 219.
18. *Ibid.*
19. *Ibid.*
20. William J. Goode, *World Revolution and Family Patterns* (Glencoe, 1963), p. 105.
21. Edwin Terry Prothro and Lutfy N. Diab, *Changing Family Patterns in the Arab East* (Beirut, 1974), p. 71.
22. Louise E. Sweet, "Reconstituting a Lebanese Village Society in a Canadian City," in Barbara C. Aswad, ed., *Arabic Speaking Communities in American Cities* (Staten Island, N.Y., 1974), footnote 4, p. 51.
23. Prothro and Diab, *op. cit.*, p. 72.
24. *Ibid.*, p. 99.
25. See *Perspective Canada* (Ottawa, 1974), Table 2.10, p. 23.
26. Edwin Terry Prothro, *Child Rearing in the Lebanon* (Cambridge, Mass., 1961), p. 154.
27. Goode, *op. cit.*, 143.
28. Baha Abu-Laban, "The Adolescent Peer Group in Cross Cultural Perspective," *Canadian Review of Sociology and Anthropology*, 7 (1970), pp. 201-211.
29. A respondent reported that in one elementary school classroom, when faced with the task of making Christmas cards, an Arab-Canadian Muslim girl and a Jewish girl, the only non-Christian children in the classroom, banded together to produce their own versions of greetings. Amid giggles, the Jewish girl wrote the following on her card: "Roses are red. Violets are bluish. If it weren't for Christmas, we'd all be Jewish." The nine-year old Muslim girl wrote on her card: "Roses are red. Violets are blue. God doesn't forget, there are Muslims too."
30. Harold B. Barclay, "The Lebanese Muslim Family," in K. Ishwaran, ed., *The Canadian Family*. Revised Edition (Toronto, 1976), p. 103.
31. Khattab, *op. cit.*, p. 39.
32. Wassef, *op. cit.*, p. 217.

EIGHT

Linguistic and Attitudinal Adaptation

The successful adjustment of Arab immigrants requires both linguistic and psychological adaptation. It requires that they learn or improve their knowledge of one or both of Canada's official languages and, as well, that they develop new attitudes and commitments, which may be reflected in such things as acquiring Canadian citizenship, deciding to make Canada a permanent home and developing a general liking for Canadian society and culture. This chapter examines the Arab immigrants' assimilation to the English or French language, as well as their attitudes towards Canadian citizenship, permanent settlement in Canada and the Canadian and Arab Eastern ways of life. In an attempt to provide further insight into these aspects of adaptation, the final section of the chapter will discuss the advice which Arab-Canadian respondents would give to prospective immigrants from the Arab world. Differences in the adaptive experience of Arab Canadians will be considered throughout the discussion.

LEARNING ENGLISH AND FRENCH

Language has often been referred to as the greatest of social inventions. It facilitates communication and the establishment of common understanding, it serves as a vehicle for the transmission of the cultural heritage of the group and it provides a focus for development of cultural identity development. People who move from one linguistic environment to another, over which they have no control, face learning a new language, as well as adapting to the demands of the new environment. The development of new language skills among such immigrants is an important factor in their ability to harmonize their relationships with different aspects of the new social system. The following section will tell the story of how immigrants from the Arab East adapted themselves linguistically to the new Canadian environment.

THE EARLY IMMIGRANTS AND THEIR DESCENDANTS

Abraham Bounadere and many of the Arab immigrants who followed him to Canada before World War II arrived with little or no knowledge of English or French. Except for reciprocal borrowing of words, their native Arabic does not have anything in common with English or French and this makes it all the more difficult to learn the new language(s). Yet some of the early Arab immigrants went about learning a second language with amazing zeal. The experience of Abraham Bounadere, the first Syrian immigrant to Canada, is noteworthy. Relating Bounadere's experience, Karam said:

> Happily he had some knowledge of writing and reading in Arabic and when, on his arrival in Montreal, he rented a room, his kindly Irish landlady took a motherly interest in the young foreigner and spared no effort in pointing out the English names of various articles, and objects, and taught him other expressions and elementary sentences as well. Young Abe at the outset, got himself a small notebook and first writing down in his native Arabic the word he wished to learn, then wrote opposite to it the English, and sometimes also the French equivalent, in Arabic characters. After obtaining the translation of as many words at a time as he could possibly get without unduly imposing on his volunteer teacher he would sit by himself, in his spare time, and study what he had transcribed. Subsequently he would endeavour to recognize and use the words in ordinary conversation or in his business contracts. This was to be the method subsequently adopted by many a young Syrian who happened to be able to read and write Arabic. The more ambitious went further, in venturing into the English alphabet and numerals, gradually learning to sign their own names and to write other words. There were those to come who were to learn from those who came before them, and the earlier Syrians were only too willing to help, even to the extent of giving up their time for days at a time, in order to break the newcomers into the new ways of making a livelihood.[1]

Self-education in general was confined to learning the most basic language skills necessary for the management of everyday affairs, particularly in business. The primary emphasis was on speaking the language, and many early Syrian immigrants could not go beyond this stage, except to sign their names. As one Canadian-born informant expressed it, "I think the pioneers accomplished great feats in trade and business, even in the absence of good knowledge of the language. They made well using the various necessary expressions to sell their hardware." It is commonly agreed that the acquisition of a facility with the language was an important factor in the expansion of Arab-Canadian enterprise outside of Montreal in the latter part of the nineteenth and early twentieth centuries.

Not all the early Arab immigrants succeeded in learning English and/or French, and most of them were prone to use Arabic among themselves, feeling more at home with it. If an immigrant went into business and could not learn the language, he might be forced, sooner or later, to call on a close relative (e.g., son) to manage the business for him, or select a partner, or even sell the budding enterprise. Another way of coping, followed by some ingenious souls, involved the use of personal codes for business management. Commenting on this technique, Hitti observes: "I have personally known a number of Syrians in this country who keep stores and run their business without being able to read and write. Some have had the ingenuity to devise some system of transcribing, by means of dashes and dots, which they alone can decipher."[2]

How far did the learning of English and French penetrate the early Arab-Canadian community? The earliest reliable figures, based on the 1931 Canadian Census, show that 11.5% of Canadians of Arab origin could not speak English, and 4.6% were unable to speak English or French.[3] These figures do not tell us how well the early pioneers knew English or French, but they indicate a high degree of linguistic assimilation.

The figures also indicate that the immigrants were more inclined to integrate with the anglophone than the francophone stream. Outside of Quebec, the pioneer Arab immigrants seem to have little or no incentive to learn a new language other than English. In Quebec, a relatively small minority of them learned French, and an equal or slightly larger minority learned both English and French. The majority, concentrating in Montreal, learned English, the dominant language of business and commerce. As one second generation Montreal Arab Canadian interviewed in this study remarked, echoing the observations made by several other respondents, "the pioneer immigrants found their integration into the anglophone stream to be profitable to their business."

The Canadian-born descendants of the early pioneers were introduced to English and, in addition, to French in Quebec, early in life. Their proficiency was developed more fully in these languages than in Arabic. English was the more popular of the two official languages. In Quebec, as a general rule, the children of Syrian origin, particularly those of the Orthodox faith, tended to enrol in English (Protestant) schools because they were denied entry into the French (Catholic) school system. However, many of them learned French and became trilingual (English, French and Arabic). Only in recent years have Arab Quebeckers begun to enrol, in substantial numbers, in French schools and universities. To a large degree, this trend may be attributed to Quebec's determined efforts to strengthen its national identity through language legislation and other

183

TABLE 17

Knowledge of English and French Among Canadian-Born
Respondents by Province of Residence

Degree of Linguistic Facility	Knowledge of English		Knowledge of French	
	Quebec	Ontario	Quebec	Ontario
Very well	85%	97%	76%	9%
Well	12	00	17	13
Not so well, or not at all	2	3	7	78
Total %	100%	100%	100%	100%
(N)	(41)	(31)	(41)	(32)

measures. Today, one may encounter both English and French educational backgrounds within the same family, the older siblings (or generation) tending to be a product of the English and the younger ones of the French school system.

Table 17 provides information regarding the linguistic assimilation of Canadian-born Arabs interviewed in Quebec and Ontario.[4] It will be observed that the Quebec descendants of early Arab immigrants are almost as fluent in English as their Ontario counterparts. A negligible percentage of them, in either province, have little or no knowledge of English. This finding emphasizes the continued importance of English to the Arab-Canadian ethnic group, regardless of place of residence.

With reference to French, the table shows that 93% of Arab-origin Canadians in Quebec, compared to 22% of those in Ontario, know French either "very well" or "well."[5] Clearly, fluency in French is more common among Arab Quebeckers than Ontarians, and among the Canadian than the foreign-born generations. Overall, the results show the group's striking ability to speak French, particularly in Quebec.

Given Arab Quebeckers' fluency in French and English, one might raise a question about their attitudes towards language legislation in Quebec. While this study did not focus specifically on this or related political issues, a few assessments can be made. Arab Quebeckers interviewed in the course of this study have emphasized the need for linguistic adaptation in the new environment. They have acknowledged the necessity of learning French without restricting opportunities for learning English – the language which has played, and still plays, an important role in their successful economic adjustment. As Quebeckers, they empathize with Quebec's political and cultural aspirations, as well as the provincial government's quest for a more equitable status for French Canadians. However, as an ethnic group they have avoided being drawn into public debates on language legislation or on other political issues affecting the life chances of non-French Quebeckers. Unlike other ethnic groups, Arab Quebeckers have not yet taken a formal stand regarding the controversial issue of language legislation.

Not all Arab Quebeckers are content with their community's silence on such a vital question. For example, the Montreal-based *Arab World Review* has criticized its client community for its failure to take a stand on the issue.[6] Also, in an article in *Le Devoir* entitled "Is the Arab-Canadian Community Dying?," an Arab Quebecker, Abdelkader Banabdallah, criticized what he considered to be lack of public involvement on the part of his ethnic group:[7]

> The Arab-Canadian community, over 150,000 [*sic*] strong, is one of the quietest, if not most lifeless, of all Arab communities in the diaspora. The events which have been shaking Canada and particularly Quebec during the past year have not been able to draw it out of its lethargy. It's enough to make one wonder if this community is not in the process of dying. . . . In an article entitled "Arabs are Conspicuous by their Absence, as Usual," *The Arab World Review* (in its July issue) which is published in Montreal, has risen up against this state of affairs.
>
> Recalling that the language bill in Quebec stirred up passionate comments and sometimes fierce reactions and that the Quebec government itself solicited the opinion of ethnic groups and linguistic communities, *The Arab World Review* underlines the fact that every single one of the groups took a stand for or against certain aspects of the legislation: 'The Jews first, the English, Italians, Greeks, Spanish, Portuguese, Israelis, Lithuanians, Latvians, Indians, Chinese, Germans, Swedish, Irish, Armenians, Haitians, Chilians – in short, the whole blessed list from this Tower of Babel which makes up 20% of Quebec's population. If there were pygmies or blue Indians of the Amazon, says the review, they would have expressed their opinion, but not the Arab community.'[8]

Banabdallah attributed what he termed the "shrinking of obligation on the part of Arab Canadians to the "fact that a great number of the Arabs settled in Canada are still traumatized by their sudden departure from their homeland, following settlings of accounts between Muslims and Christians."[9] Whether or not Banabdallah's argument is valid, Arab Quebeckers have tended to remain silent on issues affecting ethnic minorities in Quebec. In this instance, public silence has concealed the fact that many of them do not wish to be denied the opportunity to maintain strong links with the English language and culture.

To sum up, the early Arab immigrants and their descendants show signs of successful linguistic adaptation in the new environment. Overall, they have tended to follow the anglophone stream, but with increasing numbers in Quebec today becoming fluent in French as well as English. Probably because of cross-pressures resulting from loyalty to the English and French traditions in Canada, Arab Quebeckers have neither supported nor opposed language legislation in Quebec. However, a self-critical and vocal segment has been urging more active political and cultural involvement on the part of their ethnic community.

The Post-war Immigrants and their Descendants
At the time of entry to Canada, the language ability of post-war Arab immigrants was significantly greater than that of the early pioneers. A large majority of the recent Arab immigrants were highly qualified educationally and occupationally and they arrived with an already well-developed facility with at least one of Canada's official languages. A substantial portion of them knew both official languages before they came to this country.

The results of this study reveal that 81% of the foreign-born respondents (that is, immigrants) claimed good or perfect knowledge of English and 58% made similar claims regarding knowledge of French. The percentage of Arab immigrants claiming fluency in English is only slightly higher than the one found in the Department of Manpower and Immigration longitudinal survey of immigrants; however, the percentage of Arab immigrants claiming fluency in French is over five times as large as reported for other immigrants in the government survey.[10] The high rate of fluency in French among post-war Arab immigrants may be attributed to the fact that the majority of them came under French cultural influence either as subjected peoples (as in the case of Algerians and Moroccans) or as students in French-type private schools (as in the case of Egyptians and Lebanese).

Data on the linguistic facility of recent Arab immigrants are reported in Table 18. These data are based on the responses of the foreign-born portions of the sample surveyed in Quebec and Ontario. It will be observed that facility with English was as good among the Quebec-bound Arab immigrants as those destined to Ontario. In contrast, good or perfect knowledge of French was much more common among the respondents residing in Quebec than Ontario: about nine out of 10 of the former group and only three out of 10 of the latter felt that they knew French either "very well" or "well." It seems clear that Arab immigrants having knowledge of French are largely concentrated in Quebec. Comparative analysis of Tables 17 and 18 shows that among the new immigrants facility with French parallels that of the Canadian-born respondents, whereas facility with English is somewhat below that of the latter group.

The Arab immigrants' knowledge of English or French is associated with certain background characteristics in ways which are generally consistent with current research evidence.[11] For example, the results show that education, occupation, income and length of residence in Canada are associated with facility in French in the Quebec portion of the sample, and with facility in English in the Ontario portion of the sample. Considering country or region of origin, the proportion of immigrants

TABLE 18

Knowledge of English and French Among Recent
Arab Immigrants by Province of Residence

Degree of Linguistic Facility	Knowledge of English		Knowledge of French	
	Quebec	Ontario	Quebec	Ontario
Very well	45%	48%	66%	14%
Well	35	34	23	15
Not so well, or not at all	20	18	11	71
Total %	100%	100%	100%	100%
(N)	(133)	(141)	(133)	(138)

having good or perfect knowledge of French was highest (96%) among those originating from North Africa other than Egypt (i.e., Tunisia, Algeria, and Morocco), lower among immigrants originating from Egypt (71%) and lowest among those originating from the Arab Near East (51%). With reference to knowledge of English, the proportion was highest among immigrants originating from Egypt (95%), slightly lower among those originating from the Near East (84%) and lowest (48%) among those originating from North Africa (other than Egypt).

Although the proportion of post-war Arab immigrants having knowledge of English or French was high, a sizeable minority had little or no knowledge of Canada's official languages. The social adaptation of this minority was undoubtedly complicated by this handicap. Edith Ferguson's observation, made about immigrants with low economic and educational standards, seems applicable to the disadvantaged portion of post-war Arab immigrants:

Because of their language handicap and their lack of confidence in a strange new situation, many of these people have trouble in dealing with government offices on such matters as unemployment insurance, workmen's compensation, housing, and taxation. It is hard for them to communicate with employers, landlords, hospitals, and schools. When they are new in the country they are ignorant of wage laws and can be exploited by unscrupulous employers. Because they are unskilled, they are especially vulnerable to unemployment.[12]

The case records of the Arab Community Centre in Toronto illustrate many of the above problems. In addition, they reveal that scores of Arab immigrants needed translation services, letter writing, interview support, and assistance in filling out forms and applications and in dealing with the intricate government bureaucracy.

Language training courses were often taken by post-war immigrants,

Arab or otherwise, in order to acquire or improve their language skills. While self-education of the type followed by the early Syrian pioneers still plays a role, today formal language training of immigrants is the more common method of learning the language. Where this is difficult or inconvenient to obtain, television fills an important gap.

One source of evidence regarding the linguistic adaptation of second generation Arab Canadians is A.M. Khattab's study of Arab Muslims in Alberta (Edmonton and Lac La Biche). The study shows that second generation respondents tended to attribute to themselves better knowledge of English (in terms of speaking, reading and writing) than did the immigrant generation.[13] Khattab also notes that English was the language commonly used by the second generation, while Arabic was typically the one used by the first generation.[14] Further evidence regarding the language position of the new Canadian-born generation is derived from observations made by Arab-Canadian clergymen. In interviews with these religious leaders, many indicated that children of post-war immigrants have not only acquired good knowledge of English or French, but have also lost the parental language. As a consequence of this, several church groups in Toronto and Montreal, in an attempt to reach the second generation, have been introducing religious services in one of Canada's official languages.

CHANGE OF CITIZENSHIP

Naturalization of immigrants as Canadian citizens reflects their acceptance of and identification with the adopted land. It is an index of acculturation and assimilation, if only because it occurs after years of residence in Canada (formerly the legal minimum was five years; it has now been reduced to three years) during which immigrants learn the language and blend into the new environment. While, on the surface, naturalization may appear to be a major symbolic rejection of the Old Country and its ways, in actual practice it precludes neither loyalty to the ethnic heritage nor the possibility, however slim it might be, of return migration, at some future date.

For Arab Canadians, as for other ethnic groups, the issue of naturalization and return migration primarily concerns the immigrant generation, not the Canadian born. The question of return migration of Canadian-born, adult descendants of Arab immigrants has never been significant. On the contrary, in interviews immigrant parents tended to list, as one of the reasons for staying permanently in Canada, the arrival of children. For this reason, the relevant questions in the survey were confined to the foreign-born respondents, and the following discussion will be similarly confined.

The first Syrian to take out naturalization papers was Selim Sheyck, a Maronite Catholic, who became a Canadian citizen in 1892.[15] By the end of 1901, the number of Syrians naturalized as Canadian citizens did not exceed 30 out of a total of about 2,000.[16] Until then, the early Syrian immigrants tended to view their immigration to Canada as a temporary sojourn, motivated by economic interests, and they saw no reason to seek Canadian citizenship. However, their attitudes were to undergo radical transformation, slowly in the 1900's and more rapidly in the 1910's. In the first decade of this century, a new spirit of optimism began to set in, largely conditioned by economic success and increasing familiarity with English and French. The immigrants no longer felt Canada to be a strange land and with their newly acquired confidence they sought the establishment of supportive ethnic institutions.

> As further evidence of the growth of this spirit of optimism and confidence, and in distinct contrast to the condition hitherto existing, was the gradual increase in the number of permanent settlers. Indeed, this is best illustrated by the flood of applications for naturalization papers. At Ottawa in 1913, Shaker Karam, on one single occasion, led 86 men to the altar of Canadian citizenship.[17]

If any of the early Syrian immigrants still had doubts about acquiring Canadian citizenship, there were none left at the end of World War I. Those who had doubts were probably back in Syria by then, and there were many who returned. More importantly, the war did two things. First, it demanded loyalty from all Canadians, and Syrian immigrants were particularly willing to give it because they had experienced oppression under the Ottoman Turks, Canada's new enemy. Second, the war exposed the volatility of the Arab Near East, and Syria and Lebanon became too unsettled to be able to attract their native sons from abroad. Meanwhile, Syrian families were reunited in Canada, unattached Syrian immigrants got married, and the new Canadian-born generation arrived. Together, these events determined the future of the early Syrian-Canadian community. Henceforth, Canadian citizenship was sought as a matter of routine.

The situation of post-war Arab immigrants was similar in outcome, if not in detail, to that of the early pioneers. Two items in the interview schedule provided relevant information regarding these immigrants. First, if the respondent was a naturalized Canadian citizen or planned to become one, s/he was asked to give the reason(s) for this. Second, if the respondent had a landed immigrant status, but was unsure about becoming a Canadian citizen or did not plan to become one, s/he was asked to give the reasons for this. Table 19 reports the reasons given for acquiring or planning to acquire Canadian citizenship.

Of a total of 257 respondents born outside of Canada 228 (88%) had either acquired or planned to apply for Canadian citizenship. Only 29 respondents (12%) were undecided or else did not plan to apply for Canadian citizenship. Table 19 shows that a large proportion of the responses centred around "positive attitudes toward Canada" as a main reason for taking out naturalization papers. Included in this were such

189

TABLE 19

Reasons for Acquiring or Planning to Acquire Canadian Citizenship		
1. Positive Attitudes toward Canada		*28%*
a. prefer Canada, have come to stay	15%	
b. like Canada, feel at home in Canada	8	
c. facilitates adjustment, integration, and identification	5	
2. Citizenship Rights		*26*
a. freedom to travel	15	
b. social and political rights	11	
3. Better Economic Opportunities		*13*
a. easier to get a job	10	
b. better opportunities for children	3	
4. Alienation from the Homeland		*4*
5. Miscellaneous Reasons		*29*
Total %		100%
Number of Responses		(395)

expressions as "feel at home and intend to stay in Canada," "enjoy being in Canada," and Canadian citizenship would "facilitate adjustment, integration and identification with the adopted land." The second most important reason for taking out naturalization papers was "citizenship rights." Among the rights mentioned by the respondents were freedom to travel, and social and political rights. Third in rank, the perceived economic benefits of Canadian citizenship, pertained not only to the respondents, but also to their children. Finally, the results show that very few responses indicated disaffection with the Arab homeland as a reason for obtaining Canadian citizenship. Clearly, it is the appeal of Canada rather than aversion to the ancestral land that propelled immigrants from the Arab world to seek naturalization.

Other studies reveal a similarly strong tendency on the part of Arab Canadians to acquire or plan to apply for Canadian citizenship. For example, Khattab's study of Arab Muslims in Alberta shows that of a total of 251 respondents, 49% were Canadian citizens, 19% were planning to apply for Canadian citizenship, 17% were undecided, and only 14% did not plan to apply for Canadian citizenship.[18] Barclay's study of the Lac La Biche Arab community reports that "fourteen of nineteen Lebanese-born men who have been in Canada five or more years said they were now Canadian citizens."[19]

The results of the Toronto-Montreal survey show that the better educated (holders of diplomas or university degrees) and the single respondents tended to mention "citizenship rights" as a reason for

190

naturalization more frequently than their less educated or married counterparts. Incumbents of lower occupational positions tended to refer to the category "have come to stay" more frequently than those in higher occupational positions. Finally, respondents who were single, younger, or in higher occupational positions tended to mention "freedom to travel" more frequently than those who were married, older or in lower occupational positions.

Of the 29 respondents who were undecided or else did not plan to apply for Canadian citizenship, eleven said they might return to the country of origin, six said "I am an Arab and will always be an Arab," and two said that they did not like Canada or did not feel at home in this country. The remainder gave other reasons, including combinations of the above. Although the number of respondents who were undecided about Canadian citizenship is too small to establish a pattern, it is worth noting that the possibility of return migration was stronger among single than married respondents, and among Egyptians than other Arab nationals.[20] Also, identification with Arab ethnic background tended to be stronger among the lower than higher educated respondents, and among those who were married rather than those who were single.

RETURN MIGRATION

An undetermined number of turn-of-the-century immigrants returned to Syria. According to most of the early pioneers interviewed, the proportion of circular migrants was very small. Only one respondent from Montreal placed the volume of return migration at about one-half: "Many of those who were here wanted to go back to Lebanon after making some money. Those who actually succeeded in making some money indeed went back and lived in their villages. About one-half went back. Those who were left behind were the ones who did not have the means to go back." Judging from official immigration statistics, the return migrants could not have approached one-half the size of the Syrian community. The respondents generally were in agreement that the large majority remained in Canada for the same reasons as those given for seeking Canadian citizenship. One respondent, answering a specific question about the return of Syrians, added: "The Syrian immigrants did not return because their goals got larger, then one would say 'I don't have friends in Syria,' then one would plan a trip for two months but would stay for two weeks, and, finally, after the second trip one would not want to go back anymore."

Regarding return migration, post-war Arab immigrants to Canada and the United States are facing an experience which their predecessors did not face, that being encouragement from many Arab states for the immigrant to return to the native homeland and assist in its social and economic development. The region's need is for highly skilled, technical and professional manpower. In the context of this new experience the following question was asked of all the foreign-born respondents covered in the survey: "Do you plan to reside permanently in Canada, or do you intend to go back to the 'old country'?" Three response categories were provided: "reside permanently in Canada," "go back to the 'old country'," and "undecided." The respondents were then asked to give their reasons for the category selected. The results showed that about one-half of the respondents endorsed the category "reside permanently in Canada," one-fourth endorsed the category "go back to the 'old country'," and one-fourth were undecided about their future plans.

There was a slightly stronger tendency among those with higher educational and occupational qualifications to check the category "reside permanently in Canada." However, among those with diplomas or university degrees, the results show that of those with postgraduate degrees (master's degrees or higher), 50% endorsed the category "reside permanently in Canada," 30% endorsed the category "go back to the 'old country'," and 20% were undecided, while of those with diplomas or bachelor's degrees, 52% endorsed the category "reside permanently in Canada," 17% endorsed the category "go back to the 'old country'," and 32% were undecided about their future plans. Hence, both groups are about equally likely to view Canada as a permanent home; however, the respondents with high educational qualifications were more likely than those with diplomas or bachelor's degrees to plan return migration.

Likewise, the tendency to view Canada as a permanent place of residence was positively associated with naturalization, length of residence, income and age. Specifically, of those who were naturalized Canadian citizens, 55% wanted to reside permanently in Canada, compared to 45% of non-Canadians endorsing that category. Of those who have been in Canada five years or less, 36% viewed Canada as a permanent home, compared to 59% of those with longer residence viewing Canada as a permanent place of residence. With reference to income, the respondents were grouped into four classes: less than $5,000 annually, $5,000-$9,999 annually, $10,000-$19,999 annually, and $20,000 or more annually. The proportions of those who checked the category "reside permanently in Canada" in each of these respective income categories were 41%, 44%, 51%, and 63%. Hence, the more affluent were more likely to view Canada as a permanent place of residence than the less affluent. The respondents were also grouped into four age categories: 30 years of age or less, 31-40 years, 41-50 years, and 51 years of age or over. The corresponding proportions of those who viewed Canada as a permanent place of residence were, respectively, 40%, 48%, 64%, and 78%. Hence the older the respondent the more likely Canada is to be viewed as a permanent home.

The reasons advanced for the choice to reside permanently in Canada included: getting used to Canada – feeling at home (26%), employment opportunities (14%), getting established here (12%), being with family (11%), political stability in Canada (6%), unsettled situation in the Middle East (6%) and limited economic opportunities in the Arab country of origin (2%). The balance of the respondents (23%) listed miscellaneous reasons for viewing Canada as a permanent place of residence. The reasons advanced for the choice to go back to the Old Country, advanced by a minority of the respondents, were: prefer it there – don't like it here (24%), belong there – should be there (16%), family and/or friends are there (15%) and wish to contribute to the homeland (12%). The remainder of the responses (33%) gave other reasons, including business plans, for their choice to return to the Arab world.

To conclude, while about nine out of 10 respondents have either acquired or plan to apply for Canadian citizenship, about one-half of them have decided to reside permanently in Canada. The factor of time appears to be particularly important. As the young Arab immigrant spends more time in Canada away from the homeland, he or she is likely to feel increasingly more at home away from "home," to feel increasingly more established and secure, and to be deterred from return migration by marriage and family obligations as well as widening kinship and friendship ties.

Educationally, occupationally and in other respects the respondents who planned to return to the Arab world were a mixed group. On the average they did not possess the same high qualifications, expertise and wide experience as did those who planned to reside permanently in Canada, although some of them had postgraduate degrees. The evidence further suggests that those who planned to return to the ancestral homeland did so more for socio-emotional reasons than for motives of personal achievement or social mobility.

ATTITUDE TOWARDS CANADA AND THE ARAB WORLD

Immigrants to Canada have to adapt to a new way of life. They have to undergo a process of resocialization in adult years in order to harmonize their relationships with different aspects of the new social system. They must make a new home, give up the familiar, relinquish old ties and make a series of adjustments, the ramifications of which reverberate throughout a lifetime. In an attempt to assess Arab immigrants' attitudes towards the adopted and ancestral lands, four open-ended questions were asked of the foreign-born respondents: What three things do you like most about the Canadian way of life? What three things do you like least about the Canadian way of life? What three things do you like most about the way of life in the country of your origin? What three things do you like least about the way of life in the country of your origin? Tables 20 through 23, respectively, report statistical summaries of the responses to these questions.

Table 20 shows that the thing liked most about the Canadian way of life is the way society is organized socially and politically. Several aspects

193

TABLE 20

Things Most Liked About the Canadian Way of Life

1. Social and Political Organization		*48%*
a. freedom	20%	
b. justice, respect for the law, human rights	7	
c. the political system	6	
d. social amenities	6	
e. organized society	4	
f. cleanliness, sanitation	3	
g. social life and recreation	2	
2. Economic and Educational Opportunities		*18*
3. The People and Their Traits		*14*
a. happy, hard working, honest, simple, sense of humor	10	
b. people here mind their own business, they do not talk too much	4	
4. Technology and Modern Conveniences		*7*
5. Other		*12*
Total %		100%
Number of Responses		(714)

of Canadian social organization were singled out for praise by the respondents: freedom, justice, respect for the law, human rights, democracy, social amenities, cleanliness and good sanitary conditions, and social and recreational life. A further 18% of the responses emphasized the respondents' attraction to economic and educational opportunities in Canada. There were, in addition, certain things that the respondents liked about the Canadian people: having a sense of humour, being happy, hard working, honest, simple, and mindful of their own business. The remaining responses showed attraction to Canada's high level of industrial and technological development, including availability of modern appliances and conveniences, or were miscellaneous.

The above view of the Canadian way of life was quite general among the respondents, with few noteworthy differences in emphasis among them. For example, single respondents tended to emphasize "freedom" more frequently than their married counterparts. Likewise, respondents from Egypt, perhaps because of the conditions underlying their emigration, tended to mention "freedom" and "economic and educational opportunities" more frequently than other Arab nationals.

On the other hand, there were certain things about the Canadian way of life for which the respondents had little liking. Table 21 shows that a plurality of all the negative responses centred around the category

TABLE 21

Things Least Liked About the Canadian Way of Life

1. Social and Cultural Organization		*25%*
a. lack of social life	7%	
b. weak family bonds	6	
c. absence of social controls over youth	6	
d. fast pace of life	4	
e. absence of cultural traditions	2	
2. The People and Their Traits		*18*
(lack of warmth, individualistic, superiority complex, etc.)		
3. Climate		*13*
4. Prejudice Against Immigrants & Strangers		*7*
5. Materialism		*6*
6. Other		*30*
Total %		100%
Number of Responses		(655)

"social and cultural organizations." The respondents were averse to weak ties within the Canadian family, the fast pace of life, and deficiency in sociability, cultural traditions, and social controls over youth. Other responses attributed to Canadians such negative characteristics as lack of warmth, individualism, and a feeling of superiority. The severity of Canada's climate was particularly salient to some respondents accustomed to the moderate climate of the Mediterranean region. Finally, they were averse to prejudiced attitudes encountered against immigrants in Canada, and materialistic orientations in the new environment.

On the whole, respondents with diplomas or university degrees tended to be more critical of aspects of Canadian culture and social organization of the Canadian people, and of materialism than were their less educated counterparts. On the other hand, the less educated tended to complain of climate, and yet at the same time to claim that there was nothing that they did not like about the Canadian way of life. Also, younger respondents (30 years of age or less) tended to be more critical of the Canadian people and of the materialistic nature of Canadian society than were the other respondents.

Turning to things liked most about the Arab world, Table 22 shows that nearly one-half of the responses referred to the category "social and cultural organization." The specific items singled out for praise by the respondents included sociability, rich cultural traditions, strong family bonds, and slower pace of life. Significantly, these items are exactly the opposite of those believed to characterize Canadian society (as shown

195

TABLE 22

Things Most Liked About the Arab Way of Life

1. Social and Cultural Organization		*46%*
a. rich, friendly social life	20%	
b. strong family bonds	10	
c. slower pace of life	8	
d. culture, traditions	8	
2. The People and Their Traits		*20*
(warm, caring, concerned, etc.)		
3. Climate		*19*
4. Other		*16*
a. I was born there	3	
b. food	3	
c. miscellaneous	10	
Total %		100%
Number of Responses		(711)

under the same category in Table 21). The results also show that 20% cf the responses attributed to the Arab people such positive characteristics as warm, caring and concerned, and a further 19% of the responses praised the moderate climate of the Arab East. The remainder of the responses referred to a multitude of things, including food and mere attraction to one's birthplace.

Again, correlation analysis shows that respondents with diplomas or degrees tended to refer more frequently to positive characteristics of the people and of social organization (such as strong family bonds and slower pace of life) and less frequently to climate. Perhaps because of things they miss in the Canadian environment, respondents with master's or higher degrees (M.D.s or Ph.D.s) were most likely to underline positive characteristics of the Arab people. In addition to the less educated respondents, the older respondents (particularly those 50 years of age or over) and relative newcomers to Canada with equal frequency praised the climate in the Arab world. Moreover, younger respondents and recent arrivals (residents for five years or less), compared to their respective counterparts, tended to emphasize strong family bonds and positive aspects of social life in the Arab country of origin.

Table 23, listing the things liked least about the way of life in the Arab country of origin, shows that the majority of the responses revolved around certain aspects of social and, more particularly, political organization. The latter, referring to political instability, lack of freedom, political party organization and, more generally, traditional political orientations, accounted for 33% of the responses. Many

196

TABLE 23

Things Least Liked About the Arab Way of Life

1. Social and Political Organization		*54%*
a. the political system and political instability	24%	
b. lack of freedom	9	
c. traditionalism	9	
d. disorganized society	8	
e. poor sanitary conditions	4	
2. Lack of Economic and Educational Opportunities		*11*
3. Underdevelopment		*10*
4. The People and Their Traits		*9*
a. emotional, hypocrites, lacking in initiative	7	
b. they interfere with other people's business	2	
5. Religious Discrimination		*4*
6. Other		*12*
Total %		100%
Number of Responses		(648)

respondents were in addition averse to traditionalism, social disorganization, and poor health and sanitary conditions, all of which were believed to characterize the Arab world. To a large degree, the preceding items are the opposite of those attributed to Canadian society (as shown in Table 20). There were other things about the Arab way of life for which the respondents had little liking, but they were mentioned far less frequently than was the first category: "lack of economic and educational opportunities", "underdevelopment", "the people" and "religious discrimination."

Aversion to the way politics are run and to political instability in the Arab East tended to characterize men more than women, younger (40 years of age or less) more than older (over 40 years of age) respondents, incumbents of lower occupational positions more than those occupying higher positions, the less educated more than those with higher education, and nationals of Jordan, Syria, Lebanon and Palestine (grouped) more than other Arab nationals.[21] The category "lack of freedom" was mentioned more frequently by the better than the less educated respondents, and by the younger than the older respondents. From this evidence, it appears that the better educated Arab immigrants in Canada are more tolerant of deficiencies in the political systems of Arab states than loss of freedom, which they believe to be non-existent, or at least limited, in those states.

Further examination of the results shows that the better educated

TABLE 24

Arab Canadians' Advice to New Arab Immigrants

Advice Area	Percentage
Work related advice	25
Encouragement to adjust	19
Learn the official language	12
Education related advice	9
Don't give up Arab identity	6
Miscellaneous	29
Total %	100
(N)	(623)

respondents, the younger respondents, and those in higher occupational positions tended to refer more frequently to the negative characteristic of "traditionalism" than did their respective counterparts. Finally, the middle aged (31-50 years of age), the better educated and those in higher occupational positions mentioned "disorganization" more frequently than the less educated, the younger (30 years of age or less) or older (above 50 years of age) respondents, or those in lower occupational positions.

ADVICE TO NEW IMMIGRANTS

The cultural values and personal experiences salient to Arab Canadians are of importance in this study for two reasons. First, they provide valuable insights into the nature of Arab Canadians' adaptation to the new environment. Second, they are often transmitted by relatives, friends, or ethnic institutions as advice to new generations of Arab immigrants. The following question was asked of all the respondents covered in the survey: "If you were asked, what kind of advice would you give Arab immigrants in order for them to do well in Canada?" There were no restrictions on the kinds of answers to be given. A total of 623 separate responses (some respondents providing more than one piece of advice) were given in answer to the question and these are summarized in Table 24.

The one single area which claimed a plurality of the responses was that of work. Content analysis of the responses revealed emphasis on hard work, self-help and independence, frugality, resourcefulness, honesty, free enterprise and, if necessary, acceptance of any kind of work as a start. Following are a few examples of the statements made by the respondents:

"Work hard and depend on yourself."
"Work hard, stick together with other Arab Canadians in

cooperation and harmony, be social and try to get involved in your community."
"Save money, work hard."
"Be smart and look after yourself."
"Push yourself through, try to open your own business."
"Don't work for a salary. Have your own business."
"Take any job at the beginning."
"Be honest and be patient if you couldn't find a job to fit your qualifications."

It is noteworthy that the respondents' admonitions in the area of work reflect elements of the "Levantine ethic" discussed in Chapter Six.

Table 24 shows that the second area of advice, that of adaptation to the new environment, claimed about 19% of the responses. The areas of adaptation covered by the respondents were varied, but the direction of the admonitions was clear. For example, one respondent advised: "Try to accept the different way of life in Canada and adapt." Another interviewee said: "Obey the law and be a trustworthy citizen." A third one added: "Make friends with Canadians."

Next in frequency of mention was advice regarding the acquisition of language skills (12%) and getting an education (9%). Quebec residents, almost uniformly, emphasized the importance of bilingualism, whereas the Ontario portion of the sample emphasized "learning the English language very well." The value of education, on the other hand, was important enough to lead many respondents to say: "Get an education while working."

About six per cent of the responses centred around retention of ethnic identity, the fifth main area of advice. "Try to assimilate," said one of the respondents, "but do not lose your identity." Another respondent advised: "Think of yourself as an Arab as well as a Canadian – since you will be working and living in Canada under a Canadian government."

Finally, the category of "miscellaneous" in Table 24 includes different pieces of advice which were not mentioned frequently enough to allow classification as a separate category, or else represented a combination of different things including reference to the preceding categories. Examples of statements included under this category are:

"Come as young as possible and don't come if you are over fifty."
"Don't occupy yourself with women and drinking."
"Don't bother coming to Canada if you aren't skilled."

There were a few noteworthy differences among different categories of respondents. For example, incumbents of higher occupational positions, compared to those in lower occupations, tended to emphasize "adaptation" and "education." Also, Canadian-born respondents tended to emphasize linguistic adjustment and retention of ethnic identity more than naturalized Arab Canadians. This evidence suggests the resurgence of interest in ethnicity among the second and succeeding generations, although more research is needed in this area. In contrast to their native-born counterparts, naturalized Canadian citizens tended to focus more on work-related advice and on advice pertaining to education. Finally, immigrants from Egypt, perhaps reflecting on their recent experiences in Canada, tended to emphasize the importance of taking any kind of job as a start.

SUMMARY

The overwhelming majority of the early Arab immigrants came to Canada with little or no knowledge of either English or French; this was also true for a much smaller, but nevertheless sizeable, portion of the postwar wave of immigrants. Typically, self-education among the earlier immigrants and formal or informal language training in the latter group have helped to mitigate the severity of the language handicap, allowing them to perform essential economic and social functions. The second and succeeding generations of Canadians of Arab origin are more assimilated linguistically than the immigrant generation. However, most groups have tended to integrate with the anglophone stream. Arab Quebeckers, being in a unique situation today, tend to be oriented – in ideology and practice – toward bilingualism in French and English, rather than toward integration into the French language alone.

There has been a strong tendency for immigrants from the Arab East to be favourable to permanent residence in Canada and to the acquisition of Canadian citizenship. There is no doubt about their generally positive feelings towards the new way of life, despite attachment to certain aspects of the Arab heritage. Having experienced both East and West, and having chosen the West, Arab immigrants see acculturative change as desirable, yet they and their descendants have continued to maintain links with the ancestral heritage.

NOTES

1. Elias Karam, "Syrian Immigration to Canada," in Elias Karam, ed., *The Syrian Canadian National Review* (Ottawa, 1935), pp. 19-20.
2. Philip K. Hitti, *The Syrians in America* (New York, 1924), p. 30.
3. W. Burton Hurd, *Ethnic Origin and Nativity of the Canadian People* (Ottawa, 1941), Table LX, p. 127.
4. Table 17 is based on responses to the following question: "How well do you know the Arabic, English and French languages?" Five response categories were provided: "very well," "well," "not so well," "very little," and "not at all." The responses regarding Arabic are discussed in the next chapter.
5. Throughout the discussion, "good" or "perfect" knowledge of the language means knowing it "well" or "very well." The latter categories ("well" and "very well") were the ones used in the survey. In much of

200

the discussion on language, the percentages are based on the combined responses to "well" and "very well," on the one hand, and to "not so well," "very little," and "not at all," on the other.

6. See article entitled "Arabs are Conspicuous by their Absence, as Usual," *Arab World Review*, July, 1977.

7. Abdelkader Banabdallah, "Is the Arab-Canadian Community Dying?," *Le Devoir*, 2 August, 1977, p. 4. (Author's translation)

8. *Ibid.*

9. *Ibid.*

10. After three years of residence, 80% of the immigrants covered in the longitudinal survey had good or perfect knowledge of English, and only 11% had an equivalent knowledge of French. See *Immigration and Population Study: Three Years in Canada: First Report of the Longitudinal Survey on the Economic and Social Adaptation of Immigrants* (Green Paper on Immigration, Vol. 4) (Ottawa, 1974), p. 102.

11. *Ibid.*, pp. 101-105.

12. Edith Ferguson, *Immigrants in Canada* (Toronto, 1974), p. 22.

13. Abdelmoneim M. Khattab, "The Assimilation of Arab Muslims in Alberta," M.A. Thesis, Department of Sociology, The University of Alberta, 1969, p. 30.

14. *Ibid.*, pp. 31-32.

15. Karam, *op. cit.*, p. 26.

16. *Ibid.*, p. 29.

17. *Ibid.*, p. 30.

18. Based on unpublished statistics provided by A.M. Khattab.

19. Harold B. Barclay, "An Arab Community in the Canadian Northwest: A Preliminary Discussion of the Lebanese Community in Lac La Biche, Alberta," *Anthropologica*, N.S., 10 (1968), p. 154.

20. Since my survey was conducted in 1974, it is possible that the Egyptian immigrants' attitudes were influenced by President Anwar Sadat's unfolding open-door policy (*infitah*) and its distinctly anti-socialist flavour.

21. In view of the above-noted negative relationship between education or occupation and expression of dissatisfaction with the political system, immigrants from Egypt, having relatively high educational and occupational qualifications, were not as averse to the shortcomings of the political system as those originating from the Fertile Crescent region. President Sadat's political posture following the 1973 Arab-Israeli war may have tempered the dissatisfaction underlying their immigration to Canada in the 1960's and early 1970's.

NINE

Cultural Preservation
and Identity

The Arab-Canadian cultural identity is not a fixed entity. Dynamic, changing, a configuration made up of many parts, it is in continuous interaction with the social environment. In general terms, ethnicity in Canada is influenced by many factors, such as government policies, public attitudes, the group's will to survive, traditions from the ancestral heritage, distance from the immigrant experience and the inflow of new immigrants. The role played by such factors may vary from time to time and from one group to another. Also, these factors may operate in opposing directions, some enhancing ethnicity, others forcing it to recede. Together, however, they determine its direction and intensity.[1]

At the level of the individual, Arab ethnicity in Canada may include one or more of the following: affiliation with a distinctive Eastern Christian church or with an Islamic sect, facility with and usage of Arabic, participation in Arab-Canadian associations, informal association with kinsmen, endogamy, maintenance of social and cultural links with the Arab heritage (e.g., through food, customs, music, exposure to ethnic media). At the group level, ethnicity may involve community solidarity, collective efforts at teaching the ancestral language or cultural heritage, or joining to combat prejudice and discrimination against the group.

The last three chapters, dealing with the adaptation of Arab immigrants and the development of ethnic institutions have, of necessity, considered aspects of Arab ethnicity, both at the individual and group levels. This chapter focuses on culture preserving tendencies among Arab Canadians, specifically considering language maintenance, sociocultural links with the Eastern heritage, antecedents and consequences of cultural identity.

LANGUAGE MAINTENANCE

Arabic was the chief idiom among the vast majority of the early and the post-war Arab immigrants to Canada. It is a language which, in spoken and written form, is distinctly different from Canada's official languages. Judging from available evidence, there are both similarities and differences between the two waves of immigrants and their descendants in usage and maintenance of the native Arabic.

The Early Period

The language of everyday conversation among the early Syrian immigrants to Canada was Arabic. Many of the early pioneers managed to learn English and/or French, but their facility with the new languages was often minimal. Once away from their main business and social transactions with the host society, they returned to their native Arabic. There were exceptions, to be sure, particularly within mixed marriages and among Syrians who lived in isolated areas, but such exceptions did not interfere with the generally frequent use of Arabic by the early immigrants.

There were several reasons underlying the survival of Arab among these immigrants. First, business transactions were carried out not only between them and the host community, but also among themselves. Thus there were strong economic interests binding together members of this ethnic community. Second, the early wave of Syrian immigration lasted for about 30 years, well into the second decade of this century, with the result that the native language was being constantly revived. Third, the ethnic rooming houses, organized for new Syrian immigrants during the early period, tended to reinforce ethnic and linguistic identities and encourage the use of Arabic. Finally, the increasing stability and permanence of the early Arab-Canadian community involved the development of ethnic institutions (e.g., the church, the mosque, voluntary associations and language schools) which, together, made some contribution towards the survival of Arabic in the new environment.

To date, some of the early pioneers have greater facility with Arabic than either English or French and, as a result, they feel more comfortable using their native language. In formal functions of Arab-Canadian organizations, there are often Arab translations of the main proceedings, largely for the benefit of the early pioneers and some of the recent post-war immigrants. Also, guest speakers are often asked to use *simple* English in addressing their Arab-Canadian audiences to ensure that their message will be generally understood.

The Canadian-Born Generations: The survival of Arabic among the early pioneers and their descendants was far from complete. While a precise determination of language loss is not feasible, some assessments can be made. Perhaps the most important factor accounting for the loss of Arabic among the second and succeeding generations is the Canadian educational system. The entry of Canadian-born Arabs into the school system coincided with the geographical dispersal of the early pioneer community in Montreal. Facility with Arabic began to decline, first slowly and then more rapidly. The following excerpt, appearing in an early Arab-Canadian publication, illustrates the situation:

203

Modified emigration laws [in Syria] have strictly limited the influx of new settlers. The old settlers here were advancing in age and their children are married. Most of the latter – if not all – cannot read Arabic, and in fact the great majority can hardly speak it. The new generation have no vivid conception of the old country or of their grand-parents and kin whom they have never seen except in their mind's eye. On the other hand, the old folks back home are being succeeded by new generations, to whom relatives in the new world are an abstract theory.[2]

Confirming the above suspicions, a well-placed Canadian-born respondent in Montreal revealed, in the course of an interview, his lack of knowledge of the countries which form the Arab world. He asked me if the people in Iraq spoke Arabic (they do, of course)!

Two observations regarding the pioneers' attempts to transmit Arabic to their offspring are worth noting. The first observation concerns the uneven teaching of Arabic at home. Usually it was the older children who were taught the ancestral language. According to one informant, "in families where there were several children, the last child did not know Arabic, mainly because his older siblings knew English or French and the youngest did not have to learn Arabic." The informant went on to give the example of his own family. He said, "I read and write Arabic, my younger brother reads it, my two sisters know it, but the rest of my brothers and sisters do not know Arabic. The third and fourth generations do not speak or understand the language."

The second observation regarding the transmission of Arabic to children of early immigrants concerns language schools which were established quite early in the Arab-Canadian community. The first school was started in Montreal in 1917, at the urging of some immigrants who wished to perpetuate the ancestral language. The first teacher, a well-educated pioneer now in his eighties, indicated that the school was discontinued shortly after it had started, due to declining enrollment and insufficient community support. A similar fate met the church-sponsored language school established in Montreal in 1924. Renewed attempts in succeeding years were also short-lived. In separate interviews, several older respondents indicated that the community at that time was financially unable to support language instruction.

The experience of Toronto's early Arab community with language schools was not much more successful than that of Montreal. The first Arabic-language school in Toronto was started by a Maronite priest, Father Sabalany, in 1922. At the beginning, over 40 pupils enrolled in the school, but attendance soon began to decline due to the Arab immigrants' movement away from the inner city. In fact, the Maronite Church of Toronto, originally located at Shuter and Victoria Streets, eventually went out of existence, language instruction disappearing with it.

Clearly, a large portion of the newly arrived second generation did not have the benefit of sustained, formal language instruction. The fear of language loss in the new environment was a main theme of an article appearing in a 1937 issue of the Toronto-based *The Syrian-Lebanese Mercury*:

> There are a few Arabic newspapers in North America which, I am afraid I must admit, can hardly live beyond a limited number of years – say fifty – if things continue in their present trend. They must die because there will soon be no one able to read them.
>
> Our mother tongue is being pitifully neglected on this continent. This condition could be remedied by establishing schools where children could learn to read and write. This would not interfere with their public schooling and higher education. . . .[3]

In a subsequent issue, the journal editor observed that "the spirit that made the Arabic school possible years ago has been weakened by the natural process of Canadianization."[4] In the late 1930s, Arabic-language instruction was at its lowest ebb, only reviving about a quarter century later among post-war Arab immigrants.

The impact of language schools on language maintenance, as compared to home instruction, among the descendants of the early Arab immigrants is not easy to determine. The combined effects of both of these institutions, however, account for the fact that a sizeable proportion of the Canadian-born respondents contacted in this study knew the ancestral language. About 25% of them claimed to know Arabic "very well" and an equal proportion claimed to know it "well." The balance, about one half, had little or no facility with Arabic. The differences between the Quebec and the Ontartio portions of the sample were minimal.

Despite their moderate fluency in Arabic, the children of early immigrants apparently have relatively limited opportunities for using this language. As Table 25 shows, about two out of 10 Canadian-born respondents used Arabic with high frequency at home and outside the home. Another five out of 10 used it "occasionally" or "rarely." The balance did not use Arabic at all in their private life.

Finally, of the 11,857 Arabs living in Canada in 1941 (the earliest year for which the Canadian Census provided relevant information on mother tongue), about 68% (8,111) claimed Arabic as the mother tongue. Since approximately 66% (7,853) of the Arabs were Canadian-born,[5] Arabic was the mother tongue of at least 51% of those born in Canada. The proportion of those who would have claimed knowledge of Arabic would probably be appreciably larger than that. In 1951, the proportion who claimed Arabic as the mother tongue declined to about 45%. This figure reflects the limited immigration during the 1940s, deaths among first generation people and the increase in the size of the second and subsequent generations. In contrast, in 1961 the proportion who claimed Arabic as the mother tongue rose to 67% as a result of the influx of new

205

immigrants. No comparable information is available for 1971, but immigration statistics suggest that this percentage will likely remain high for some time.

The Post-war Period

Between 1946 and 1975, a total of 48,619 immigrants from the Arab world were admitted to Canada. The early pioneers who were fearful of losing the Arabic language did not foresee the possibility of a revival of the ancestral language by Arab immigrants yet to come. The 1951 Canadian Census signified a total of 5,535 persons claiming Arabic as mother tongue.[6] This figure rose to 12,980 in 1961, and 28,550 in 1971.[7] It is believed that *knowledge* of Arabic would be claimed by an even larger number of persons in each of the noted census years. Today, it is estimated that about two-thirds of Canadians of Arab origin, or about 50,000 persons, know Arabic.

Clearly, the vast majority of post-war Arab immigrants had good or perfect knowledge of their native Arabic. The survey results show that nine out of 10 foreign-born respondents knew Arabic either "well" or "very well." The balance (one out of 10) is made up largely of persons who came to Canada as dependent children with limited knowledge of Arabic. In terms of fluency in Arabic, the early pioneers and their post-war counterparts were alike. However, the early pioneers were forced to use Arabic among themselves because of their limited facility with Canada's official languages. The post-war immigrants, in general, were not as limited to the use of their native Arabic. To what extent, then, did the post-war immigrants' superior knowledge of English or French limit the use of Arabic in their private life? Discussed below are the survey results bearing on this question.

Use of Arabic at Home and Outside the Home: The respondents were asked two questions relevant to the use of their native language: "Do you use the Arabic language at home?" and, "Do you use the Arabic language outside your home?" For each question, five response categories were provided: "no," "yes, but rarely," "yes, occasionally," "yes, frequently," and "yes, very frequently." Table 25 summarizes the responses to these questions, by country of birth (Canadian-born vs. foreign-born). For ease of presentation, the categories "rarely" and "occasionally" were combined under the term "sometimes," and the categories "frequently" and "very frequently" were combined and labelled "often."

It will be observed that a majority of the foreign-born respondents used Arabic "often" at home, and the remainder were about evenly divided between using it "sometimes" and not using it at all. The use of Arabic outside the home was quite prevalent as 35% of the immigrant generation used it "often," 53% used it "sometimes," and only 12% did not use it at all. There were wide differences between the foreign-born

TABLE 25

Use of Arabic at Home and Outside the Home
Among Arab-Origin Canadians, by Birthplace

	Place			
	Home		Outside the Home	
Frequency of Use*	Canadian-Born	Foreign-Born	Canadian-Born	Foreign-Born
Not at all	31%	22%	32%	12%
Sometimes	49	20	50	53
Often	21	57	18	35
Total %	100%	100%	100%	100%
(N)	(72)	(276)	(72)	(275)

*"Sometimes" combines the response categories of "rarely" and "occasionally", while "often" combines the response categories of "frequently" and "very frequently."

and Canadian-born respondents. The table shows that the foreign-born respondents were about three times as likely as the Canadian-born to use Arabic "often" at home, and twice as likely to use it "often" outside the home.

Further analysis shows that the frequent use of Arabic, both at home and outside it, was more common among immigrants from the Fertile Crescent region and Egypt than those originating from Tunisia, Algeria and Morocco; more common among the respondents with lower than higher occupational positions; and more common among immigrants with five or more years of residence than those with less than five years of residence.

These findings indicate that the home remains the most significant place for the majority of immigrants to utilize their facility with the native Arabic. Second, judging from the best available evidence, it appears that post-war Arab immigrants were not as inclined to use Arabic in their private lives as their turn-of-the century counterparts. Among the factors accounting for this difference is the fact that at the time of entry to Canada, the post-war immigrants' facility with English and French was superior, both in relative and absolute terms.

The Canadian-Born Generations: For several reasons, the post-war immigrants, compared with their earlier counterparts, appear to be less successful in teaching Arabic to their Canadian-born children. First, they tend to have good facility with English (and/or French) and thus there is less pressure on their children to learn Arabic in order to communicate with their parents. As indicated above, only about one-half of these immigrants use Arabic often at home. Second, the recent arrivals, com-

207

pared to the early pioneers, are more likely to be salaried employees and thus have less discretionary time to spend with their own families or to teach their children the ancestral language. Third, plans for return migration are not as prevalent among Arab immigrants today as in the past and, as a result, there is less pressure on parents to teach their children the language, although they might very much like them to learn it.

Nor are language schools today necessarily more effective than they were in the past. Their existence is far from being stable and attendance tends to be irregular. Under the multiculturalism policy, to which many provincial governments have been responsive, government financial support has alleviated but has not eliminated the financial problems of second-language schools. The residential dispersal of the Arab ethnic group causes equal problems. With expansion of Canada's cities and urban centres, where most of the Arab Canadians live, even the inner city (in Montreal, Toronto, Edmonton, and Vancouver) where language schools tend to locate is too long a drive (or a ride) for many families. This, together with the school's potential to interfere with children's extra-curricular activities, has been a main factor in irregular attendance. A further impediment to the learning of Arabic is relative lack of opportunities for youth to utilize newly acquired language skills in their immediate environment.

The results of the comparative study of Arab Muslims in Lac La Biche and Edmonton, Alberta, illustrate some of the above points. In both communities, the respondents were asked questions about their knowledge of Arabic in terms of speaking, reading and writing. They were instructed to endorse, in each instance, one of five response categories: "very well," "above average," "average," "below average," and "not at all." The results regarding the second generation, made up largely of descendants of post-war immigrants, were that in Lac La Biche about 80% spoke Arabic (average or better) and only 40% could read and write Arabic (average or better). In contrast, only 27% of Edmonton's second generation Arab Muslims spoke Arabic (average or better) and none of them had even average knowledge or reading or writing.[8] What factors were responsible for the observed differences between the two groups?

Factors in the ethnic group, as well as the host community, had a determining influence on the results. For example, the Arab Muslim group in Lac La Biche is much smaller, more homogeneous, and more close-knit than the one in Edmonton, and the residences of its members are physically close to each other. There are fewer distractions facing the Arab-Canadian youth in the smaller community of Lac La Biche than in Edmonton. In combination, these group and host-community factors seem to account for a large part of the differences between the two groups. Whatever the full explanation of these differences may be, it should be noted, in conclusion, that even in the smaller setting of Lac La

Biche, only four out of 10 second generation respondents could speak, read and write Arabic.

The results of this study show that many Arab-Canadian parents and institutional leaders (e.g., priests, imams) were aware of the second generation's limited facility with Arabic. No precise figures are available but this much can be said: knowledge of Arabic among the descendants of post-war Arab immigrants to Canada, in general, is not sufficiently well developed to perpetuate the linguistic tradition of this ethnic group. Barring unexpected developments, the perpetuation of this tradition in Canada will require the steady inflow of immigrants from the Arab world.

INFORMAL RELATIONSHIPS

In the early years of Arab immigration to Canada, the pioneers, according to a Montreal respondent, "were socially very close and they lived close to each other." This is understandable in view of their common cultural, linguistic, religious and economic interests. The security and fellowship which the ethnic community provided its members were invaluable for their adaptation. The increase in Syrian immigration to Canada at the turn of the century did not appreciably change the situation. As new immigrants arrived, Syrian communities were established outside of Montreal in other Canadian cities and towns. For their local residents, the new communities played a role similar to that of the parent Syrian community of Montreal.

The Syrian immigrants' business interests and frequent geographical mobility helped establish links between these developing communities. But it was at the local level that social relationships and friendships were cemented by time. It was also at that level that initiatives were taken to establish churches, mosques, Arabic-language schools and other ethnic institutions. These institutional developments further buttressed the social bonds among the early Syrian Canadians.

It would be misleading to give the impression of complete solidarity in the evolving Syrian communities or in the total early Syrian-Canadian community. There were differences and factions among the early pioneers, sometimes based on village of origin, sometimes on religious background, and sometimes on the personal inclinations of individual immigrants. As time passed, as the Canadian-born generations arrived, and as the post-war Arab immigrants were received, intra-group differences widened. Thus, social relationships, and more particularly friendships, in the Arabic-speaking communities in Canadian cities, became much more segmented.

The bases of segmentation include education, occupation, religion and country of origin. More important than these, perhaps, is the line that separates the pioneers and their descendants, on the one hand, and the post-war immigrant generation, on the other. With reference to this, the following quotation from an older, Montreal-born respondent, is illuminating:

> You go to different places and you don't see the same faces. And like everything else, when you are more numerous there is less affiliation with the group. The new groups stay together as the old immigrants stayed together. They stand as a separate group from the early immigrants.
>
> There is a gap today based on education. Today's immigrants are well educated and there is a superiority feeling among them. They come here and carry with them their problems and conflicts, while this country is not concerned about these problems and conflicts. The new immigrants are emotional, and they are biased in certain ways, until they become used to the ways of the country by taking part in government and politics.

Post-war immigrants in turn are at times critical of the earlier generations of Arab Canadians because of the latter's apparent lack of concern about social, economic and political issues facing the ancestral homeland. As a result of the generational and other dissociative factors, the Arab-Canadian community may be characterized as a loose federation of different interest and status groups with varied world views.

There are occasions for social gatherings which encompass a broad spectrum of the Arab ethnic group. Among these occasions are banquets *(haflahs)* and community meetings organized by local, regional and national Arab-Canadian associations, religious services, financial campaigns to collect funds for a worthy cause, and defense of the ethnic group against discriminatory treatment.

One of the questions asked in this study pertained to friendship patterns: "Considering your closest friends in Canada, are many of them of Arab origin?" Four response categories were provided: "No," "yes, some of them," "yes, most of them," and "yes, all of them." Table 26 shows the extent to which friendships among members of this ethnic community were group-oriented. The results were consistent with expectations: within-group primary relations were prevalent. But there were differences. For example, the immigrant generation was more inclined than the Canadian born to confine friendships to the ingroup: Arab immigrants were twice as likely as native-born Arab Canadians to have all their close friends of the same ethnic origin. Contrariwise, the Canadian-born respondents were almost four times as likely as the foreign-born ones not to have among their closest friends any of the same ethnic origin.

There were other differences among the respondents, but not as wide as those shown above. For example, ingroup orientation tended to decline slightly with longer Canadian residence and higher occupational standing. We have no information regarding differences in ingroup orientation among later generations of Arab Canadians. It would be ex-

TABLE 26

**Ethnic Origin of the Respondents' Close Friends
in Canada, by Birthplace**

Proportion of Closest Friends of Arab Origin	Birthplace	
	Canadian Born	Foreign Born
None	18%	5%
Some	39	30
Most	34	46
All	9	19
Total %	100%	100%
(N)	(71)	(275)

pected, however, that within-group friendships would decline with each succeeding generation.

SOCIAL AND CULTURAL LINKS WITH THE EASTERN HERITAGE

Language is only one aspect of the Arab cultural heritage. Arabic traditions, music, songs, dances, poetry and food can survive independently of language maintenance. Indeed, the cardinal assumption underlying the federal government's multiculturalism policy is that language and culture are two different things, and that the latter can be kept alive with or without the former. The following discussion attempts to shed further light on the extent to which Arab Canadians have kept in touch with their origins.

With each succeeding generation of Arab Canadians less and less is retained and known about the ancestral heritage. Likewise, with the passage of time there is a sharp decline in contacts with kinsmen. These issues were the subject of both comment and lament in several interviews with early Syrian pioneers and even some of the post-war Arab immigrants. *The Syrian-Lebanese Mercury* contained many articles which lamented the widening gap between the Canadian-born generations and the ancestral land, and exhorted the Arab-Canadian community to keep in touch with its heritage. For example, in 1936, in the first issue of this paper, the editorial read, in part:

> By retaining the language and culture of the old-country and adding them to the strong and admirable heritage of Canada, with her time-tested traditions and customs of French and British, we do not detract from our ability as Canadian citizens and British subjects but we are the stronger for it. This amalgamation of the two cultures is the basis of a true liberal education.[9]

211

Despite the above expressions of loss of holdings from the past, in the adopted land certain aspects of the Arab cultural heritage have endured. For example, Canada's ethnic kaleidoscope includes the Eastern Christian and Islamic traditions, however modified they have been in order to fit into the new environment. Other more or less enduring elements from the ancestral heritage include familistic orientations, kinship ties, respect for elders, traditional wedding celebrations, exchange of visits during certain feasts and holidays and many social arrangements prevalent in the ancestral community. With reference to the last point, Louise Sweet, having studied both the home village in Lebanon and the immigrant Druse community in Edmonton, notes:

> . . . that the networks, segments, styles, manners and customs of the people of 'Ain ad-Dayr as a Lebanese village continue to flourish in a western Canadian city, and that economic, social, and ideological functions of greater security for all are so enhanced. . . . A more extensive study would show some few occasions of conflict with the Canadian 'system,' but to a very remarkable degree the village of 'Ain ad-Dayr is successfully reconstituted in a Canadian city without friction, almost invisibly, unless one has been a member of it, by almost more than a change of costume in public.[10]

Canadians of Arab origin have also kept alive a unique aspect of the literary heritage. In this connection, a short article appearing in another 1936 issue of the *Mercury* is worth quoting:

> A remarkable feature about the Arabic literature is the superabundance of poetry. One may find an ode or lyric in the most insignificant story, and the poetry is of a high standard. It seems that the language is so poetic that every man, who is thoroughly educated in it, can write excellent poetry at will.
> The literature of Arabia has its origin in the improvisations, recitations, stories and chiefly in the songs and poems of pre-Mohammedan times. The language of these poems, as of all best Arabic literature, was that of the desert Arabs of Central Arabia.
> A custom which is perpetuated even today among us is the art of the previously mentioned improvisation, whereby opposing teams, representing two tribes, villages or families, seek by improvising in song to outdo each other in their display of wit, humor and wisdom. Often at such a contest feeling reaches a high peak as the audience drinks in with a keen intellectual appreciation the ready repartee of the singers, lending their sympathies to one team or the other.[11]

Contests of the type suggested above, though not frequent, continue to this day among those versed in the language.

The survey results shed further light on the degree to which this ethnic

TABLE 27

Social and Cultural Links With the Eastern Heritage, by Birthplace

Selected Activity

Frequency	Eating Arabic food	Corresponding with relatives or friends	Sending money to relatives	Listening to Arabic music and songs	Reading Arabic journals or books	Listening to Arabic broadcasts	Watching Arabic films	Visiting the old country
			Canadian Born					
Not at all	4%	56%	77%	10%	80%	53%	55%	57%*
Rarely	1	12	7	14	5	19	16	18
Occasionally	10	22	14	42	8	19	27	14
Frequently	44	10	1	22	5	7	1	8
Very frequently	41	—	**	13	1	1	—	3
Total %	100%	100%	100%	100%	100%	100%	100%	100%
(N)	(73)	(73)	(73)	(72)	(73)	(73)	(73)	(73)
			Foreign Born					
Not at all	10%	9%	49%	16%	32%	44%	46%	55%*
Rarely	4	9	9	13	15	20	26	27
Occasionally	16	22	25	26	31	21	20	8
Frequently	26	34	16	23	11	8	5	5
Very frequently	44	25	**	22	11	6	2	5
Total %	100%	100%	100%	100%	100%	100%	100%	100%
(N)	(275)	(275)	(275)	(274)	(274)	(274)	(275)	(273)

*With reference to "visiting the old country," "rarely" means once; "occasionally" means twice; "frequently" means three times; and "very frequently" menas four or more times.

**This item had four rather than five response categories. In the Interview Schedule, the last category read "regularly."

213

group has kept in touch with its past. Leaving aside those parts of the survey which have already been examined, the following discussion will focus on responses to questions dealing with Arabic food, correspondence with relatives or friends, sending money to relatives, listening to Arabic music and songs, reading Arabic newspapers and books, listening to Arabic broadcasts, watching Arabic movies, and visiting the Old Country. Table 27 shows the responses to these questions, by country of birth (Canada vs. other).

Considering the Canadian-born respondents, by far the strongest link with the past was Arabic food. In response to a question, "Do you eat Arabic food at your home?", about 85% of them endorsed the category of "frequently" or "very frequently." The second most frequent link the Canadian-born respondents had with the past was "listening to Arabic music and songs." As Table 27 shows, about 35% of the Canadian-born respondents checked the response category "frequently" or "very frequently"; another 42% checked the category "occasionally"; and the remainder were divided between the categories of "rarely" and "not at all."

About four out of 10 descendants of Arab immigrants visited the Old Country at least once, and as many as 25% of the visitors did so three or more times. The results also show that in at least two respects the links with relatives and friends were maintained: about 33% of the Canadian-born respondents corresponded with relatives or friends "occasionally" or "frequently," and about 15% sent money to relatives on an occasional basis. The mass media provided the weakest link between these respondents and the Arab Near East, but nonetheless about one out of four Canadians of Arab origin listened to Arabic broadcasts and an equal proportion watched Arabic films at least occasionally. A slightly smaller portion read Arabic newspapers or books "occasionally" or "frequently."

The foreign-born respondents (i.e., immigrants), were similar to their Canadian-born mates on two items, "eating Arabic food" and "visiting the old country." On all the other items, however, they kept in touch with the past more frequently than the native-born respondents. It is worth noting over 50% of the foreign-born respondents were more or less involved in all eight of the selected activities, except "visiting the old country" where less than 50% visited the country of origin at least once.

To sum up, the respondents maintained frequent social and cultural links with the Eastern heritage.[12] There were differences in the expected direction between the Canadian-born and foreign-born portions of the sample. Generally speaking, the higher the generation, the less frequent contact was with certain aspects of the ancestral heritage. With reference to apparently enduring aspects of the Arab ethnicity, such as music, songs, food and visits to the Old Country, the differences between the two portions of the sample tended to disappear.

ANTECEDENTS OF CULTURAL IDENTITY

There are differences within the Arab-Canadian community both in retention of cultural identity and in acculturative and assimilative change. These differences are a product of many interacting conditions, some unique to this ethnic group and others shared by many ethnic groups. It should be emphasized that the existence of a strong cultural identity both at the individual and group levels is not a hindrance to assimilation, for ethnicity and assimilation are not necessarily mutually exclusive alternatives. Rather, they may represent two sides of the same coin, linked together by dynamic processes of social life. Yet where it exists with some strength cultural identity does make a difference. Under certain conditions, for example, it may influence the development of distinctive attitudes and forms of behaviour.

Drawing on the results of the national survey as well as the existing literature, the discussion will first consider factors influencing Arab cultural identity, such as generation, socio-economic status, age, marital status and spouse's ethnic background, religion and country of origin, and then selected forms of behaviour and attitudes believed to arise from ethnic identity.

The Generational Factor

For Arab immigrants to Canada in general, the generational factor is one of the most important influences on cultural identity and assimilation. The gap between the first or immigrant generation and the second and succeeding generations is indeed wide. Members of the latter group have been born, raised and educated within the context of Canadian culture and institutions. They have no past memories of a "foreign" homeland to glorify and no memories of, or regrets for, broken friendship and kinship ties. The native-born offspring of Arab immigrants are Canadian, and they want to behave like Canadians. The adage which seems to rule supreme in the lives of the Canadian-born generations is "to be liked is to be alike." Consider, for example, the following excerpt from a 1937 article written just before the coronation of King George VI:

> The Syrian-Lebanese community in Toronto are just as interested in this Coronation as English-born citizens are. The Syrian-Lebanese people in Canada live tranquilly and thrive and prosper with this, their adopted country. When George VI is crowned King on May 12th, he will be able to rely as much on his Syrian-Lebanese Canadians as he will on Londoners.[13]

Despite the strength of identification shown in the above passage, the editorial policy of the journal in which it appeared was to maintain Arab cultural identity – a reminder that acculturation and ethnicity need not be mutually exclusive alternatives.

TABLE 28

**Strength of the Respondent's Cultural Identity,
by Generation**

Strength of Cultural Identity	Generation	
	Canadian-born Generations	Immigrant Generation
High	6%	23%
Medium	36	47
Low	58	30
Total %	100%	100%
(N)	(72)	(273)

Using a multi-dimensional measure of cultural identity, the present study shows that 23% of the first generation and only six per cent of the Canadian-born respondents were classified as "high" on ethnic identity. (Table 28).[14] Contrariwise, 30% of the former group and 58% of the latter were classified as "low" on ethnic identity. The existence of a wide gap between the immigrant and native-born generations should not obscure the fact that a substantial portion of respondents from the latter group exhibited some form of ethnically-based behaviour.

Canadian-born Muslims are no more immune to a decline in cultural identity than their Christian counterparts. Speaking of the Lac La Biche Arab (Muslim) community, Barclay states:

Inevitably contrasts between first and second generation in Lac La Biche will widen and become more magnified as the second generation in the public schools acquire English as their first language or at least become bilingual. They readily acquire non-Lebanese friends. . . . As the old generation, already weakened in its allegiance to the past, retreats to the background, the hold of tradition will become feeble indeed.[15]

That there are exceptions to the above-noted trends is shown by the results of Sweet's study of the Arab Druse community in Edmonton. She found, transplanted in the Canadian setting, a wide range of social and cultural patterns which paralleled, even in the finest detail, those in existence in the home village of Lebanon. She explained, "The strength of Druse identification, ideology (even among the essentially uninstructed), and kinship and the advantages of maintaining such solidarity seem to override deep assimilation or complete acculturation. There is, so far as I have been able to discover, very little erosion from the community."[16] She further argued that the "preindustrial bonds survive because they have no competitive or counteractive mechanisms in the Canadian system: it is the latter system which can provide 'nothing better.' "[17]

Should the bonds that bind this community erode and family security disappear, the likely alternative would be vagrancy and welfare.[18] Sweet's study focused specifically on the immigrant generation, a large majority of whom were post-war immigrants. The underlying theme of the article suggests the likely persistence of adaptive patterns in succeeding Druse generations.

There are differences in the maintenance of cultural identity not only between the first and subsequent generations, but also between the second and third generations. As one religious leader put it, "the second generation tends to retain a basic knowledge of Arabic, while the third generation tends to lose the language especially if they intermarry. Intermarriage has happened in a large number of cases. However, a vast majority have retained spiritual affiliation with the church and this commitment is probably more important than their commitment to their ethnicity (Arab heritage)." In a similar vein, an older respondent in Montreal remarked: "Lebanese children *today* go to Canadian schools and mix freely and their mentality has become typically Canadian." Differences between the second and third generation were also observed in the area of sports some 40 years ago:

> We notice lately that the third generation of Syrians and Lebanese have taken to sports more than we the second generation. Our parents who came from the old country played absolutely no sports at all and made strenuous objection to their children's participation in games which they saw to be in the least degree rough or dangerous. Thus these children had to play hockey, skate and swim in secret. . . . The writer was quite surprised the other day when, as he walked through a city park, he saw a hockey game in progress whose teams were composed entirely of Syrian and Lebanese boys. . . . This thing is without precedent among us in Toronto. Our beloved parents thought that death would be our instant lot the moment we stepped upon ice or entered a swimming tank. . . . Let's continue to indulge in sports ourselves and see to it that our children be given every encouragement and opportunity to do likewise.[19]

Although, as one might expect, differences between the first and second generation sometimes led to conflict and disavowal of ethnicity, the conflict was not very intense for two reasons. First, among the early immigrants, the older children (who had to learn Arabic and become familiar with the Eastern heritage) tended to play the role of mediator between the immigrant generation and the host community and also between the elders and their younger siblings. This role had an integrative effect on the Syrian community, containing the traditional rebelliousness of the second generation. Second, in the post-war period, the intensity of the conflict was mitigated by the immigrants' higher educational and occupational background and, often, prior knowledge of the language and

217

culture. In view of this, one should be careful not to confuse among Arab Canadians conflict which may exist anywhere between parents and children with the conflict arising from exposure to two cultural patterns.

Finally, a word needs to be said about the third generation's return to or rediscovery of the ancestral past. There is evidence that this process occurs, for reasons that are unique to the Arab-Canadian ethnic group. As indicated above, cultural identity was steadily eroded among the Canadian-born generations. Following the 1967 Arab-Israeli war, in which the Arab states suffered a humiliating defeat, a feeling of gloom and dejection permeated the Arab-Canadian community. There were reports of concealment, at times denial, of ethnicity even by members of the first generation. Those Arab-origin Canadians who were separated from the past by one or more native-born generations were probably strengthened in their resolve to pay only the scantest attention to their ethnicity. Six years later, however, the 1973 Arab-Israeli war, in which the Arab states were not defeated, revitalized commitment to Arab ethnicity and a feeling of pride in cultural identity. As my survey was carried out in 1974, many respondents, representing different generations, affirmed the resurgence of ethnicity among descendants of the early Arab immigrants. Whether or not this return to the past, however symbolic, will last for a long time remains to be seen.

Socio-Economic Factors

The few available studies of Arab Canadians do not reflect a consistent pattern of relationships between socio-economic factors and assimilation.[20] For example, according to Khattab's study of Arab Muslims in Alberta (Edmonton and Lac La Biche), there was a clear, positive relationship between assimilation and both education and income. The relationship held for older as well as younger respondents. In contrast, Barclay's study of the Lac La Biche Muslim community reports that the poorest Muslims were said to be the most highly assimilated, and their children were said to be best integrated into the larger community.[21] However, in what appears to be a self-contradiction, Barclay notes that for the more prosperous Muslims,

> . . . there is an ambivalence over the loyalty to the past ties and the lure of financial success wrought by full compromise with the dominant cultural milieu. It is out of loyalty to kin and confession that they support a *Qur'an* school and want their children to read and write Arabic. It is out of the lure of finance that they increasingly succumb to middle class Canadian values.[22]

Considering the full range of findings from Khattab's and Barclay's studies, available evidence seems to indicate a positive relationship between assimilation and socio-economic status.

In this survey, it was cultural identity rather than assimilation that was under investigation. Because of the importance of the generational factor, it was held constant in the statistical analyses of the data. The results show that, among the Canadian-born respondents, there was a negative relationship between cultural identity and education, and positive relationships between cultural identity and both occupational status and income. The pattern of relationships was slightly different among the foreign-born respondents: cultural identity was negatively related to both education and occupation and almost unrelated to income.

Other Background Factors
Because life experiences and attitudes are often tied to such personal characteristics as sex, age and marital status, it will be worth while to examine the relationship between such factors and cultural identity. The results show that among both the native- and foreign-born respondents there were no sex differences in allegiance to the past. Religion was related to ethnicity among the Canadian-born but not the foreign-born respondents. Among the Canadian-born, 25% of the Muslim-Druse respondents had strong (i.e., "high") ethnic identity, compared to only four per cent of their Christian counterparts. Contrariwise, 25% of the Muslim-Druse and 60% of the Christian respondents had weak ("low") ethnic identity. For both the Canadian-born and foreign-born portions of the sample, there was a low, positive relationship between age and cultural identity. Among first generation respondents, age at the time of entry into Canada and length of residence were unrelated to ethnic identity.

Generally speaking, the married respondents, regardless of generation (whether first, second or higher), were more likely than their single opposites to be high on cultural identity. An even stronger association was found between the ethnic origin of the respondent's spouse and cultural identity, for both the Canadian- and foreign-born portions of the sample: marriage to a non-Arab tended to weaken cultural identity appreciably. Allegiance to the past was strongest among the respondents who were married to Arabs from the Old Country, weaker among those who were married to Canadian-born Arabs, and weakest among the respondents who were married to non-Arabs.

As indicated previously, the post-war Arab immigrants to Canada came from virtually all parts of the Arab world. What differences are there in the strength of cultural identity among those immigrants of diverse origins? Considering the first generation respondents, cultural identity was strongest among immigrants from the Near East, i.e., Syria, Lebanon, Jordan, Palestine and Iraq, with 80% of them being classified as "high" or "medium" on ethnic identity; weaker among immigrants from Egypt, with 57% being classified as "high" or "medium" on ethnic identity; and weakest among immigrants from North Africa other than Egypt, i.e., Tunisia, Algeria and Morocco, with none of them scoring "high" on ethnic identity and only 43% being classified as "medium." These differences may be explained at least in part by the

219

political and economic estrangement of immigrants from Egypt, and by the disruptive impact of the French colonial system on Arab North Africa.

The longitudinal survey on the economic and social adaptation of immigrants asserts that an immigrant's knowledge of English or French "may not have a strong influence on the preservation of his culture, but it undoubtedly affects the ease with which he adapts and the speed of his adaptation to the new cultural environment."[23] The present study shows that in the foreign-born portion of the sample there was a negative relationship between knowledge of English or French and cultural identity. In the Canadian-born portion of the sample, on the other hand, there was a strong positive relationship between facility with Arabic and cultural identity. It seems that the relationship between language and cultural identity is complex.

SOME CONSEQUENCES OF CULTURAL IDENTITY

In the three previous sections, the discussion focused on the influence of different factors on cultural identity. In this section, the influence of cultural identity on certain attitudes and forms of behaviour will be considered. The discussion will necessarily be confined to a few questions investigated in the survey.

Table 29 shows the relationship between cultural identity and attitudes towards the preferred ethnic origin of the spouse of an Arab Canadian. For both the Canadian- and foreign-born portions of the sample, ethnicity makes a considerable difference in the structuring of attitudes towards endogamy. Considering the upper half of the table, 33% of the Canadian-born respondents who scored "high" on cultural identity and only eight per cent of those who had a "medium" score indicated preference for a mate from the Old Country. None of those who were "low" on cultural identity indicated a similar preference. Also, 67% of the Canadian-born respondents who scored "high" on cultural identity, 54% of those who had a "medium" score and only 26% of those with weak ethnic identity indicated a preference for an Arab-origin person brought up in Canada. The trend is reversed in the third category – the one which combines "to be married to a non-Arab Canadian" and "ethnicity of spouse is of no importance." Of those who were "low" on cultural identity, 74% endorsed the third category, compared to 39% of those who had a "medium" score and none of those who were "high" on ethnic identity making a similar preference.

The trends in the lower half of Table 29 are in the same direction as those reported above, although the percentages are different. Also, it should be noted that there was a stronger tendency among the foreign-born than the native-born respondents to indicate preference for someone from the Old Country. The latter group in general tended to favour "an Arab person brought up in Canada."

TABLE 29

Relationship Between Cultural Identity and the Preferred Ethnic Origin of The Spouse of an Arab-Canadian by Birthplace

Preferred Ethnic Origin of Spouse	Strength of Cultural Identity		
	Canadian-born Respondents		
	High	Medium	Low
From the old country	33%	8%	—
Canadian-born Arab	67	54	26
Ethnicity of no importance	—	39	74
Total %	100	100	100
(N)	(3)	(26)	(42)

	Foreign-born Respondents		
	High	Medium	Low
From the old country	58%	40%	24%
Canadian-born Arab	23	17	15
Ethnicity of no importance	19	43	60
Total %	100	100	100
(N)	(62)	(124)	(78)

The replies to two other questions were also analysed holding cultural identity constant. The questions were: "In your judgment, how do Canadians generally regard people of Arabic-speaking origin?" (Response categories: "very highly," "highly," "average," "below average," and "poorly,") and "In your judgment, how fair are the mass media (newspapers, radio, and TV) in their treatment of Arabic-speaking people?" (Response categories: "very fair," "somewhat fair," "somewhat unfair," and "very unfair.") The results are shown in Tables 30 and 31, respectively.

In Table 30, only two Canadian-born respondents are "high" on cultural identity and these will be omitted from the discussion. The upper half of the table shows no clear pattern of the relationship between cultural identity and perception of Canadians' evaluation of Arabs. In comparison, among the foreign-born respondents, there was a negative relationship between cultural identity and perception of Canadians' evaluation of Arabs. Thus, about 53% of the respondents classified as "high" on cultural identity, 41% of those classified as "medium" and only 30% of those classified as "low" on ethnic identity felt that Canadians evaluated Arabs below average or poorly. Contrariwise, of the respondents who had strong allegiance to the past, only five per cent felt

221

TABLE 30

Relationship Between Cultural Identity and Perception of Canadians' Evaluation of Arabic-Speaking People, by Birthplace

Perception of Canadians' Evaluation	Strength of Cultural Identity		
	Canadian-born Respondents		
	High	Medium	Low
Very highly or highly	50%	22%	10%
Average	50	48	70
Below average or poorly	—	30	20
Total %	100	100	100
(N)	(2)	(23)	(40)
	Foreign-born Respondents		
	High	Medium	Low
Very highly or highly	5%	22%	17%
Average	42	36	53
Below average or poorly	53	41	30
Total %	100	100	100
(N)	(55)	(121)	(70)

TABLE 31

Relationship Between Cultural Identity and Perception of Mass Media Treatment of Arabic-Speaking People, by Birthplace

Perception of Media Treatment	Strength of Cultural Identity		
	Canadian-born Respondents		
	High	Medium	Low
Generally fair	—	33%	23%
Generally unfair	100	67	78
Total %	100	100	100
(N)	(3)	(24)	(40)
	Foreign-born Respondents		
	High	Medium	Low
Generally fair	7%	17%	23%
Generally unfair	93	83	77
Total %	100	100	100
(N)	(58)	(124)	(77)

TABLE 32

Relationship Between the Immigrant's Cultural Identity and Residence Plans

	Strength of Cultural Identity		
Residence Plans	High	Medium	Low
Reside Permanently in Canada	32%	53%	55%
Return to the Old Country	41	25	15
Undecided	27	22	30
Total %	100%	100%	100%
(N)	(59)	(117)	(80)

that Canadians evaluated Arabs highly or very highly, compared to 22% of those classified as "medium" and 17% of the ones classified as "low" endorsing the same categories. These results suggest that the foreign-born respondents' perceptions of how Canadians evaluated them influenced and, in turn, were influenced by commitment to their ethnic group.

According to Table 31, of the Canadian and foreign-born respondents, the large majority felt that the mass media in general were unfair in their treatment of Arabs. Because of this, the respondents who were "high" on ethnic identity were only slightly more likely to attribute unfairness to the mass media than those whose ethnic identity was moderate or low. The important point is that ethnicity was not irrelevant to the way the respondents perceived fairness or unfairness on the part of the Canadian mass media.

To obtain some measure of their commitment to the adopted land, the immigrants in the sample were asked, "Do you plan to reside permanently in Canada, or do you intend to go back to the 'old country'?" The response categories provided were the same as those shown in Table 32. This table shows the relationship between cultural identity and residence plans. The data show that the tendency to return to the Old Country was strongest among the respondents with "high" cultural identity, weaker among those classified as "medium," and weakest among the respondents with "low" cultural identity. The pattern is reversed in relation to plans to reside permanently in Canada. The percentages associated with the "undecided" category do not reflect the same pattern as in the other two categories.

In addition to being related to such attitudes and beliefs as shown above, cultural identity was also related to those forms of behaviour examined in Table 26 (eating Arabic food, corresponding with relatives or friends in the Old Country, listening to Arabic music, etc.) The only exception was "visiting the old country" which, in the foreign-born portion of the sample, was unrelated to cultural identity. Thus, regardless of the direction of attitudes towards the country of origin, post-war immigrants would not hesitate to go back for a visit. There were variations in the strength of the relationship between cultural identity and each of the behaviours previously examined but the tendency to engage in these activities was always stronger among those with "high" rather than "low" cultural identity. This was as much true of the foreign-born as the Canadian-born portion of the sample.

SUMMARY

The Arab-Canadian cultural identity is a complex cluster of traits, attitudes and behaviours, varying by time and other factors. It is shaped by pressures from within and without the host society, and its strength is influenced by the size of the immigrant generation. A sense of Arab ethnicity was invigorated at the beginning of this century and after its mid-point, when the volume of Arab immigration to Canada was relatively large. During these two time periods in particular, emphasis was placed on linguistic tradition, which is a major component of cultural identity. Over the years, with varying degrees of effectiveness, the family and the community language school have played a role in language maintenance. But the transmission of language to the descendants of Arab immigrants has been far from complete and language loss has increased with each succeeding generation.

Whether or not an Arab Canadian knows Arabic, links with the ancestral heritage can be, and have been, maintained through such things as Arabic food, music, dances, mass media exposure, visits to the Old Country, and correspondence with friends and relatives left behind. Generally speaking, the immigrant generation was more likely to maintain links with the cultural heritage than its Canadian-born counterpart, but the differences tended to disappear in relation to three things: eating Arabic food, listening to Arabic music and visiting the Old Country.

In this study cultural identity was measured by a scale comprised of several items. The results show that the great divide is between the foreign-born and the Canadian-born generations and, within each group, cultural identity is related in a complex way to socio-economic status and other background characteristics. Further, there are behavioural and attitudinal differences between those who scored high and those who scored low on the cultural identity scale.

Arab cultural identity in Canada is not likely to be reduced to a uniform configuration among Arab Canadians, and we will probably always encounter patterned variations in its strength. Because of the relative youthfulness of the immigrant generation, coupled with its numerical dominance, Arab ethnicity will probably continue to be vigorously manifested, especially if immigration from the Arab world continues. Also, the federal government's policy of multiculturalism and the relatively tolerant public attitude towards ethnic differences, if continued, will probably enhance the development and preservation of ethnic identity without diminishing loyalty to Canada as the chosen land.

224

NOTES

1. For recent considerations of ethnicity in Canada, see Paul M. Migus, ed., *Sounds Canadian* (Toronto, 1975), particularly W.W. Isajiw, "The Process of Maintenance of Ethnic Identity," pp. 129-38; M. MacGuigan, "Constitutional Aspects of Ethnic Identity in Canada," pp. 123-28; and W. Kalbach, "Demographic Aspects of Ethnic Identity," pp. 139-46. See also Leo Driedger, ed., *The Canadian Ethnic Mosaic*, (Toronto, 1978), particularly Ch. 1.
2. Aziz Salloum, "Keep in Touch with the Old Land," *The Syrian-Lebanese Mercury*, Vol. 1, No. 5, January 15, 1937, p. 2.
3. *Ibid.*
4. *The Syrian-Lebanese Mercury*, Vol. II, No. 18, February 25, 1938, p. 2. The relevant article, entitled "New Arabic School founded in Brooklyn," provides a brief account of Toronto's first Arabic-language school.
5. Cf. W. Burton Hurd, *Ethnic Origin and Nativity of the Canadian People* (Ottawa, 1941), Table 18, p. 210, and Table 21, p. 211.
6. This figure represents 45% of 12,301.
7. The 1961 figure represents 67% of 19,374, while the 1971 figure was so reported in the census.
8. Abdelmoneim M. Khattab, "The Assimilation of Arab Muslims in Alberta," M.A. Thesis, Department of Sociology, University of Alberta, 1969, pp. 31-32.
9. *The Syrian-Lebanese Mercury*, Vol. 1, No. 1, September 7, 1936, p. 3.
10. Louise Sweet, "Reconstituting a Lebanese Village Society in a Canadian City," in Barbara C. Aswad, ed., *Arabic Speaking Communities in American Cities* (Staten Island, N.Y., 1974), p. 50.
11. *The Syrian-Lebanese Mercury*, Vol. I, No. 2, October 6, 1936, p. 2.
12. Many respondents felt that the 1973 Arab-Israeli war produced in the Arab-Canadian community a feeling of pride in ethnic identity and a stronger commitment to ethnicity. Since the survey was carried out in 1974, it is possible that the responses to survey questions were influenced by this new attitude. The likely effect of these events would have been to strengthen the links with the ancestral heritage.
13. *The Syrian-Lebanese Mercury*, Vol. 1, No. 8, April 15, 1937, p. 7.
14. In this study, ethnic identity was measured by a scale comprised of four items. The questions, in the Interview Schedule, which correspond to these items were: 1) Considering your closest friends in Canada, are any of them of Arab origin? (Response categories: "no," "yes, some of them," "yes, most of them," and "yes, all of them"); 2) Do you use the Arabic language at home? (Response categories: "no," "yes, but rarely," "yes, occasionally," "yes, frequently," and "yes, very frequently"); 3) Do you use the Arabic language outside your home? (Response categories: same as in "2" above); 4) Are you a member of any Arab-Canadian organizations? (Response categories: "no," "yes,

one organization," "yes, two organizations," "yes, three organizations," and "yes, four or more organizations") The scoring procedure followed was that of summated scales. Since the last three items had five response categories each, scores of 1, 2, 3, 4, and 5 were assigned. The first item, having only four response categories, received scores of 1, 2, 3, and 5. A value of 1 was assigned to the first response category, "no," and the succeeding values were assigned to the remaining categories in the order in which they appeared. The final score for each respondent was obtained by summating the values assigned him on each of the four items. The respondents receiving scores of 4-9 were classified as "low" on ethnic identity; those receiving scores of 10-13 were classified as "medium"; and the respondents receiving scores of 14-20 were classified as "high" on ethnic identity.

15. Harold B. Barclay, "An Arab Community in the Canadian Northwest: A Preliminary Discussion of the Lebanese Community in Lac La Biche, Alberta," *Anthropologica* N.S. 10 (1968), p. 155.
16. Sweet, *op. cit.*, p. 50.
17. *Ibid.*
18. *Ibid.*
19. *The Syrian-Lebanese Mercury*, Vol. 1, No. 5, January 15, 1937, p. 3.
20. Socio-economic factors are usually defined in terms of education, occupation, and income. In statistical analyses, these factors may be treated separately or else combined to form a socio-economic status (SES) index.
21. Barclay, *op. cit.*, pp. 154-155.
22. *Ibid.*, p. 154.
23. Department of Manpower and Immigration (Canada), *Immigration and Population Study: Three Years in Canada: First Report of the Longitudinal Survey on the Economic and Social Adaptation of Immigrants* (Green Paper on Immigration, Vol. 4) (Ottawa, 1974), p. 101.

TEN

Conclusions

Two waves of Arab immigration to Canada, coming from markedly different social and political contexts, define the origins of today's Arab-Canadian community. From the turn of the century on, this community has been in a state of flux. Neither in size, constitution, nor in general position in Canadian society has it remained static. Within this ethnic group, over time, religious, economic and social differences have actually increased. At present, the label Arab Canadian does not refer to a fixed religious affiliation, social or economic standing, occupation, Arab country of origin or distance from the immigrant generation. Rather, it encompasses a wide range of these characteristics and draws attention to the mixture of what some 80,000 Canadians of Arab origin have inherited from the past and what they have acquired in the Canadian experience; it is a dynamic ethnic identity in constant interaction with the new environment.

The contrasts between the turn of the century and post-war generations are significant. The former generation was composed of young, Christian, Syrian-Lebanese seeking freedom from poverty and the Ottoman Empire's oppressive colonial regime. Despite limited educational, linguistic and other resources, the pioneer immigrants dreamed of economic success in Canada. The post-war immigrants, on the other hand, consisted of a broader mixture of Christian groups and a substantial portion of non-Christians (Muslims and Druses). Now numerically dominant in the Arab-Canadian community, the post-war immigrants were highly qualified, both educationally and occupationally, and they came not only from Syria and Lebanon but also from many regions of the Arab world. Above all, their political socialization and ethnic identifications, acquired in a decolonized Arab world, were, on the average, markedly different from those of the early pioneers.

Typically, the immigrants who came in the first wave started their careers in low status occupations such as industrial labour or in self-employment as peddlers and vendors. Many of those who went into ped-

227

dling succeeded in expanding the enterprise, becoming prosperous and thereby experiencing, within a lifetime, a high degree of upward social mobility. With such an advantaged background, their children did not face as restricted a range of occupations as had the immigrant generation, thus as the Canadian-born generation entered the labour force, the early Arab-Canadian community began to experience further occupational differentiation. The post-war immigrants, in contrast, arrived in Canada with a considerably higher average level of formal education which made it possible for six out of 10 of them to start their careers in professional and other white collar occupations; others went into wage employment as blue collar or service workers; and a smaller number entered self-employment in a variety of fields. This resulted in a dispersal of the Arab ethnic group throughout the Canadian occupational structure.

Contemporary Canadian society, in contrast to Canada at the turn of the century, places far more emphasis on formal education as a prerequisite for advancement in the occupational structure. Hence, the minority of post-war Arab immigrants whose formal schooling is limited face quite different conditions than did their turn-of-the-century counterparts, who were also educationally disadvantaged. While both waves of immigrants probably had similarly high levels of aspiration for personal advancement, the opportunities for dramatic upward mobility are far less for the recent immigrant with a low educational background. Similarly, given that family background influences the mobility opportunities of children, the second generation of this specific disadvantaged group of post-war immigrants may not only be less advantaged in comparison with the children of better educated immigrants, but, as well, they may also be disadvantaged compared to the second generation Arab Canadians of some 50 years ago. Accordingly, their acculturation experience may evolve differently. Research is needed to explore the implications of this for the character of the Arab-Canadian community of the future.

Overall, the economic adaptation of Arab immigrants and their descendants, from the early days of immigration to the present, has been successful. Arab Canadians have contributed significantly to the development of this country; this is as much true of the early peddlers as of the skilled labourers, business people, professionals and semi-professionals of today. The names of Arab Canadians who have achieved prominence in their respective occupations are to be found in virtually all fields. In return, Canada has contributed towards the realization of what was a dream for many Arab Canadians or their immigrant forebears: economic well-being and financial security.

The economic adaptation of immigrants, particularly those from non-Western countries, usually demands social and cultural adaptation. The degree to which differences are narrowed or eliminated can be a matter for both individual and group concern. In the early part of this century, the analogy of a "melting pot" was commonly used to characterize what appeared to be the on-going process of assimilation of vast numbers of immigrants into American society. Influenced by this analogy, social scientists and lay people alike predicted the rapid passing of ethnic groups and any traces of ethnicity. But the course of history proved otherwise. There has been a recent resurgence of ethnicity in North American society and this has led to questioning of the adequacy of the original evidence on which the "melting pot" ideology was based. In Canada, as in the United States, where power relationships between the host and the immigrant population are asymmetrical, assimilation in practice involves immigrant conversion, in varying degrees, to the way of life of the dominant group. But it need not mean the total absorption of immigrants or the total loss of contact with their past.

Arab Canadians have been subject to two sets of social forces: one encouraging acculturation, or even assimilation, into the larger society, and the other encouraging group maintenance. Each of these tendencies will be considered briefly.

With reference to acculturative change, it may be noted that the Canadian socio-cultural system has been not only an effective but also an unavoidable source of change. It is effective because it is highly organized, overwhelming in its totality, and also because it is the socio-cultural system of the dominant group. It is unavoidable because the Arab-Canadian community, from the start, has been urban, desegregated, relatively small, spread across the country, and hence vulnerable. Moreover, many of the post-war Arab immigrants were presocialized into the Western way of life, in that they knew English and/or French and were familiar with Western culture and institutions before entry into Canada.

For the Canadian-born generations, there is the added influence of the Canadian school system, which is one of the most effective mechanisms of acculturative change. Clearly, at all times, the second generation Arab Canadian, compared to the first, has gone farther on the acculturation-assimilation continuum. There are differences within the second generation, but the differences between generations have been consistently wide.

A second source of acculturative change is internal; that is, subject to individual or group control. Arab immigrants have been movitated to learn the new language (English and/or French) and adapt, as well as possible, to the new environment. Part of this motivation is economic, of course, but the larger part seems to be based on personal inclinations and preferences. Generally speaking, Arab immigrants have developed positive attitudes towards Canada, particularly the Canadian political system and many aspects of social and cultural organization. They tend to take out naturalization papers as soon as they become eligible, and to regard Canada as home. Also, the arrival of the second generation tends to strengthen the immigrants' allegiance to the adopted land. Perhaps because of these factors, the ethnic institutions which the Arab immigrants have established have not been insular but rather supportive of adaptive change.

It is clear that Arab immigrants have had to integrate themselves into the new system not only at the socio-economic but also at the cognitive and affective levels. In the process, they have established supportive kin and friendship networks, supplanting many of those left behind, and they have discarded many of the norms and modes of behaviour which appeared to be detrimental to their well-being in the new Canadian environment. A large majority of Arab Canadians are now established in a relatively stable interrelationship with their larger community, having carved a secure niche for themselves in what used to be an unfamiliar setting.

For Arab Canadians, living in Canada has meant the adoption of many Canadian norms and values. To be sure, they have also retained, in varying degrees, their ethnic identity and elements of the cultural heritage; but the demands of the new socio-cultural system have necessitated the development of new orientations and modes of behaviour. As a consequence, they now have in common the experience of having abandoned, or even rejected, some of the ways of the Old Country, in the process of embracing the ways of the new land. This process appears to intensify with each succeeding generation and with economic advancement.

At the same time, there are also pressures towards group maintenance, reflected in part in a moderate degree of institutional development within the Arab-Canadian community. The ethnic institutions developed include churches, mosques, secular associations, and newspapers. In addition, the Arab-Canadian family has played a role in maintaining aspects of the ancestral heritage. In all other spheres, Arab Canadians have been, and still are, integrated with the institutions of the larger society.

The development of religious institutions was given first priority by the early and post-war immigrants in order to preserve the traditions of Eastern Christianity and Islam. Once the second generation increased in number and advanced in age, language maintenance and the preservation of cultural traditions became a concern and language schools were often developed through churches and mosques. Secular associations were established, partly to transcend the confining boundaries of religious institutions and partly to respond to challenges faced by the Arab-Canadian community at large. As adaptive mechanisms, these associations have been an important factor in group maintenance and social control, as well as in the sharing of aspects of group culture with the larger Canadian society.

The political dimension of group maintenance became more salient in the post-war period, and some organizations consider this to be the major thrust of their programmes. Two basic concerns are involved here: presenting and explaining the Arab viewpoint, which they often feel to be either ignored or misrepresented on various social, economic and political matters, such as the Palestine question and the Arab-Israeli conflict, the energy crisis, the civil war in Lebanon, and economic development needs of the Arab States; and defending the Arab-Canadian community and protecting its integrity against discriminatory treatment, bias and prejudice in various institutional spheres, particularly the mass media. As a partial response to these problems, Arab-Canadian organizations have tended to support the publication of their own multi-language (Arabic, English and French) periodicals.

The last point to be made under group maintenance concerns the family. The Arab-Canadian family, in general, provides an important socio-cultural link with the ancestral heritage. Arabic food, music, songs, traditions, values, cultural artifacts, and direct or indirect contact with the Old Country are often part of the Arab-Canadian family experience. The role of the Arab-Canadian family in group maintenance continues to be important, in view of the fact that a large majority of Arab Canadians are either immigrants themselves or else second generation Canadians; further, a large number of recent immigrants came as intact family units. The reported differences among Canadians of Arab origin in the degree of tradition preserved in family life appear to be influenced by such factors as parents' education, occupation, religion and distance from the immigrant experience.

The Arab-Canadian ethnic identity has been nourished by the institutions developed by the group, and more specifically by exposure to the linguistic and cultural heritage. An undetermined number of Canadians of Arab origin have probably lost contact with the past, but the majority are aware and proud of their ethnic origins. While they are in agreement that they and their ancestral heritage ought to be respected and treated fairly in the Canadian media and the institutions of the larger society, there are important differences in the pattern of ethnic concerns.

For example, some Arab Canadians have kept alive, in varying degrees, the narrower symbols of ethnic identity such as aspects of the expressive domain of Arab culture, the Eastern religion to which they belong, and memories of the country of origin or even a specific village. Other Arab Canadians, coming mostly from the ranks of post-war immigrants, have expressed broader symbols of ethnicity rooted in a pan-Arab identity. For this group, the commonalities and interests that bind the inhabitants of the entire Arab world, be they social, cultural or political, are a main component of Arab-Canadian ethnicity. Hence, the heavy emphasis which this group places on political events and developments in the Middle East, particularly the Arab-Israeli conflict. Given the complexity and pluralism of the Arab ethnic group in Canada, there are forms of ethnic identification within it which fall on a continuum ranging from the narrow to the broad. The development, possible transformation or resurgence of these identifications from generation to generation constitutes a fruitful area for future research.

231

The Arab-Canadian community today is radically different from the parent community which emerged at the turn of this century. Its evolution has been influenced by the early pioneers and their descendants, as well as the large wave of post-war Arab immigrants, each in their own way leaving an indelible mark. Its future position in Canada will bear the stamp of the new second and subsequent generations of Canadians of Arab origin who are now reaching maturity. It will be for them to ensure that the olive branch will remain an integral graft on the Canadian family tree.

Appendix

DEPARTMENT OF SOCIOLOGY
TELEPHONE (403) 432-5234

THE UNIVERSITY OF ALBERTA
EDMONTON, CANADA
T6G 2E1

SURVEY OF ARABIC-SPEAKING COMMUNITIES
IN CANADA

This questionnaire is part of a national study of Arabic-speaking communities in Canada. The study is supported by a research grant from the Department of the Secretary of State, Ottawa, under the Ethnic Histories Project.

The purpose of the study is to investigate the socio-economic development and adjustment of Arabic-speaking Canadians from the early days of immigration to the present time, as well as the adjustive role which their social, cultural and religious organizations play in Canadian society.

All information obtained in this study will be treated confidentially, and the published results will maintain the anonymity of the respondents.

Your cooperation would be most appreciated.

Yours sincerely,

Baha Abu-Laban, Ph.D.
Professor of Sociology
and Project Director

Interviewer _____   Date _____

Interview Number _____   Time _____

233

SURVEY OF ARABIC-SPEAKING COMMUNITIES
IN CANADA

1. Current place of residence: _____ _____

City or town   Province

2. Place of birth: _____ _____

City or town   Province or country

IF YOU WERE BORN OUTSIDE OF CANADA:

2.1 How did you come to Canada?

____(1) As a sponsored immigrant   ____(3) As a student

____(2) As an independent immigrant ____(4) As a visitor

3. What is the Arab country of your (or, if Canadian-born, your father's) origin? (check one)

____(1) Lebanon   ____(4) Jordan

____(2) Syria   ____(5) Egypt

____(3) Palestine   ____(6) Other (What? _____)

4. Citizenship: (check one)

____(1) Canadian by birth   ____(5) Palestinian

____(2) Naturalized Canadian   ____(6) Jordanian

____(3) Lebanese   ____(7) Egyptian

____(4) Syrian   ____(8) Other (What? _____)

   4.1 IF YOU ARE A NATURALIZED CANADIAN CITIZEN OR PLAN TO BECOME ONE, please give the reason(s) for this:

   1._____

   2._____

   3._____

   4.2 IF YOU HAVE A LANDED IMMIGRANT STATUS, BUT YOU ARE UNSURE ABOUT BECOMING A CANADIAN CITIZEN, OR DO NOT PLAN TO BECOME ONE, please give the reasons for this:

   1._____

   2._____

   3._____

5. How many years of formal education have you had? (check one)

____(1) 6 years or less   ____(4) 13-15 years

____(2) 7-9 years   ____(5) 16 years or more

____(3) 10-12 years

6. Do you hold any diplomas or university degrees? (check one)

____(1) Yes ____(2) No

6.1 If "Yes," please specify:

Diploma or Degree	Institution	Year	Specialty Area

7. How well do you know the Arabic, English and French languages? (check one in each column)

I. ARABIC	II. ENGLISH	III. FRENCH
____(1) Very well	____(1) Very well	____(1) Very well
____(2) Well	____(2) Well	____(2) Well
____(3) Not so well	____(3) Not so well	____(3) Not so well
____(4) Very little	____(4) Very little	____(3) Very little
____(5) Not at all	____(5) Not at all	____(5) Not at all

8. Have you ever returned to visit the Arab country from which you (or your parents) came? (check one)

____(1) No   ____(4) Yes, three times

____(2) Yes, once   ____(5) Yes, four times

____(3) Yes, twice   ____(6) Yes, five or more times

8.1 If "Yes," what year did you visit the "old country" last?

_____

8.2 If "No," are you planning to visit the "old country" in the near future? (check one)

____(1) Yes   ____(2) No

9. Do you correspond with relatives or friends in the "old country"? (check one)

____(1) No   ____(4) Yes, frequently

____(2) Yes, but rarely   ____(5) Yes, very frequently

____(3) Yes, occasionally

10. Have you ever assisted or sponsored any relatives or friends from the "old country" to immigrate to Canada? (check one)

____(1) No   ____(3) Yes, three of four times

____(2) Yes, once or twice   ____(4) Yes, five or more times

11. Do you send money to relatives in the "old country"?

____(1) No   ____(3) Yes, occasionally

____(2) Yes, but rarely   ____(4) Yes, regularly

12. Considering your closest friends in Canada, are any of them of Arab origin? (check one)

___(1) No   ___(3) Yes, most of them

___(2) Yes, some of them   ___(4) Yes, all of them

13. Do you read the Arabic press (newspapers, magazines and/or books)? (check one)

___(1) No   ___(4) Yes, frequently

___(2) Yes, but rarely   ___(5) Yes, very frequently

___(3) Yes, occasionally

14. Do you listen to Arabic music and songs? (check one)

___(1) No   ___(4) Yes, frequently

___(2) Yes, but rarely   ___(5) Yes, very frequently

___(3) Yes, occasionally

15. Do you listen to Arabic broadcasts? (check one)

___(1) No   ___(4) Yes, frequently

___(2) Yes, but rarely   ___(5) Yes, very frequently

___(3) Yes, occasionally

16. Do you watch Arabic films? (check one)

___(1) No   ___(4) Yes, frequently

___(2) Yes, but rarely   ___(5) Yes, very frequently

___(3) Yes, occasionally

17. Do you use the Arabic language at home? (check one)

___(1) No   ___(4) Yes, frequently

___(2) Yes, but rarely   ___(5) Yes, very frequently

___(3) Yes, occasionally

18. Do you use the Arabic language outside your home? (check one)

___(1) No   ___(4) Yes, frequently

___(2) Yes, but rarely   ___(5) Yes, very frequently

___(3) Yes, occasionally

19. Do you eat Arabic food at your home? (check one)

___(1) No   ___(4) Yes, frequently

___(2) Yes, but rarely   ___(5) Yes, very frequently

___(3) Yes, occasionally

20. Are you a member of any Arab-Canadian organizations? (check one)

___(1) No   ___(2) Yes

21. Are you a member of any social, religious, political, professional organizations or unions? (check one)

___(1) No   ___(2) Yes

22. IF YES TO QUESTION 20 OR QUESTION 21: In the appropriate columns below, please list all such organizations and, for each one, give additional information as requested.

Name of Organization	Length of membership (in years)	Are you (or were you) a member of any committees? (Yes or No)	What offices, if any, do you (or did you) hold in the organization? What year(s)?
ARAB-CANADIAN ORGANIZATIONS			
OTHER ORGANIZATIONS			

QUESTIONS 23 THROUGH 34 APPLY TO THOSE WHO WERE BORN OUTSIDE OF CANADA. FOR CANADIAN-BORN RESPONDENTS, PLEASE SKIP TO QUESTION 35, page 7.

23. For how long have you been living in Canada? (check one)

____(1) 5 years or less   ____(4) 21-30 years

____(2) 6-10 years   ____(5) 31 years and over

____(3) 11-20 years

24. How old were you when you came to Canada? (check one)

____(1) 14 years or less   ____(4) 36-50 years

237

____(2) 15-20 years   ____(5) 51-65 years

____(3) 21-35 years   ____(6) 66 years and over

25. For what reason(s) did you come to Canada? (List as many as may apply)

_____

_____

_____

26. Before you came to Canada, did you consider your financial situation in the "old country" to be:

____(1) Below average   ____(3) Above average

____(2) Average   ____(4) Wealthy

27. To which city or town did you go when you first came to Canada?

_____   _____

City or town   Province

27.1 Why did you go there?

_____

_____

28. What kind of work did you do when you came to Canada? _____

Job or occupation

29. From which of the following sources, if any, did you receive help at the time of arrival in Canada? (check as many as may apply)

____(1) Relatives in Canada   ____(4) Arab organizations in Canada

____(2) Arab friends in Canada   ____(5) Other (specify): _____

____(3) Persons from my hometown in Canada

     ____(6) None of the above

29.1 What kinds of help did you receive?

_____

_____

30. Do you plan to reside permanently in Canada, or do you intend to go back to the "old country"? (check one)

____(1) Reside permanently in Canada   ____(2) Go back to the "old country"

     ____(3) Undecided

WHY? _____

_____

APPENDIX

31. What three things do you like most about the Canadian way of life?
    1. _____
    2. _____
    3. _____

32. What three things do you like least about the Canadian way of life?
    1. _____
    2. _____
    3. _____

33. What three things do you like most about the way of life in the country of your origin?
    1. _____
    2. _____
    3. _____

34. What three things do you like least about the way of life in the country of your origin?
    1. _____
    2. _____
    3. _____

35. What would you say is better for a person of Arabic-speaking origin in Canada: (check one)
    ____(1) To be married to someone from the "old country"
    ____(2) To be married to an Arab person brought up in Canada
    ____(3) To be married to a non-Arab Canadian, or
    ____(4) Ethnicity of spouse is of no importance
    WHY? _____
    _____

36. If you were asked, what kind of advice would you give Arab immigrants in order for them to do well in Canada?
    _____
    _____
    _____

37. In your judgment, how do Canadians generally regard people of Arabic-speaking origin? (check one)
    ____(1) Very highly   ____(4) Below average

239

____(2) Highly   ____(5) Poorly

____(3) Average

38. In your judgment, how fair are the mass media (newspapers, radio, and TV) in their treatment of Arabic-speaking people? (check one)

____(1) Very fair   ____(3) Somewhat unfair

____(2) Somewhat fair   ____(4) Very unfair

39. Have you ever faced any discrimination or ill treatment because of your national or ethnic origin? (check one)

____(1) No   ____(3) Yes, sometimes

____(2) Yes, but rarely   ____(4) Yes, often

39.1 If "Yes," in what areas have you faced discrimination or ill treatment?

_____

_____

_____

_____

40. In general, do you feel that the unsettled political situation in the Arab world, and the Arab-Israeli conflict, have created special problems for the Arab-Canadians? (check one)

____(1) No   ____(4) Yes

40.1 If "Yes," what are these problems?

_____

_____

_____

_____

41. In general, do you feel that the unsettled political situation in the Arab world, and the Arab-Israeli conflict, have created special problems for you personally? (check one)

____(1) No   ____(2) Yes

41.1 If "Yes," What are these problems?

_____

_____

_____

_____

42. It is sometimes said that success in business depends heavily on good relations with influential Jewish businessmen.
Do you agree or disagree with this? Why?

_____

_____

_____

_____

BACKGROUND DATA

43. Sex: ___(1) Male   ___(2) Female

44. Age:

    ___(1) 20 years or less   ___(4) 41-50 years

    ___(2) 21-30 years   ___(5) 51-65 years

    ___(3) 31-40 years   ___(6) 66 years and over

45. What is (or was) your father's occupation? (Please be specific)

_____

46. What is your present occupation? (Please be specific) (If retired, what was your occupation before retirement?)

_____

47. How long have you been in this occupation? _____years

48. In which of the following broad income categories did your total family yearly income from all sources fall last year? (check one)

    ___(1) $4,999 or less   ___(3) $10,000-19,999

    ___(2) $5,000-9,999   ___(4) $20,00 or more

49. In what religion were you raised? (check one)

    ___(1) Maronite   ___(5) Coptic

    ___(2) Catholic   ___(6) Moslem

    ___(3) Greek Orthodox   ___(7) Druse

    ___(4) Protestant   ___(8) Other (What? _____)

50. Marital status: (check one)

    ___(1) Single   ___(4) Divorced

    ___(2) Married   ___(5) Separated

    ___(3) Widowed   ___(6) Other (What? _____)

IF MARRIED:

50.1 Where was your spouse (wife/husband) born? (check one)

____(1) In an Arab country

____(2) In Canada, of Arab background

____(3) In Canada, of non-Arab background

____(4) Other (Where? _____)

50.2 In what religion was your spouse raised? (check one)

____(1) Maronite   ____(5) Coptic

____(2) Catholic   ____(6) Moslem

____(3) Greek Orthodox   ____(7) Druse

____(4) Protestant   ____(8) Other (what? _____)

50.3 Is your spouse employed? (check one)

____(1) No

____(2) Yes (What is her/his occupation? _____)

50.4 How many children, if any, do you have? (please circle one number)

0   1   2   3   4   5   6   7   8   9 or more

Bibliography

Abu-Laban, Baha. "The Arab-Canadian Community," in Elaine C. Hagopian and Ann Paden, eds., *The Arab Americans: Studies in Assimilation.* Wilmette, Ill.: Medina University Press International, 1969, 18-36.

_____. "Social Change and Local Politics in Sidon, Lebanon," *Journal of Developing Areas*, 5 (1970), 27-42.

_____. "The Adolescent Peer Group in Cross Cultural Perspective," *Canadian Review of Sociology and Anthropology*, 7 (1970), 201-211.

_____. "The Arab Community in the Canadian Mosaic," *Rikka*, 3 (1976), 30-31.

_____. "Middle East Groups," in *The Canadian Family Tree*, Revised Edition. Ottawa: Information Canada, 1979.

Abu-Laban, Baha and Sharon McIrvin Abu-Laban. "Educational Development," in Abdeen Jabara and Janice Terry, eds., *The Arab World: From Nationalism to Revolution.* Wilmette, Ill.: Medina University Press International, 1971, 32-54.

_____. "Education and Development in the Arab World," *Journal of Developing Areas*, 10 (1976), 285-304.

Abu-Laban, Baha and Faith T. Zeadey, eds. *Arabs in America: Myths and Realities.* Wilmette, Ill.: Medina University Press International, 1975.

Abu-Laban, Sharon McIrvin. "Stereotypes of Middle East Peoples: An Analysis of Church School Curricula," in Baha Abu-Laban and Faith T. Zeadey, eds., *Arabs in America: Myths and Realities.* Wilmette, Ill.: Medina University Press International, 1975, 149-69.

Abu-Laban, Sharon and Baha Abu-Laban. "Women and the Aged as Minority Groups: A Critique," *Canadian Review of Sociology and Anthropology*, 13 (1976), 103-116.

Abu-Lughod, Ibrahim. *Arab Rediscovery of Europe.* Princeton, N.J.: Princeton University Press, 1963.

Abu-Lughod, Ibrahim and Baha Abu-Laban, eds. *Settler Regimes in Africa and the Arab World.* Wilmette, Ill.: Medina University Press International, 1974.

Abu-Lughod, Janet. *Cairo: Thousand and One Years of the City Victorious.* Princeton: Princeton University Press, 1971.

———. "Cairo: Perspective and Prospectus," in L. Carl Brown, ed., *From Medina to Metropolis: Heritage and Change in the Near Eastern City.* Princeton: Darwin Press, 1973, 95-113.

Adachi, Ken. *The Enemy That Never Was: A History of the Japanese Canadians.* Toronto: McClelland and Stewart Limited, 1976.

Al-Hamdani, Muwaffak and Baha Abu-Laban. "Game Involvement and Sex Role Socialization in Arab Children," *International Journal of Comparative Sociology*, 12 (1971), 182-91.

Al-Qazzaz, Ayad. *Women in the Middle East and North Africa.* Austin: University of Texas Press, 1977.

Alvi, Sajida. "Options Beyond the Home," *Islam Canada*, 2 (October 1973), pp. 9 and 4.

Anderson, Grace M. and David Higgs. *A Future to Inherit: The Portuguese Communities of Canada.* Toronto: McClelland and Stewart, 1976.

Antiochian Orthodox Christian Archdiocese of New York and All North America. *Twenty-Ninth Annual Convention.* Montreal, August 19-25, 1974.

Antonius, George. *The Arab Awakening.* London: Hamish Hamilton, 1938.

Arab-Canadian Delegates. "Brief No. 16." Presented to Heritage Ontario, June 2-4, 1972.

Aruri, Naseer. "The Arab-American Community of Springfield, Massachusetts," in Elaine C. Hagopian and Ann Paden, eds., *The Arab Americans: Studies in Assimilation.* Wilmette, Ill.: Medina University Press International, 1969, 50-66.

Aswad, Barbara C., ed. *Arabic Speaking Communities in American Cities.* Staten Island, N.Y.: Center for Migration Studies and Association of Arab-American University Graduates, 1974.

Atalla, Theophile. "People of Lebanese Origin." *Encyclopedia Canadiana*, Vol. 6. Toronto: Grolier of Canada Limited, 1968, 108-109.

Atiyah, Edward. *The Arabs.* Revised Edition. Harmondsworth, Middlesex: Penguin, 1958.

Avery, Donald. "Canadian Immigration Policy and the 'Foreign' Navvy: 1896-1914," in Jay Atherton, ed., *Historical Papers 1972.* Montreal: The Canadian Historical Association, 1972, 135-56.

Awan, Sadiq Noor Alam. *The People of Pakistani Origin in Canada.* Ottawa-Hull: Canada Pakistan Association, 1976.

Baker, Peter. *Memoirs of an Arctic Arab.* Yellowknife, N.W.T.: Yellowknife Publishing Co., 1976.

Barclay, Harold. "An Arab Community in the Canadian Northwest: A

Preliminary Discussion of the Lebanese Community in Lac La Biche, Alberta," *Anthropologica* N.S., 10 (1968), 143-56.

Barclay, Harold. "The Perpetuation of Muslim Tradition in the Canadian North," *Muslim World*, 59 (1969), 64-73.

____. "A Lebanese Community in Lac La Biche, Alberta," in Jean Leonard Elliott, ed., *Minority Canadians: Immigrant Groups.* Scarborough: Prentice-Hall of Canada, 1971, 66-83.

____. "The Lebanese Muslim Family," in K. Ishwaran, ed., *The Canadian Family.* Revised Edition. Toronto: Holt, Rinehart and Winston of Canada, Limited, 1976, 92-104.

Becker, Jane. "The Scramble for Arab Money," *Executive*, September, 1974, 31-36.

Belkaoui, Janice Monti. "Image Creation in the Prestige Press: A Case Study of Arab and Israeli Images." M.A. Thesis, Department of Sociology and Anthropology, Carleton University, 1976.

Berry, John W., Rudolf Kalin and Donald M. Taylor. *Multiculturalism and Ethnic Attitudes in Canada.* Ottawa: Supply and Services Canada, 1977.

Blishen, Bernard R. "A Socio-Economic Index of Occupations," *Canadian Review of Sociology and Anthropology*, 4 (1967), 41-53.

Blood, Robert O. and Donald M. Wolfe. *Husbands and Wives.* Glencoe: The Free Press, 1960.

Bonds, Joy, *et al. Our Roots are Still Alive: The Story of the Palestinian People.* San Francisco: Peoples Press, 1977.

Bradwin, Edmund. *The Bunkhouse Man.* Toronto: University of Toronto Press, 1972. (The original edition of this work appeared in 1928.)

Breton, Raymond. "Institutional Completeness of Ethnic Communities and the Personal Relations of Immigrants," *American Journal of Sociology*, 70 (1964), 193-205.

Brockelmann, Carl, trans. Joel Carmichael and Moshe Perlman. *History of the Islamic Peoples.* New York: Capricorn Books, 1960.

Burnet, Jean. *Next-Year Country: A Study of Rural Social Organization in Alberta.* Toronto: University of Toronto Press, 1951.

Canada. Citizenship Branch. "Middle East Groups," in M. Storey and B. Pearson, eds., *The Canadian Family Tree.* Ottawa: Citizenship Branch, 1967, 237-43.

____. Manpower and Immigration. *Immigration and Population Study: Immigration Policy Perspectives.* (Green Paper on Immigration, Vol. 1) Ottawa: Manpower and Immigration, 1974.

____. Manpower and Immigration. *The Immigration Program.* (Green Paper on Immigration, Vol. 2) Ottawa: Manpower and Immigration, 1974.

____. Manpower and Immigration. *Immigration and Population Study: Immigration and Popula-*

tion Statistics. (Green Paper on Immigration, Vol. 3) Ottawa: Manpower and Immigration, 1974.

———. Manpower and Immigration. *Immigration and Population Study: Three Years in Canada: First Report of the Longitudinal Survey on the Economic and Social Adaptation of Immigrants.* (Green Paper on Immigration, Vol. 4) Ottawa: Manpower and Immigration, 1974.

Canadian Arab Friendship Association of Edmonton. *A Salute to the Pioneers of Northern Alberta.* Edmonton: Canadian Arab Friendship Association, 1973.

Canadian Society of Muslims. "Report: On the Image of Islam in School Textbooks in the Province of Ontario, Canada," unpublished manuscript, n.d.

"Canadians of Syrian and Armenian Origins," *Citizen*, Vol. 6, No. 5 (December 1960), 1-5.

Clarke, Alfred C. "An Examination of Residential Propinquity as a Factor in Mate Selection," *American Sociological Review*, 17 (1952), 17-22.

Corbett, David C. *Canada's Immigration Policy: A Critique.* Toronto: University of Toronto Press, 1957.

Creighton, Donald. *A History of Canada.* Revised Edition. Boston: Houghton Mifflin, 1958.

Cresswell, Robert. "Lineage Endogamy among Maronite Mountaineers," in J.G. Peristiany, ed., *Mediterranean Family Structure.* Cambridge: Cambridge University Press, 1976, 101-114.

Delvoie, L.A. "Growth in Economic Relations of Canada and the Arab World," *International Perspectives*, November/December(1976), 29-33.

Driedger, Leo, ed. *The Canadian Ethnic Mosaic: A Quest for Identity.* Toronto: McClelland and Stewart Limited, 1978.

El-Idd, Jose. *Jowlat fi Al-'Alam Al-Jadid.* (Travels in the New World) Buenos Aires: Rustom, 1959. (Arabic)

Elkholy, Abdo A. *The Arab Moslems in the United States.* New Haven: College and University Press, 1966.

Epp, Frank H. *Whose Land is Palestine?* Grand Rapids, Mich.: William B. Eerdmans Publishing Company, 1970.

———. *The Palestinians: Portrait of a People in Conflict.* Toronto: McClelland and Stewart Limited, 1976.

Fathi, Asghar. "Mass Media and a Moslem Immigrant Community in Canada," *Anthropologica* N.S., 15 (1973), 201-30.

———. "The Arab Moslem Community in the Prairie City," *Canadian Ethnic Studies* (Third Bibliographical Issue), 5 (1976), 409-426.

Fathi, Asghar and B. Hunter Smeaton. "Arabic-Canadian Periodical Publications," *Canadian Ethnic Studies* (Third Bibliographical Issue), Vol. 5, No. 1-2, 1976, 1-4.

Ferguson, Edith. *Immigrants in Canada.* Toronto: Guidance Centre, Faculty of Education, University of Toronto, 1974.

246

Forrest, A.C. *The Unholy Land.* Toronto: McClelland and Stewart Limited, 1972.

Gibran, Gibran Kahlil. *Collection of Complete Works, Vol. III.* Beirut: Sader Press, 1955.

Goode, William J. *World Revolution and Family Patterns.* New York: Fress Press of Glencoe, 1963.

Gordon, Milton M. *Assimilation in American Life.* New York: Oxford University Press, 1964.

Haavio-Mannila, Elaine. "Convergences between East and West: Tradition and Modernity in Sex Roles in Sweden, Finland, and the Soviet Union," in Martha T. Shuch Mednick, Sandra Schwartz Tangri, and Lois Wladis Hoffman, eds., *Women and Achievement: Social and Motivational Analyses.* New York: Halsted Press, 1975, 71-84.

Hagopian, Elaine C. "The Institutional Development of the Arab-American Community of Boston," in Elaine C. Hagopian and Ann Paden, eds., *The Arab Americans: Studies in Assimilation.* Wilmette, Ill.: Medina University Press International, 1969, 67-83.

Hagopian, Elaine C. and Ann Peden, eds. *The Arab Americans: Studies in Assimilation.* Wilmette, Ill.: Medina University Press International, 1961.

Haiek, Joseph R., ed. *The American Arabic Speaking Community: 1974 Almanac.* Los Angeles: The News Circle, 1974.

Hawkins, Freda. *Canada and Immigration, Public Policy and Public Concern.* Montreal: McGill-Queen's University Press, 1972.

Hayani, Huda. "Arab Women in Canada," *Arab Dawn*, Vol. 4, No. 4 (June, 1972), 9-10.

Hayani, Ibrahim. "The Petrodollar Problem: Adjusting to Change," *Canadian Business*, (March, 1975).

____. "Investment Opportunities in Iraq," *Canadian Business*, (September, 1975), 34, 36 and 38.

____. "Saudi Arabia – The Land of Oil and Money," *Canadian Business*, (November, 1975), 28-29.

____. "How to do Business in the Middle East . . .," *Foreign Affairs*, (March, 1977), 53-66.

Helal, Joseph. "Resumé of the History of the Syrian Canadian Association – Montreal," in Elias Karam, ed., *The Syrian Canadian National Review.* Ottawa: The Syrian Canadian National Committee of St. Elijah's Church Society, 1935, 38-39.

Hitti, Philip K. *The Syrians in America.* New York: George H. Doran Company, 1924.

____. *The Arabs: A Short History.* Fourth Edition. London: Macmillan & Co. Limited, 1965.

____. *Lebanon in History, from the Earliest Times to the Present.* Third Edition. London: Macmillan, 1967.

____. *History of the Arabs.* Tenth Edition. London: The Macmillan Press Limited, 1970.

House of Commons Debates. December 17, 1945.

Hurd, W. Burton. *Ethnic Origin and Nativity of the Canadian People.*

Ottawa: Dominion Bureau of Statistics, 1941.

Isaacs, Harold R. *Idols of the Tribe: Group Identity and Political Change.* New York: Harper and Row, Publishers, 1975.

Isajiw, Wsevolod. "The Process of Maintenance of Ethnic Identity," in Paul M. Migus, ed., *Sounds Canadian.* Toronto: Peter Martin Associates Limited, 1975, 129-38.

_____. ed. *Identities: The Impact of Ethnicity on Canadian Society.* Toronto: Peter Martin Associates Limited, 1977.

Ismael, Tareq Y. *Government and Politics of the Contemporary Middle East.* Homewood, Ill.: The Dorsey Press, 1970.

_____. *Canada and the Middle East.* Toronto: Canadian Institute of International Affairs (*Behind the Headlines*, Vol. 32, No. 5), December, 1973.

_____. *The Arab Left.* Syracuse: Syracuse University Press, 1976.

Ismael, Jacqueline S. and Tareq Y. Ismael. "The Arab Americans and the Middle East," *Middle East Journal*, 30 (1976), 390-405.

Johnson, Gilbert. "The Syrians in Western Canada," *Saskatchewan History*, 12 (1959), 31-32.

Kalbach, Warren E. *The Impact of Immigration on Canada's Population.* Ottawa: Dominion Bureau of Statistics, 1970.

_____. "Demographic Aspects of Ethnic Identity," in Paul M. Migus, ed., *Sounds Canadian.* Toronto: Peter Martin Associates Limited, 1975, 139-46.

Karam, Elias, ed. *The Syrian Canadian National Review.* Ottawa: The Syrian Canadian National Committee of St. Elijah's Church Society, 1935.

_____. "Syrian Immigration to Canada," in Elias Karam, ed., *The Syrian Canadian National Review.* Ottawa: The Syrian Canadian National Committee of St. Elijah's Church Society, 1935, 19-37.

Kayal, Philip M. "Religion and Assimilation: Catholic 'Syrians' in America," *International Migration Review*, 7 (1973), 409-426.

Kayal, Philip M. and Joseph M. Kayal. *The Syrian-Lebanese in America.* Boston: Twayne Publishers, 1975.

Kenny, L.M. "The Middle East in Canadian Social Science Textbooks," in Baha Abu-Laban and Faith T. Zeadey, eds., *Arabs in America: Myths and Realities.* Wilmette, Ill.: Medina University Press International, 1975, 133-47.

_____. "The Modern Arab World," in R.M. Savory, ed., *Introduction to Islamic Civilization.* Cambridge: Cambridge University Press, 1976, 147-59.

Khattab, Abdelmoneim M. "The Assimilation of Arab Muslims in Alberta," M.A. Thesis, Department of Sociology, University of Alberta, 1969.

Khuri, Fuad. "Parallel Cousin Marriage Reconsidered: A Middle Eastern Practice that Nullifies the Effects of Marriage on the Intensity of Family Relationships," *Man*, 5 (1970), 597-618.

Landau, Rom. *Arab Contribution to Civilization*. San Francisco: The American Academy of Asian Studies, 1958.

Leslie, G. *The Family in Social Context*. New York: Oxford University Press, 1976.

Lewis, Bernard. *The Arabs in History*. Third Edition. London: Hutchinson University Library, 1964.

Longrigg, Stephen H. *The Middle East*. Chicago: Aldine Publishing Co., 1963.

Lovell, Emily Kalled. "A Survey of the Arab-Muslims in the United States and Canada," *Muslim World*, 63 (1973), 139-54.

Lower, Arthur R.M. *Colony to Nation: A History of Canada*. Don Mills: Longman, 1971.

Lutfiyya, Abdulla M. *Baytin: A Jordanian Village*. The Hague: Mouton, 1966.

Lutfiyya, Abdulla M. and Charles W. Churchill, eds. *Readings in Arab Middle Eastern Societies and Cultures*. The Hague: Mouton, 1970.

MacDonald, Norman. *Canada: Immigration and Colonization, 1841-1903*. Toronto: Macmillan of Canada, 1966.

MacGuigan, M. "Constitutional Aspects of Ethnic Identity in Canada," in Paul M. Migus, ed., *Sounds Canadian*. Toronto: Peter Martin Associates Limited, 1975, 123-28.

Markotic, Valdimir. *Ethnic Directory of Canada*. Calgary: Western Publishers, 1976.

Massoud, Muhammad Said. *Al-'Arab wal Kuwwat Al-Ajnabiya*. (The Arab and the Foreign Forces) Beirut: Dar Al-Ra'ed Al-'Arabi, n.d. (Arabic)

——. *I Fought As I Believed*. Montreal: M.S. Massoud, 1976.

McDiarmid, Garnet and David Pratt. *Teaching Prejudice*. Toronto: The Ontario Institute for Studies in Education, 1971.

Meissner, Martin, *et al*. "No Exit for Wives: Sexual Division of Labour and the Cumulation of Household Demands," *Canadian Review of Sociology and Anthropology*, 12 (1975), 424-39.

Menuhin, Moshe. *The Decadence of Judaism in Our Time*. New York: Exposition Press, 1965.

Miller, Lucius Hopkins. *Our Syrian Population: A Study of the Syrian Population of Greater New York*. Columbia University Library, N.Y., and New York Public Library, Widener Collection, Harvard University, 1904.

Millet, David. "The Orthodox Church: Ukrainian, Greek and Syrian," in Jean Leonard Elliott, ed., *Minority Canadians: Immigrant Groups*. Scarborough: Prentice-Hall of Canada Ltd., 1971, 47-65.

Moughrabi, Fouad and Naseer Aruri, eds. *Lebanon: Crisis and Challenge in the Arab World*. Detroit: Association of Arab-American University Graduates, 1977.

O'Bryan, K.G., J.G. Reitz and O.M. Kuplowska. *Non-Official Languages: A Study in Canadian Multiculturalism*. Ottawa: Minister Responsible for Multiculturalism, 1975.

Palmer, Howard, ed. *Immigration and the Rise of Multiculturalism.* Toronto: Copp Clark Publishing, 1975.

Peristiany, J.G., ed. *Honour and Shame: The Values of Mediterranean Society.* London: Weidenfeld and Nicolson, 1965.

Peters, James and Habeeb Salloum. *Arabic Contributions to the English Vocabulary.* Toronto, 1973.

Porter, John. *The Vertical Mosaic.* Toronto: University of Toronto Press, 1965.

_____. *Canadian Social Structure: A Statistical Profile.* Toronto: McClelland and Stewart Limited, 1967.

Prothro, Edwin Terry. *Child Rearing in the Lebanon.* Harvard Middle Eastern Monograph Series. Cambridge, Mass.: Harvard University Press, 1961.

Prothro, Edwin Terry and Lutfy Najib Diab. *Changing Family Patterns in the Arab East.* Beirut: American University of Beirut, 1974.

Radecki, Henry with Benedykt Heydenkorn. *A Member of a Distinguished Family: The Polish Group in Canada.* Toronto: McClelland and Stewart, 1976.

Reed, Denys R. "The Arab Community in Toronto," unpublished manuscript, 1973.

Reid, W. Stanford, ed. *The Scottish Tradition in Canada.* Toronto: McClelland and Stewart Limited, 1976.

Richmond, Anthony. *Post-War Immigrants in Canada.* Toronto: University of Toronto Press, 1967.

_____. "Sociology of Migration in Industrial and Post-Industrial Societies," in J.A. Jackson, ed., *Migration.* Cambridge: At the University Press, 1969.

Rosenstock, Janet and Dennis Adair. "Multiculturalism in the Classroom: A Survey of Interracial Attitudes in Ontario Schools," unpublished manuscript, September, 1976.

Saati, Hassan and Gordon K. Hirabayashi, *Industrialization in Alexandria: Some Social and Ecological Aspects.* Cairo: American University, 1959.

Sabella, Lily. "En remontant le cours de l'histoire," *Trait d'Union,* Vol. 4, No. 4, 1967, p. 5.

Said, Edward. "Shattered Myths," in Naseer H. Aruri, ed., *Middle East Crucible: Studies on the Arab-Israeli War of October 1973.* Wilmette, Ill.: Medina University Press International, 1975, 408-447.

Said, Edward and Leila Meo. *Lebanon: Two Perspectives.* Detroit: Association of Arab-American University Graduates, 1975.

St. George Orthodox Church of Montreal. *Twenty-Fifth Anniversary.* Montreal, May 30, 1965.

Salloum, Aziz. "Keep in Touch with the Old Land," *The Syrian-Lebanese Mercury,* Vol. 1, No. 5, January 15, 1937, p. 2.

Savory, R.M., ed. *Introduction to Islamic Civilization.* Cambridge:

Cambridge University Press, 1976.

Sayegh, Fayez A. *Arab Unity.* New York: The Devin-Adair Company, 1958.

Scott, Frank and Michael Oliver, eds. *Quebec States Her Case.* Toronto: Macmillan of Canada, 1964.

Scott, W.L. "The Eastern Christian Churches," in Elias Karam, ed., *The Syrian Canadian National Review.* Ottawa: The Syrian Canadian National Committee of St. Elijah's Church Society, 1935, 42-54.

Shibli, Jabir. *Our Palestine: Conflict - Or Cooperation?* Montreal: The Canadian Arab News Service, 1946.

Statistics Canada. *Perspective Canada.* Ottawa: Information Canada, 1974.

Storey, M. and B. Pearson, eds., *The Canadian Family Tree.* Ottawa: Canadian Citizenship Branch, 1967.

Sweet, Louise E., "Reconstituting a Lebanese Village Society in a Canadian City," in Barbara C. Aswad, ed., *Arabic Speaking Communities in American Cities.* Staten Island, N.Y.: Center for Migration Studies and Association of Arab-American University Graduates, 1974, 39-52.

Szalai, Alexander, ed. *The Use of Time.* The Hague: Mouton, 1972.

de Tocqueville, Alexis. *Democracy in America.* New York: New American Library, 1956.

Vallee, F.G., M. Schwartz and F. Darknell. "Ethnic Assimilation and Differentiation in Canada," *Canadian Journal of Economics and Political Science,* 23 (1957), 540-49.

Wakin, Edward. *A Lonely Minority: The Modern Story of Egypt's Copts.* New York: William Morrow and Company, 1963.

Ware, Timothy. *The Orthodox Church.* Harmondsworth, Middlesex: Penguin Books Ltd., 1963.

Wassef, Nadia Hanna. "The Egyptians in Montreal: A New Colour in the Canadian Ethnic Mosaic," M.A. Thesis, Department of Geography, McGill University, 1977.

Weber, Max, trans. Talcott Parsons. *The Protestant Ethic and the Spirit of Capitalism.* New York: Charles Scribner's Sons, 1958. (The original German edition of this work appeared in 1904-5.)

Wickens, G.M. "Introduction to the Middle East," in R.M. Savory, ed., *Introduction to Islamic Civilization.* Cambridge: Cambridge University Press, 1976, 1-4.

Wirth, Louis. "The Problem of Minority Groups," in Ralph Linton, ed., *The Science of Man in the World Crisis.* New York: Columbia University Press, 1945, 347-72.

Woodsworth, J.S. *Strangers Within Our Gates.* Toronto: Toronto University Press, 1972. (The original edition of this work appeared in 1909.)

Zarbatany, Michael. "History of C. Aboud's Family," unpublished calligraphic manuscript, Montreal, 1912. (Arabic)

251

———. "A Short History of Syria," in Elias Karam, ed., *The Syrian Canadian National Review*. Ottawa: The Syrian Canadian National Committee of St. Elijah's Church Society, 1935, 8-15.

Archival Sources Relating to Syro-Lebanese Canadians

Records of the Immigration Branch (Record Group 76): RG 76, Vol. 522, File No. 801591, Pts. 1, 2, 3: "Immigration from Syria and Lebanon, 1910-1949." RG 76, Vol. 431, File No. 64239: "Immigration from Syria and Lebanon, 1905-1910, 1913."

Records of the Department of External Affairs (Record Group 25): RG 25, 61(a), Vol. 1845, File No. 766: "National Status of Syrians and Lebanese, 1937-38."

Records of the Department of Labour (Record Group 27): RG 27, Vol. 289, File No. 1-26-50: "Immigrants from Beirut, 1949."

Records of the Department of the Secretary of State (Record Group 6): RG 6, D1, "Certificates of Release from Internment"; arranged alphabetically by surname – World War I: Vol. 22 A-C, 23 D-G, 24 H-K, 25 K-M, 26 M-O, 27 P-R, 28 S, 29 T-V, 30 V-Z.

Records of the Department of Justice (Record Group 13): Mainly fragments of files dealing with individual cases, 1910, 1919-1920: Vol. 159, File No. 93; Vol. 235, File No. 1006; Vol. 239, File No. 1835; Vol. 246, File No. 373; Vol. 240, File No. 2095.

Sir Wilfrid Laurier Papers (Manuscript Group 26 G): MG 26, G, Vol. 541, pp. 146733-146735: letter of congratulations from the Syrian Liberal Club of Winnipeg, 30 Oct. 1908.

Sir Robert Borden Papers (Manuscript Group 26H): MG 26 H, Vol. 191, pp. 106720-106721: telegram from the Canadian Lebanon Association, Vancouver, 30 May 1916.

Index

Abu Bakr: 13-14
Acceptance: See *Reception*
Acculturation: 3, 60, 188, 228
Aden: 9
Adjustment: 3, 98-125, 128-151, 181-200, 217, 220, 227; Economic: 98-125; Religious: 141-144; Language: 181-188; Attitudes: 188-200
Afghanistan: 15
Age Composition: 71, 197, 198
Al-'Alamein: 151
Algeria: 5, 8, 20, 38, 40, 43, 44, 58, 67, 71, 117, 118, 186, 187, 207
Al Rashid mosque: 139
Al-Shehab: 132, 150
American University of Beruit (Syrian Protestant College): 39
Anglo-Egyptian Treaty (1936): 40
Antiochian Orthodox Christian Archdiocese of New York and All North America: 131, 132, 155n
Antiochian Orthodox Church: See Syrian Orthodox Church
Arab Community Centre (Toronto): 63, 119-120, 150, 154, 166-167, 179n, 187
Arab Community Newsletter: 154
Arab Canadian Professional Association: 149

Arab Dawn: 153-154
Arab Folklore Group: 149-150
Arab-Israeli conflicts: 41, 91, 150, 153, 154, 176-177, 201n, 218, 225n
Arab national movement: 39-41
Arab Palestine Association: 149, 154
Arab World Review: 153, 185
Arabian Knights: 150
Arabian Muslim Association: 139
Arabic Reinforcement Culture: 154
Arabisation: 15-19, 26n, 38, 177
Art: 22
Assimilation: 3, 60, 83, 84, 94, 128-151, 183, 184, 188, 199, 215, 218, 228, 229
Association Québec-Palestine: 149, 154
Associations: See *Organizations, Institutions*

Bahrain: 8, 58, 117, 118
Bashir, Archbishop Anthony: 143-144
Bedouins: 9, 11, 12, 43, 50n
Bois-de-Boulogne Community Centre: 134
Boosamra, Salim: 87, 106

253